DE

Other books in the Virgin True Crime series

KILLERS ON THE LOOSE
CROSSING TO KILL
LONE WOLF
I'LL BE WATCHING YOU
UNSOLVED MURDERS
MY BLOODY VALENTINE

DEATH CULTS
Murder, Mayhem and Mind Control

Edited by Jack Sargeant

First published in Great Britain in 2002 by

Virgin Books Ltd
Thames Wharf Studios
Rainville Road
London W6 9HA

A catalogue record for this book is available from the British Library

ISBN 0 7535 0644 0

Typeset by TW Typesetting, Plymouth, Devon
Printed and bound in Great Britain by
Mackays of Chatham PLC

CONTENTS

ACKNOWLEDGEMENTS   vii

DARKNESS RISING   1
Introduction by Jack Sargeant

1. KALI'S KILLER THUGS   9
Chris Barber

2. DEATH SPIRAL OF THE ASSASSINS   36
Monte Cazazza and Marzy Quayzar

3. CUT 'EM OFF   56
Michael Spann

4. ACID FASCISM   78
Michael Spann

5. JONESTOWN   103
John Harrison

6. FAMILY TIES   124
Mikita Brottman

7. WACO AND THE FINE ART OF KILLING   131
John Harrison

8. APOCALYPSE OM   162
Andrew Leavold

9. BURNT OFFERINGS   187
Mikita Brottman

10. THE WEST END LESBIAN VAMPIRES   207
Andrew Leavold

11. BLOOD AND SAND   225
    Jack Sargeant

12. WHAT THE WORLD NEEDS NOW IS FEAR   247
    Lance Sinclair

    THE CONTRIBUTORS   265

ACKNOWLEDGEMENTS

My thanks to the following individuals who have helped shape this volume: all the contributors to the present volume for rising so admirably to the challenge and deadlines laid before them, and especially Monte Cazazza and Michael Spann, who have both aided beyond the call of duty. To Kerri Sharp at Virgin for her unwavering endorsement and support of this project. Thanks to all who have tolerated my own rantings and have offered suggestions during the writing and editing of this book: Stephanie Watson, Julian Weaver, Simon Kane, and Angus Carlyle. To those writers with whom I have discussed parts of this volume: Peter Sotos and Jack Hunter. Thanks also to those bookstores and booksellers who have assisted in my quest for research materials, and to Dan at Koma Books On Line, and to those shop assistants in my local branches of the larger book chains who have helped.

Special thanks to those who have encouraged and supported me, driven me to airports and libraries, and welcomed me into their homes, and especially Lawrence English, Andrew Leavold, Helen Bernhagen, Kristy Matheson and the Kids, Phillipa Berry, Marisa Giorgi, Tyler Hubby, Stuart Swezey, Melissa Hoffs, Tessa Hughes Freeland, Carlo McCormick, John Harrison and Amanda Swinton and, of course, the Mumesons: Jamie Leonarder, Aspasia, and Michael Williams.

Also to James Pyman, Caspar Williams, Stewart Cain, Karen Howl, Joe Coleman, Whitney Ward, and Jason Williams, and no doubt several erroneous omissions.

Many thanks for permission to quote from the following sources:

Madness & Civilization, Michel Foucault, London: Routledge, 2001; *Castration and the Heavenly Kingdom*, Laura Engelstien, New York: Cornell University Press, 1999; *Manson: The Unholy Trial of Charlie and The Family*, John Gilmore & Ron Kenner, Los Angeles: Amok Books, 2000; *Spirits, Blood and Drums: the Orisha Religion in Trinidad*, James T Houk, Philadelphia: Temple University Press, 1995; *Buried Secrets, A True Story of Serial Murder, Black Magic, and Drug-Running on the U.S. Border*, Edward Humes, New York: Dutton, 1991; *Current Affair*, Channel Nine Network, Australia; *Ritual Sacrifice: A Concise History*, Brenda Ralph Lewis, Thrupp: Sutton Publishing, 2001; *The Autobiography of a Runaway Slave*, Esteban Montejo, translated by Dr Miguel Barnet, The Bodley Head, 1968, reprinted by permission of the Random House Group Ltd, New York and London; *Battle for the Mind*, William Sargant, Pan/Macmillan, 1959, London.

My God, my God, why hast thou forsaken me?
– Matthew 27:46

If you're doing business with a religious son of a bitch,
get it in writing. His word ain't worth shit.
– William S Burroughs

DARKNESS RISING

JACK SARGEANT

... these horsemen of the Apocalypse, sent by God Himself; these are no angels of triumph and reconciliation; these are no heralds of serene justice, but the dishevelled warriors of a mad vengeance. The world sinks into universal Fury. Victory is neither God's nor the Devil's: it belongs to Madness.

— Michel Foucault, *Madness And Civilization*

What fools these mortals be.

— Puck, *A Midsummer Night's Dream*

Then said Jesus, Father, forgive them; for they know not what they do.

— Luke 23:34

It is the knowledge of the infinite blackness of death, the certainty of physical destruction and the corporality of the material world, that, together, have become one of the defining aspects of our humanity. We taste the possibility of the infinite in teasingly brief ecstatic moments, in the *petite mort* of orgasm, knowing that the darkness of the infinite will eventually swallow us in death. Religious belief emerges as a way in which, both as individuals and as societies, humanity can negotiate the uncertainty of existence and the cold terror of the inevitability of death.

That the world's major religions promise a triumph of life eternal over death is clearly their prime attraction.[1] Yet the guarantee of metaphysical immortality is not without its price, invariably following a process of specific religious devotion, and, in the Judeo-Christian tradition, following the final conflict between good and evil, infidel and devotee, faithful and heathen:

Armageddon. To enter the afterlife the immortal soul must be correctly prepared; we can achieve our rightful position in the sacred world only by following the correct behaviour in the profane world; those who are found wanting – infidels or sinners – either endure eternal punishment or are condemned to fleeting mortality.

Death and suicide cults generally betray a series of recognisable phenomena, although a cult does not have to exhibit all of these characteristics to be classified as such. While it is all too easy in our society to label all cults as intrinsically 'bad', as delinquent manifestations that have sprung from the minds of those for whom mainstream religion offers no promise, the term 'cult' also functions to fulfil a degree of sociopolitical control. The last two decades of the twentieth century saw various evangelical Christian groups deriding many, if not all, other religious groups as dangerous cults. Further, some of these evangelical Christian groups have posited the existence of a massive underground satanic society aimed at overthrowing Christianity.

This volume does not seek to engage in such paranoia, recognising it as merely a means by which one religion can re-enforce its supposed cultural dominance over different belief systems. To label all cults as inherently 'other' or 'evil' is an act of pointless discrimination, and, for those who wish to explore such notions, this volume will be entirely unsatisfactory. It is not our intention here to disparage any single religious belief, but to draw attention to those particular cults whose beliefs are by their nature violent.[2]

While the specific religious, metaphysical and philosophical beliefs behind these death cults vary, they tend towards a conviction in the culmination of religious history; they embrace the notion of the completion of a temporal cosmological cycle, of apocalypse now, of Armageddon, of the end. These beliefs are frequently manifested through often unconventional readings of religious texts, supplemented with other information, gleaned from what cult leaders and followers deem to be potent signs of the end: the temporal millennium, strange or rare natural phenomena (for example the arrival of the Hale-Bop comet), always-imminent conflict (such as a forthcoming race war or massive geopolitical nuclear conflagration), or any other of a number of manifestations of supposed 'divine revelation'.

Often these cults are led by a charismatic figure, who has, or at least claims to have, specialised knowledge regarding the forthcoming rapture. The leader exhibits a unique relationship with both the metaphysical world and the material world and is able to synthesise the two into a believable *Weltanschauung*. The leaders are able to attract and keep followers, seducing them via a combination of visionary sermons and through control of their physiological needs and desires. Cult rulers have been known to dictate the diets of members (both nutritional and narcotic, depending on the nature of the cult), the awards that devotees receive, the punishments they endure and the modes of sexual behaviour in which they are permitted to engage. Relinquishing control and responsibility to a single leader, or an established (and thus appearing to be naturalised) chain of command, is also common among cults. Such a relationship between power and devotion has, in some cases, led to reports that cult leaders have performed miracles before stunned and malleable adherents.

In many cults devotees typically feel disenchanted with dominant, socially acceptable modes of religion;

often they believe that there is a spiritual lack in their lives that the cult's belief system fulfils. Followers are frequently able to find new converts, whether through approaching similarly disenfranchised souls, or through more seductive techniques, such as 'flirty fishing', where attractive female cult members are dispatched to attract new members via titillating promises of a new sensual nirvana.[3]

Cult leaders often appeal to their followers' sense of disenfranchisement, and their perceived dislocation from the common herd. Excommunicated from the mainstream of society, many cult members finally feel they belong when they are indoctrinated into the group. Moreover, this sense of belonging to a special elite group is emphasised by the separation of the cult members from society. In the cases of several cults, this distance becomes increasingly pronounced as the perceived apocalyptic climax nears, frequently as a direct result of actions undertaken by the chosen few, and groups often retreat both psychologically and geographically in order best to face – and to survive – the forthcoming tribulations.

The moment at which some cults become snuff-fixated is impossible to predict. Gurus may become increasingly irrational, paranoid and obsessed with pushing the group into abyss, even while trying to survive their interpretation of end-time eschatology. For the Manson Family it was the move to Death Valley; for Jim Jones and the People's Temple the paranoia led to Guyana. Onwards and downwards. The balance tilts, the end is nigh, blood flows.

However, attempting to second-guess the behaviour of a secluded cult is potentially hazardous. When the American government became interested in the Branch

Davidians group who had bunkered down in their fortified compound in Waco, Texas, much of the ensuing blood that was spilled was that of cult members who perished in the final battle. The increasing societal fear of cults almost certainly contributed to this grisly conflagration. Of course, a martyr's death – dying in an eruption of flaming violent glory – is also a trademark of many charismatic cult leaders.

The edition you hold in your hands offers some insight into the most notorious of cults, such as Aum, and the People's Temple, as well as lesser-known cults, such as Brisbane's lesbian vampire killers and the Mexican Matamoros murderers. But these cults all belong to the chaotic turbulence of the twentieth century; earlier cults, whose violent religious philosophies and blood lust often exceeded those of their contemporary manifestations, are also included within this volume.

To see cults purely as a modern phenomenon is a failure of thinking: modern men and women are no more corrupt than their ancestors. Humanity has never had an age of innocence: rather, every genealogical moment driven by unquestioning belief is drenched in blood. Our history is marked by folly far more frequently than progress, and is characterised more by fear and hate than by understanding.

Further, it is not merely the bastardised forms of Christianity – or uniquely twisted interpretations of the Bible – that inform the cults included in this volume. Cults have manifested across the globe, with their beliefs reflecting twisted versions of all manner of faiths and indigenous beliefs. In recognition of this, also included are chapters on the Kali-worshipping Thuggee and the murderous Islamic assassins.

As the twentieth century entered its final years, the irrational fear of cults led to the absurdity of a number of Christian writers and some so-called therapists suggesting that there were vast secret satanic cults procuring and killing children. Some of these fundamentalists went as far to suggest that a majority of serial killers belonged to an elite occult movement dedicated to some suitably arcane satanic cause. Such conspiracies are a psychic salve, allowing groups ranging from Christian fundamentalists and self-proclaimed 'survivors' to black-clad snuff-driven teens the luxury of believing in some greater meaning. But, of course, human folly and blank stupidity need no elucidation: rather it is the swirling vortex of chaos that beckons and seduces even while it escapes easy interpretation and ready definition.

For the reader who is searching for meaning, for reason, for the light of the 'human spirit' in the darkness, this volume offers little in the way of hope. However, for those willing to dive into the abyss, the following volume contains descriptions of enough mindless folly, human stupidity and ugly brutality to offer a tragic yet gleeful *schadenfreude*. In the end, then, this volume is dedicated to the few avatars of liberty, for whom unquestioning adherence to thoughtless belief is an enemy, and willing obedience a distraction from life's true pleasures and the soul's true potential.

A note on the text: Where possible full references and bibliographic information is included within the essay; however, the nature of some archives, cuttings and online databases sometimes excludes full publishing data. All Japanese, Persian, Arabic and Hindi words are presented in the most common Anglicised spelling.

The opinions and beliefs expressed in this volume do not necessarily reflect those of the editors or publishers. Readers are assumed to be mature adults.

NOTES

1. Of course, religion also offers spiritual content for many, who have a personal relationship to their god(s) that fulfils them. However, in its manifestation as organised doctrine, religion often appears to focus less on metaphysical contemplation and philosophical exploration and more on dogma.
2. Further, of course, it is a truism that the dominant religions of today, including Christianity, have been at various times and in various cultures viewed as dangerous cults.
3. 'Flirty fishing' refers to the tactical strategy of sending eager female followers to seduce potential adherents and has occurred in numerous cults. The term was coined – and possibly best realised – by the Children of God (see Chris Mikul, 'Hookers For Jesus! The Strange Saga of the Children of God', in David Kerekes and David Slater (eds) *Critical Vision: Random Essays & Tracts Concerning Sex, Religion, Death*, Stockport: Critical Vision/Headpress, 1995).

'everything was a blank'.

1. KALI'S KILLER THUGS

CHRIS BARBER

Worshippers of Kali – the monstrous goddess of destruction and demon-slayer – initiated India's Thug cult, who sacrificially strangled many thousands of victims, becoming the original killer cult. Thugs existed as a clandestine sect for almost a thousand years, longer than any other known killer cult. The full body count of Thuggee victims, like its real origins, remains an unsolved mystery, but the cult spread across India like a plague. Their modus operandi grew increasingly gruesome and ruthless, involving the joyful massacre of women, children and babies. This reign of terror terminated only when the British army hunted down and hanged some four thousand prototype, group serial killers. Incredibly, even now this cult remains shrouded in secrecy, yet they created a terrorist conspiracy with international links. Today this legacy is more relevant than ever.

You must go much further back for the full story, to the dawn of time, prehistory, the age of mythology . . .

KALI'S ETERNAL DEATH DANCE

Our planet was being laid waste by evil demons, Shumbha and Nishumbha, whose power proliferated. They were fearless and ruthless, possessing divine protection, and mere mortals could not kill them. The finest generals led massive armies into battle against them but all were routed. Even the gods were powerless against them and fled heaven as the demons advanced.

9

In a last bid for salvation, the gods summoned the goddess to save the universe from demonic tyranny and destruction.

Parvati – the goddess – bathed in the Ganges and heard their prayers; she magically created another goddess from her body. Ugly, blackened and grotesque in appearance, she was named Kalika. After vowing to exterminate the demons, she was approached by Shumbha's messenger, offering the goddess Shumbha's hand in marriage. Kalika replied she would marry whoever defeated her in battle. Shumbha was infuriated and sent another envoy. Kalika hummed and sighed as she roasted him alive.

Suddenly an army of raging demons attempted to storm Kalika's Calcutta fortress. But her mighty lion saw them off. Then demon generals, Chunda and Munda, manoeuvred their armies to outflank Kalika and besiege her. Kalika assessed the logistics and changed tactics. While she chanted herself into a trance, her forehead was torn open and a new goddess crawled out. Clad in tight-fitting tigerskin, she held aloft a shimmering sword and noose. Her fierce onslaught caught the enemy off-guard and they retreated in disarray. Amid confusion, Chunda and Munda were captured, and decapitated at Kalika's command.

The strongest demon – Raktabij – protected Shumbha from Kalika's advance. But Kalika was not daunted and engaged Raktabij in savage combat. As she slashed deeply into the demon's flesh, blood oozed from his wounds. When each drop hit the earth, it exploded and mutated into another raging demon. Warrior demons proliferated and Kalika realised that, the more she wounded Raktabij, the more demons amassed against her. Again, Kalika deployed Chamunda to extend her gigantic tongue and lick up every drop of Raktabij's cursed blood before any could touch the ground. Having accomplished this, they watched Raktabij scream in agony and die. His multitudes of bloody offspring were maddened and approached Kalika, who sweated profusely. She wiped her brow and from her sweat two loyal disciples arose. To each she handed a noose. They charged the demons, strangling all without spilling a drop of blood; for this service, Kalika rewarded them with the right to kill in perpetuity and benefit from the spoils, but warned them to observe her omens.

Meanwhile, Shumbha's and Nishumba's armies ambushed Kalika, riding defiantly atop her lion. The gods looked on helplessly as their champion prepared to meet her fate; although their powers were depleted, they realised one chance remained. If they all pooled together their remaining abilities and invested it in Kalika, she might muster enough strength for a final struggle. Bramhadev evoked his power on a swan; Shankar's purveyor rode on a bull. A peacock represented Kartikaya's virginal force, while an eagle soared with Vaishnavi's strength, and Aindri's power came via an elephant. Kalika felt rejuvenated, and another ferocious battle raged as Kalika's new strengths mercilessly massacred demon hordes. Shumbha watched fearfully as his superior tactical ability and combat experience were outmanoeuvred. Then reconnaissance reported Nishumbha had been slain.

The demon overlord was enraged, taunting Kalika for deploying the gods' occult powers. Kalika – Dark Mother, as she was also known – grinned, revealing her rotten, blood-drenched teeth, proclaiming that her allies were diverse expressions of her own nature. At that moment all her powers were spectacularly submerged into her body and she stood alone. Shumbha grabbed Kalika and flew into the sky. Their mortal combat emblazoned the heavens, two towering warriors matching blow for blow. Shumbha tired and the goddess twisted her adversary around before hurling him at the ground. At last he was dead and his demonic army retreated to hell!

Kalika was enraged beyond control, and her dance of death and destruction continues into eternity.

CHARRED REMAINS

Many millennia later, India was effectively under British rule. What started as trading posts, where the British East India Company could wheel and deal, became the jewel in the crown of the British Empire.

In October 1812, John Maunsell – a British officer in the 23rd Native Infantry of the Bengal Army – ventured across country from Agra to Ettawah (100 kilometres southeast) on a routine ordinance mission. He was on horseback, armed with a revolver and sword, and accompanied by two sepoy orderlies. The journey should have taken three days. As dusk fell on the second day, they erected a camp near Sindhouse village.

Three days later, they had not arrived in Ettawah, so a cavalry search party set out. In a wayside grove among the ashes and scorched earth of a smouldering fire, charred regimental buttons and insignia were discovered. These were identified as Maunsell's, but his body was never found.

Without bothering to open an official investigation, an army unit took reprisals, destroying villages and randomly selecting civilians, who were tried for murder. A proper investigation could have alerted the British to the Thug threat. Instead the East India Company ignored rumours as native superstition, and refused to get involved. Maunsell's mysterious disappearance and probable murder were recorded as misadventure.

Violent highway robbery was commonplace throughout India: every year an estimated forty thousand people were murdered by Thugs.[1] Strangely, Maunsell was the only Briton they killed.

LONE INVESTIGATOR

British reluctance to get involved in what were deemed local affairs was compounded by sloppy bureaucratic and military incompetence. Robbery and murder by Thugs was rife – even with the Raj in charge. With one known exception, the cult avoided British targets – conveniently escaping British attention.

A British army captain, William Henry Sleeman, had served in India since 1806; he was fascinated by Indian culture and studied Hinduism. Appointed to investigate the mysterious murders of several wealthy businessmen in the Nerbudda Valley (Northern India), he immediately noticed various bizarre coincidences pertaining to the crime scenes. Their attackers had savagely mutilated all the victims' corpses before burial. Graves were similarly dug and well camouflaged, the bodies in varying stages of putrefaction. Sleeman noted the careful destruction of identification marks, combined with extensive wounds that quickened decomposition, and remote burial sites, serving to destroy evidence. But he also noticed a macabre ritualistic quality, particularly considering that each victim was strangled before being mangled. All the murders took place within the same period – autumn. Various forensic police reports exhibited notable reluctance towards rigorous investigation. Unable to deduce a coherent explanation, Sleeman approached his superiors to sanction a wider investigation, but they refused. He discussed matters with Indian acquaintances, who talked openly about esoteric religious sects and human sacrificial cults, dedicated to the goddess – Kali.

Spooked but unsure what to believe, Sleeman visited the Kali temple in Calcutta during a festival of devotees; he was shocked by what he witnessed. The aisles were caked with blood from the sacrificial slaughter of animals to appease the goddess, whose monstrous, naked effigy towered over the congregation. Around her neck was a garland of human skulls, and her four arms were outstretched, one brandishing a *talvar* (sword), another the *shul* (pike), her third held a *chakra* (wheel) and the remaining hand grasped a *parshu* (axe). Her gaping mouth revealed rotting teeth dripping human blood. In frenzied adoration, priests beat the backs of worshippers and selected worthy individuals to have hooks stabbed through their muscles and attached to ropes, tied to poles. As the poles swung around, the victim was raised overhead and whirled over the frantic assembly, spraying everyone with blood as they chanted, 'Victory to Mother Kali!'

By tracing the Kali connection, Sleeman's investigation began to make sense. He was told about a clandestine killer cult known as Thugs. Their modus operandi was to infiltrate groups of travellers by deceit, gang up on and strangle them, offering these sacrificial victims to Kali. Victims were robbed of all cash and possessions, the booty divided among the Thug group. Initiation was passed down from father to son, through generations. Apparently, the sect dated back to AD 760–800 and was inspired by sacred paintings on cave walls at Kailasa Ellora, depicting human sacrifices to the goddess.

TRADE SECRETS

In 1820, a feature appeared in *Asiatic Researches*[2] called 'On the Murderers Called Phansigars' by Robert Sherwood, a British doctor working in Madras. *Phansi* is Hindustani for noose, and Sherwood began researching the phenomenon in 1816, after persuading some rogue bandits to reveal their religious practices. He gathered evidence from across southern India and alleged that Phansigars form gangs of ten to fifty members, who seek smaller parties of travellers (on horse or foot) en route between towns. Aware of potential danger, travellers generally congregated on the edge of town, seeking others to accompany them, relying on safety in numbers.

Phansigars were adept in these situations, priding themselves on their ability to con and cajole strangers to trust them. First advance reconnaissance was collected, via a network of local town officials who kept their ears to the ground, knowing a cut from the proceeds awaited whoever provided the hottest tip. This might include selecting the wealthiest travellers, head counts and intended destinations. The Thug cell split into pairs or trios, delegated a mission controller and strategically dispersed along the predicted route. When the tourists approached, each robber contingent would 'fortuitously' bump into them, proclaiming their luck at avoiding bandits, and ask if the travellers minded if they all continued together, thus creating a safer group for all. This chicanery was an elaborate Thug charade. Pretending not to recognise cult brethren, fellow travellers would continue joining the growing group, until these usurpers outnumbered their hosts. Phansigars had developed a system of covert hand signals and code words, enabling secret communication among them without arousing outside suspicion. At the controller's signal,

Phansigars rose into action with meticulous efficiency, usually when the whole party had set up camp in a remote location.

Two or three thugs simultaneously pounced on each victim. Their weapon was a yellow or white silk turban or *ruhmal*, with a knot tied in one corner and a silver coin (consecrated by Kali) in another. The assassins perfected their killing technique into a ritualistic ballet. Double knots prevented the silk from slipping through fingers. While this was speedily thrust around the neck and tightened, another Phansigar grabbed the victim's legs, wrenching them from under him. A third might grip his hands by the wrists. There followed a ruthless orgy of asphyxiation, the climax of Thuggee terror. Stranglers prided themselves on ensuring no one escaped: old men, young girls, weeping babies, even pet dogs – all were massacred. Only one exception might be granted this strict no-survivors policy: boys aged between seven and twelve, after watching their parents die, could be adopted by stranglers as apprentices.

After the killing frenzy came the carnage of necromania – dismembering, mutilating and carving up the corpses. Slashes were cut in the torso, from shoulders to hands and to feet; the abdomen was split open, joints hacked apart and deep holes gouged into the chest between ribs. Some claimed it was ritualistic; many realised this butchery renders bodies difficult to identify and hastens putrefaction.

Sleeman was fascinated by these revelations. The implications were staggering and scary: the Thuggee represented a nationwide conspiracy that had lasted for centuries, supported by local government officials, policemen, landowners and princes, bribed with cuts from the loot. Sleeman spent ensuing years haranguing his superiors for a full investigation. But only another coincidental turn of events eventually manifested the support he needed.

British subjugation of India was initially unintentional, resulting from the power vacuum left by the collapse of the Mogul Empire. Even while consolidating control, British forces had pursued a tolerant, hands-off policy towards indigenous culture. But a new breed of zealous, Victorian Christian supremacists were winning control of British colonial affairs. They were shocked by India's 'primitive' paganism and lack of Christian values. British colonial hegemony had to be imposed, and Sleeman's exposé of the killer Kali cult was the example to prove their case.

CONFESSIONS OF A PHANSIGAR

Employing skilful mendacity and charlatanism to deceive strangers was all part of the ritual, a skill stranglers were proud of. Thugs claimed they could mimic any role required, regardless of class or profession. However, their most sacred rite was the ritualistic burial ceremony or *Tuponee*. Every initiate possessed a pickaxe, his most sacrosanct possession, believed to be Kali's tooth and consecrated by the goddess as a gift to devotees. After erecting a tent around the crime scene, participants gathered behind to propitiate Kali with their human sacrifices and prayers. Pickaxes were utilised to dig graves (usually in sand, about a metre – or just over 3 feet – deep, concealed from public paths) into which mangled corpses were stacked. These were covered with a layer of rocks to deter marauding animals and camouflaged. Where the murder scene was considered unsafe, bodies were carted off in sacks and buried later under covert conditions.

Following killings, victims were stripped of cash and valuables. This booty was divided into equal shares, the group leader taking two shares, other participants each receiving one share. Where required, additional shares were created to cover kickbacks for aides and informants. As a further precaution, Thug groups travelled away from their home turf to perform these antics (an average of 200 kilometres or 125 miles).

During their human-hunting season, Thugs were extremely superstitious, relying on divination and positive omens before embarking. For this, a silver or brazen Kali icon was erected, surrounded by a lizard, snake, pickaxe and sometimes a noose or knife, together with cakes, fruit and flowers; incense was burned and prayers were said. A sheep was sacrificed, its decapitated head with its right foot in its mouth and a burning lamp on top, and was set before the goddess, who was entreated to bless the undertaking. The sheep's mouth and nostrils were observed for convulsive animation, connoting Kali's approbation. If this was absent, the mission was aborted. Initiates wore yellow or white garments – a team-stripe of Kali's favourite colours. *Ramasee*, their codified language, combined words, signals and signs. This communication system enhanced bonding.

An animist spirit – the tiger – was adopted by Thugs as a cult mascot, admired for its stealth, strength, cunning and predatory nature; it was known as *Kankali* or man-eater, and initiates protected tigers. Accounts suggest poison or swords were occasionally used to dispatch victims, but strangulation was favoured because Kali supposedly strangled demons, to preclude spilling blood.

Another significant bonding ceremony, undertaken with relish, was shared consumption of *gur* – unrefined-sugar drink. This happened before missions, and was thought to induce hallucinogenic trances (initiation rites were essential cult activity).

Thugs engaged in killing activity for only a couple of months each year, during India's autumn Dasahara festival (October/November). The rest of the time, initiates lived ordinary lives, working conventional day jobs and raising families. So extra annual income from robberies must have provided a welcome boost to cash flows. This must have seemed all rather mundane, which may explain why cult activity was so important, an escape from tedious monotony into intense existence. Autumn ushers in dramatic environmental change, celebrated in significant religious festivals around the world.

THUG-BUSTERS
Earliest recorded reference to Thugs appears in thirteenth-century manuscripts of Jalala-d Din Firoz Khily, Sultan of Delhi, who tried a thousand captured Thugs. He would not execute them, being superstitious and concerned about their spiritual quest. Instead, he exiled them to Bengal.

In the late eighteenth century, while Britain and France fought the Napoleonic Wars, India's notorious Tipu Sultan ruled Maisaw. Tipu was a Jacobite sympathiser, renowned for statesmanship and military prowess. As such, he engineered the greatest Indian military victories against the British. Under Tipu, Maisaw became the first state successfully to outlaw Thuggee and protect citizens. Tipu was finally defeated by an Anglo-Indian alliance at Seringapatam in 1799. While storming his fortress, the East India Company recorded their first Thug arrests, soon releasing them as quasi-religious vagabonds.

In 1830, Lord William Bentinck appointed Sleeman to wipe out Thugs. Detection was helped by the decadence and corruption into which the cult had degenerated. For centuries Thuggee had rigorously preserved clandestine status by engendering fear and observing strict codes of conduct. Victims were carefully selected, some groups forbidden as targets, including women (Kali being female) and the camala caste: blind, beggars, untouchables (the lowest Hindu caste), priests, carpenters, stonemasons and gold/brass/iron smiths. However by the nineteenth century, the cult was marred by sloppy and greedy practice, and infiltration by opportunists, whose actions suggest sacrosanct traditions were secondary to the loot: women were regularly targeted, bodies poorly buried, cops and landowners bribed for protection.

Feringheea was an infamous Thug leader who was captured in 1830 and confessed his involvement. Sleeman discovered that initiates, when questioned directly, bragged with alacrity about cult activity. He claims he established friendly rapport with Thugs, regarding them as decent chaps. The British transformation of India's infrastructure – jungle clearance, modern roads and railways – made traditional Thuggee methods more difficult and tracking culprits easier.

For twenty years, Sleeman vigorously hunted down suspects, sending three to four thousand Thugs to the gallows or prison, eventually ending cult activity. He won a knighthood for his trouble.

BACK WHERE WE STARTED . . .

The goddess Kali is one of many incarnations of Parvati – Shiva's wife. Often depicted as dark, ugly and violent, she may have three eyes and four arms, each representing a different facet of her personality: one holds a sword; the second holds a severed human head; the third guards against fear; the fourth grants bliss. Other adornments include a girdle of severed arms, earrings of children's corpses and a serpent bracelet. She is among the most ancient figures in the Hindu pantheon, and her black skin acknowledges her as a defender against the (lighter) Aryan conquest. Kali remains one of the best-loved Hindu deities; only elephant-headed Ganesha surpasses her popularity. The Thug death cult represented a tiny minority of Kali followers.

Kali, or Kell, is the feminine form of the Sanskrit *Kala*, 'time' or 'dark'. She was known as Bhavani to Thugs. Calcutta (Kolkata/Kalighata) is named after Kali, who is variously known as the Dark (or Black) Mother, Durgha, Bhowani, Devi, Bhadrakali, Chandi, Mahakali; she's omnipotent and all-pervasive, the destructive Mother Goddess of Time and saviour of the universe, renowned for reconciling oppositions. Skulls represent seed syllables of the Sanskrit alphabet, sacred sounds that created the universe; the sword cuts through illusion. She has cross-gender attributes, and punishes wickedness. There are elements of the 'monstrous feminine' in depictions, drunk on blood and obstreperous, beyond moral order, a warning against uncontrolled female power. She's also a potent sexual totem, often depicted naked, carved into lewd pornographic tableaux.

When slaughtering demons, she worked herself into an interminable destructive frenzy, dancing on and eating victims' corpses, causing catastrophes – even Shiva couldn't stop her. So he threw himself under her feet, causing her to stamp him to death, this realisation finally curtailing her gyrations. She is often depicted standing on Shiva's corpse, which (like the skull garland) symbolises the remains of finite existence. Kali represents everyone's potential for both good and bad behaviour.

Just as Kali and Parvati are one, alternative characteristics of a single being, so her multifarious incarnations are manifestations of Shiva – his feminine side. As absolute night, she devours all that exists, and protects followers from fear; criminals notoriously favour her. As a Bhakti or third-path deity she demands passionate devotion: today's followers still sacrifice animals at her altar.

Kali Yuga is the current age in the Hindu four-stage cycle, which ends with death and destruction of all life by fire and flood, so the golden age can begin anew. Samsara is the endless cycle of rebirth, and the quality of one's next life depends on karma (one's fate based on actions in preceding lives). Hinduism advocates action over thought, so you can break the eternal death/rebirth cycle through rituals, or overcoming desire.

Many sects emerged during the post-Gupta period (AD 800–1800). Shaktas are devoted to female power, and likewise Tantrists who perform black mass and break social taboos. From this background, the Thugs possibly formed, attempting to escape the rebirth cycle by propitiating Kali, and claiming descent from mythological demon stranglers.

LAST RITES

The word 'Thug' is derived from the Hindi *thag* (pronounced *tag*), meaning deceiver, thief or swindler, and written in Sanskrit as *sthaga*, from *sthagati*, meaning to hide or conceal. 'Thuggee' is the generic historical term describing methods and practices pertaining to India's Thugs.

The true origin of Thugs is uncertain and unlikely to be discovered. However, recent evidence in archaeological fieldwork suggests that, among ancient cultures, human sacrifice was more common than previously believed. It is probable that most early civilisations propitiated their gods with human sacrifice. Kali is one of the oldest deities, and the Indus Valley was populated by some of the earliest cities. It is conceivable that Thugs developed as a continuation of a high-priest clan, dating back to the earliest sacrificial rites.

Many Thugs were hereditary initiates, part of a family tradition passed from father to son. Apprenticeships initially kicked off at the age of eight or nine, the first kill witnessed at twelve or thirteen. Here is part of Sleeman's interrogation of Thug Sahib Khan:

'At what age do you initiate them?'

'I was initiated by my father when I was only thirteen.'

'Have you any rule as to the age?'

'None. A father is sometimes avaricious and takes his son out very young merely to get his share of the booty, for the youngest boy gets as much in his share as the oldest man.'

'How soon do you let them see your operation?'

'The first expedition they neither see nor hear anything of murder. They don't know our trade, they get presents, bought out of their share, and become fond of the wandering life, as they are always mounted on ponies. Before the end of the journey they know that we rob. The next expedition they suspect that we kill and some of them even know it. And in the third expedition they see all.'[3]

Adolescence is well chosen to indoctrinate young Thugs. It inspires confusion, pent-up frustration, violent impulses and the need to prove oneself. When a father, without counter-guidance, raises his son to believe killing is his conventional destiny, the cult's duration is understandable.

POST-THUG CULT

There are puzzling mysteries pertaining to Thuggee, inadequately explained by recorded evidence. Exploring these in relation to developments informing today's broader understanding of killer cults can offer insights.

When a Thug fraternity ritually devoured *gur*, it's claimed a mass trance is induced, lasting throughout a mission. As if possessed by Kali, individual autonomy is lost. Bodies become vessels through which Kali's energy flows, existing purely at her bidding. Similar intense states experienced through ritualistic group bonding are widely recorded. The Olympian god Dionysus shares some chaotic attributes associated with Kali: role-playing performances are enhanced through dissolution of personal identity. Friedrich Nietzsche explores this phenomenon in *The Birth of Tragedy*:

> Excitement is able to inspire a whole mass of men with the artistic faculty of seeing themselves surrounded by such a host of spirits with whom they know themselves to be essentially one . . . to see yourself transformed before your own eyes, and then to act as if you had actually taken possession of another body and another character . . . Here we actually have the individual surrendering himself by the fact of his entrance into an alien nature. Moreover, this phenomenon is epidemic in its

manifestation: a whole throng experiences this metamorphosis . . . a chorus of transformed beings, whose civic past and social position are totally forgotten. They have become the timeless servants of their god, living apart from all the life of the community . . . a community of unconscious actors, who mutually regard themselves as transformed among one another.[4]

William Sargant's *Battle for the Mind* offers a cornucopia of relevant insights into mind control and brainwashing techniques. He recounts how quasi-religious and political sects subject congregations to dramatic sensations:

Their methods for working up group excitement were most effective: they rang bells, sang psalms, and scourged themselves until blood flowed in torrents . . . Just as Hitler's conversion of the German masses to the Nazi faith was helped by meetings where rhythmic chanting, torchlight processions, and the like, could arouse them to states of hysterical suggestibility . . .[5]

Similar states are apparent among fans at soccer matches, where fervent chanting passes from each to his neighbours in steadily rising pitch, until the crowd chant in unison. During intense group arousal, usual inhibitions are broken down by psychochemical and sensory overload. This condition opens people to suggestibility, like wiping parameters from your hard drive and substituting new configurations. Participants in psychoanalysis attempt to reach transference, a stage where the analysand projects guilt on to the analyst;

similarly in sympathetic magic such as voodoo, one's manifestations cause others to imitate them. In group dynamics, actions pass contagiously from each to others.

Enter the high priest, be it Savonarola, preaching eternal damnation for nonconformists, or Hitler's absurd ranting. This new configuration determines subsequent actions, akin to mass hypnosis. In the Middle Ages, the sheer sight of flagellants was enough to provoke citizens to massacre Jews.

The craving for adventure as an escape from routine life is a widespread need. Erich Fromm in *The Anatomy of Human Destructiveness* explores the destructive potential of deeply ingrained drives. He argues that it's one reason why relatively prosperous, ordinary people are willing to ditch security, charging off to fight wars, even when their interests aren't directly threatened. It's not just about pursuing the Nirvana Principle (of Sigmund Freud's Death Drive), or an adrenaline-hyped thrill from risk-taking.

Aggressive narcissism originates in the lack of libidinous relationships to objects in the extended world; the libido is directed towards the ego. A narcissist worships himself, impervious to the surrounding world. He can relate to others only when they support his delusions – anyone who doesn't is a threat.

Group narcissism replaces the individual with his group. The group is everything, idolised by individual members. Outsiders must confirm the group's perceived status, or represent a threat. Initiates repress personal desires if these conflict with group functions. Initiation rituals and rites of passage bond the group ever closer together, increasing alienation from those excluded. Members express feelings towards each other, each supporting all. Conformity to this self-perpetuating dynamic is demonstrated through dominating outsiders. Internal consensus constructs reality as group experience, without recourse to external reason. As cohesion tightens, members manipulate each other more easily. Self-criticism is overcome, as one is aware that one is part of something superior. Feelings of equality flow between group members, regardless of external status. The fused group

> to some extent, reverses all values . . . Encourages deep-seated human impulses . . . impulses that are stunted by the principles of egotism and competition . . . Class differences, if not absent, disappear to a considerable extent . . . Man is man again, and has a chance to distinguish himself, regardless of privileges that his social status confers upon him as a citizen . . . an indirect rebellion against the injustice, inequality and boredom governing social life . . . he does not have to fight the members of his own group . . . in a kind of perversely socialised system.[6]

Further, Fromm cites Kali as the ultimate destructive, two-faced mother image. She is cold and dispassionate in response to her child's Oedipal cravings. Her failure to respond intensifies the child's desire. Never knowing her love means that a child must try ever harder to fill that lack. But this may never be resolved and increased striving only attains greater misery. The mother-goddess is eternally two-faced, the womb where life begins and womb of the earth – death, where life must return. This lack manifests in necrophilia.

A peculiar feature of this quasi-Hindu sect of Kali worshippers is that membership included all religions, classes and castes. There were as many Muslims as Hindus, almost inconceivable today, Islam being a monotheistic, desert religion. However, secular India has a tradition of religious intermingling. After the Mogul conquest (from 1526, according to Baber) these Muslim rulers prudently encouraged religious integration. Another possibility is that Kali is associated with Fatima (as female deity). Fatima was Muhammad's much-revered daughter, who led a sectarian Muslim cult.

Curious evidence suggests formation of a joint, multinational killer cult comprising Thugs and Persia's Order of Assassins; while it sounds fantastic it is worth investigating.

The prophet Muhammad died in AD 632, leaving no clear successor. Violent feuds and schisms beset his followers. Muhammad's daughter, Fatima was a Shi'a Muslim, massacred by orthodox Sunni Muslims. Fatima's son escaped, forming a heretical sect that suffered generations of internal splits. Ismailis were an unorthodox Shi'a sect, claiming to be the rightful heirs of Fatima, supported by a sizable following and powerful empire. In the tenth century they trailblazed across the Middle East, almost defeating the Sunni, but were suddenly halted when the Turkish Seljuk joined in, supporting the Sunni caliphs.

Decades later, Hasan bin Sabbah was born, converting to Fatimid-Ismailis in 1072. He travelled, visiting rulers' courts, collecting followers and narrowly escaping execution when a tower catastrophically collapsed, freaking out his captors as a bad omen. Eventually he acquired a fortress, Castle Alamut (Eagle's Nest), high in the Elburz Mountains. Here Sabbah founded his politico-religious death cult, the Order of Assassins, inventing a new approach to warfare. His dedicated followers were trained as elite killers – a crack suicide squad brainwashed into believing eternal martyrdom waited in heaven if they assassinated Hasan's political rivals. The castle overlooked lavish, Eden-like valleys, rare amid desert. Hasan enclosed and populated them with scores of sexy women, offering lavish feasts and other luxuries. Prior to his mission, each assassin was drugged and wafted there for a few days, believing he had visited Paradise. Then came the mission.

Assassins were trained to use various weapons – including a strangler's noose. Hasan selected political, religious and military opponents, dispatching Assassins, alone or paired, to infiltrate enemy palaces (usually as service staff). Gradually they gained the ruler's trust, and, at first opportunity, strangled, stabbed or poisoned their victim. Guards then killed most Assassins, yet they assassinated dozens of rulers, spreading fear and chaos.

Despite instigating many successful missions, Hasan never won the outright victory he yearned. Occupying his castle into old age, he was known as the Old Man of the Mountain. He died, leaving his castle to a small army of Assassins. Gradually they were captured and executed, or forced to flee Persia, disappearing by 1300. However in the years following the Old Man's death, many Assassins escaped to India. It is considered likely Assassins forged links with Thugs.

SUB-THUG GENRE

Are Thugs devout worshippers, believing this path offers eternal salvation, or ruthlessly efficient killer-robbers, after the loot and murdering victims to minimise the chance of capture? Perhaps they are just bad – group sadists and prototype sociopaths, regarding other people as objects to be manipulated.

Under interrogation, a Thug told Sleeman how victims were regarded

'. . . as victims thrown into our hands by the deity to be killed – and that we are the mere instruments in her hands to destroy them – and that if we do not kill them she will never again be propitious to us and we and our families will have to endure misery and want.'[7]

Despite social prejudice and legal prerogatives, from a scientific or philosophical perspective the abdication of free will is valid. However, the crux is not whether you are personally responsible for your actions, but that society must hold you responsible.

Thugs were engaged in a murderous, profit-motivated conspiracy with powerful establishment figures in wider society. The full extent is not known, but police, civil servants, landowners and even princes tipped off Thugs when wealthy merchants passed their jurisdiction. After murders, informants received a cut from proceeds.

Fanatical religious conviction coupled with economic necessity could motivate Thugs. But devotion is not suggested by their transgression of Kali's lore. Although Thugs were forbidden from killing holy men, Sleeman recounts an '*interview*' where one recalls encountering two wretched-looking priests in Kurnal village:

Cheyne Jamadar said: 'Were we not taken in by the fine clothes of the party we murdered near Mooltan? What profit then can we expect from travellers dressed in rags?'

'Such heresy!' said Runjeet. 'The goddess has put them into our hands and we have no right to let them go.'

'True – there is no reason to spare them,' nodded Bukshir, a celebrated strangler. 'I will give 100 rupees for their ponies and whatever other property they possess.' The ponies being worth about half this sum, the offer was thought sportsmanlike. The death of the holy men was decreed.[8]

The section describes the Thugs introducing themselves, tricking the priests into trusting and accompanying them on their journey. They lodge and feast together in a hotel, happily setting off together next morning; but the Thugs escort them to a previously selected spot where Cheyne gives the *Thirnee* (killing signal). The victims are strangled and the booty sorted, then the murderers continue their trek. Sleeman concludes:

Everyone was satisfied, and even those Thugs who stubbornly brought up the fact of Kali's law were persuaded by Cheyne Jamadar that they had undoubtedly brought the holy men a speedy passage to Paradise, so that no blame could be attached to the murder.[9]

Sleeman recounts 'interviews', published by his grandson James Sleeman, as *Thug, or a Million Murders* in 1920. Sir William Henry Sleeman is acknowledged as the Thuggee expert, and his chronicles became the focus of all subsequent accounts, sometimes embellished by Dr Robert Sherwood's observations.

This creates a priori problems regarding validity and interpretation. You may have noticed that Sleeman's frequent references to 'interviews' could be more accurately termed 'interrogations'. What should we make of this account? Sleeman, a British colonial military officer and self-confirmed Christian, spent most of his life serving in India, studying the 'Oriental' religion as a hobby (confident in his superior cultural perspective). He believed that he alone had uncovered an astonishing secret. He failed to find recognition from his peers, but obsessively pursued his quest. Finally, new, partisan incumbents expediently recognised his usefulness. One wonders what status his testimony would have in a contemporary court of law.

The only other *original* and revered work evidencing *Phansigars* is an essay by Robert Sherman, a doctor of medicine. Like Sleeman, he was a British colonial official of minor importance, serving in an alien, exotic land.

Both minor officials share an obscure concern for what they regarded as a monumental conspiracy, belittled by peers, confronted by broad social indifference and lack of interest; perhaps they share something with the Thugs, whose secret lives they find so seductive. Each is alienated; both are alien to their surrounding culture. A superior, civilising, colonial and reactive perspective burdens each: one with militaristic/Christian disciplines, the other with medical science – liberalising, progressive, edifying regimes. Both sense that hidden danger and regressive forces confront them, yet each is offered abundant information when enquiring directly. Each is determined to expose, categorise and explain every uncharted detail of this cultural distraction. Like the Thugs, they live predominately mundane, ordinary lives, but are sometimes intoxicated and excited when immersed in Thuggee history. Their claims of extracting confessions recall the Spanish Inquisition – from a time when European culture was ravaged by violence, murder, conspiracy, plague and greed; taking this for granted.

Although Thug activity as outlined by Sleeman and Sherwood is broadly corroborated in numerous witness statements or 'confessions', closer reading excludes objective potential. Their reports frequently contradict each other, each offering only his own transcripts of supposed confessions. The vernacular used therein is remarkably Anglicised, suggesting more about the authors than their topic or said 'confessors'.

Maybe Thug culture was tired, decadent and dying when discovered by Europeans, an anachronism past its sell-by date, waiting to be finally put out of its misery.

NOTES

1. This is WH Sleeman's estimate. Note that George L Bruce states this as, '40,000 murders in 1812 alone . . .' in *The Stranglers: The Cult of Thuggee and its Overthrow in British India*, London: 1969. However, in the Introduction to Taylor's *Confessions of a Thug*, Oxford University Press, 1939, Sleeman is quoted as estimating Thug murders at 40,000 a year, and this figure is stated by him as his estimate in the listed reports.
2. Alternative sources claim *Madras Literary Gazette* #9.
3. George L Bruce, *The Stranglers*, op. cit. p. 54. Bruce quotes from *Thug, or a Million Murders* by James Sleeman, 1920, but does not list publisher/page details. However, James Sleeman quotes from his grandfather's recorded interviews: 'Thuggee and Dacoity File Archives', the India Office Library, Ramaseeana, or 'A Vocabulary of the Peculiar Language Used by the Thugs; Report on Budhuk alias Bagree Dacoits and other Gang Robbers by Hereditary Profession; Report of the Depredations Committed by the Thug Gangs', by William Henry Sleeman and

associates. Note that none of these books/documents are currently in print.

4. Friedrich Nietzsche, *The Birth of Tragedy*, New York: Dover Thrift Editions, 1995, pp. 26–7.
5. William Sargant, *Battle for the Mind*, London: Pan Books Ltd, 1959, p. 121.
6. Erich Fromm, *The Anatomy of Human Destructiveness*, London: Jonathon Cape, 1974, pp. 289–90.
7. George L Bruce, *The Stranglers: The Cult of Thuggee and Its Overthrow in British India*, London: Longmans, 1969, p. 49.
8. Ibid.
9. Ibid. p. 50.

BIBLIOGRAPHY

George L Bruce, *The Stranglers: The Cult of Thuggee and its Overthrow in British India*, London: Longmans, 1969.

Erich Fromm, *The Anatomy of Human Destructiveness*, London: Jonathon Cape, 1974.

Charles Malamoud, 'Indian Speculations about the Sex of the Sacrifice', in Michel Feher, *Zone – Fragments for a History of the Human Body Part One*, New York: Urzone, 1989.

Philip Meadows Taylor, *Confessions of a Thug* (semifactual novel), Oxford: Oxford University Press, 1939.

Friedrich Nietzsche, *The Birth of Tragedy*, New York: Dover Thrift Editions, 1995.

William Sargant, *Battle for the Mind*, London: Pan Books Ltd, 1959.

James Sleeman, *Thug, or a Million Murders*, 1920.

Colin Wilson, *The Mammoth Book of Murder*, London: Robinson, 1990.

Rex Warner, Foreword, *Encyclopedia of World Mythology*, London: Octopus, 1975.

The Bhagavad Gita (trans. Julian Mascaro), London: Penguin, 1962.

The Upanishads (trans. Julian Mascaro), London: Penguin, 1962.

ARCHIVES

South and Southeast Asia (leaflet), copyright the British Museum, 1998.

Thuggee and Dacoity File Archives, the India Office Library, Ramaseeana, or A Vocabulary of the Peculiar Language Used by the Thugs; Report on Budhuk alias Bagree Dacoits and other Gang Robbers by Hereditary Profession; Report of the Depredations Committed by the Thug Gangs, by William Henry Sleeman and associates.

ELECTRONIC AND INTERNET

The New Oxford Dictionary of English, CD-ROM, Oxford University Press, 2000.

Encarta, CD-ROM, Microsoft, 1996.

Mind of a Serial Killer, CD-ROM, Kozel, 1995.

The Art of Making Wolves From Human Skulls pt:7, Eugine Macer Story, 1999.

Kali, Patricia Monaghan, www.kalimandir.org.

2. DEATH SPIRAL OF THE ASSASSINS

MONTE CAZAZZA AND MARZY QUAYZAR

Nothing is forbidden, everything is permitted.
— Hasan bin Sabbah

Those who remember the past are condemned to watch others repeat it.
— Jim Morton

Peace, n. In international affairs, a period of cheating between two periods of of fighting.
— Ambrose Bierce, *The Devil's Dictionary*

What is reality? What is Illusion?
— Wizard of Gore

Assassin: a member of a secret terrorist sect of Muslims of the 11th to 13th century who killed their political enemies as a religious duty while allegedly under the influence of hashish.

History doesn't repeat itself, it's man that does.

Once upon a time in the north of Persia, hidden high in the mountains among the clouds, was an impregnable fortress called the Eagle's Nest, or Alamut. Inside this fortress resided 'the Old Man of the Mountain', Hasan bin Sabbah[1], the spiritual father and founder of an ancient secret fraternity of members of the Muhamma-dan Ismaili sect named 'The Assassins'. Hasan bin Sabbah created a 'Garden of Paradise' in a lush valley below the castle:

> Except for God's sincere servants;
> for them awaits a known provision,
> fruits — and they high honoured

in the Gardens of Bliss
upon couches, set face to face,
a cup from a spring being passed round to them,
white, a delight to the drinkers,
wherein no sickness is, neither intoxication;
and with them wide-eyed maidens
restraining their glances
as if they were hidden pearls [Koran: XXXVII: 40]

Hasan bin Sabbah convinced his followers that this magic garden was Heaven on Earth, giving them a taste of Paradise and promising them that he could return them there if they would obey his every command and sacrifice themselves if called to do so. Dressed in their white tunics and red sashes, and armed with poison and daggers of solid gold, they journeyed out into the Muslim world like the cobras and scorpions of the desert to strike terror into the hearts of Hasan bin Sabbah's enemies.

The gardens reflected the lushness of Cairo in a landscape of mostly craggy rocks constructed in a remote and well-guarded ravine. One interpretation of 'assassin' says it is derived from *Hashassin* or hashish eaters. Supposedly, young converts were given a drink spiked with hashish and slept for three days. During this time of unconsciousness they were carried into the gardens and, when they awoke, their blindfolds were removed and the drugged peasants were confronted with an intoxicating vision of running brooks, exotic plants and animals and shapely *houris* (dancing girls). It was filled with palaces and pavilions, the most elegant that could be imagined, where wine, milk and honey flowed. They were in the midst of maidens who would perform their every desire. After a few days of this they were drugged again and removed from 'Paradise'. They never knew how they entered the garden, or when they had emerged from it, and their experiences all seemed like a dream, but a vision of such power and reality that they were fully convinced that they had actually been in Paradise.

When the initiate awoke, back in the everyday world, Hasan himself announced that this world he had visited was the Paradise promised in the Koran and the initiate would be rewarded if he would follow him unto death. Initiates were told to die doing the will of Allah, as a martyrdom would automatically grant them entry back to Paradise. This created a loyal cult of followers who were willing to do anything, thus ensuring total blind obedience. There is a green valley at Alamut that still exists today.

> The old man kept at his court such boys of twelve years old as seemed to him destined to become courageous men. When the old man sent them into the garden in groups of four, ten or twenty, he gave them hashish to drink. They slept for three days, then they were carried sleeping into the garden where he had them awakened. When these young men woke, and found themselves in the garden with all these marvellous things, they truly believed themselves to be in paradise. And these damsels were always with them in songs and great entertainment; they received everything they asked for, so that they would never have left that garden of their own will. And when the Old Man wished to kill someone, he would take him and say, 'Go and do this thing. I do this because I want to make you return to paradise'. And the assassins go and

perform the deed willingly. [Marco Polo, on his visit to Alamut in 1273]

The Ancient Art of Imposture, by Abdel-Rahman of Damascus, describes another one of Hasan's conjuring tricks. Hasan had a deep, narrow pit sunk into the floor of his audience chamber. One of his disciples stood in this, so that his head and neck alone were visible above the floor. A circular dish in two pieces with a hole in the middle was fitted around the disciple's neck.

Hasan poured fresh blood around the head to make it more gruesome and this gave the illusion that there was a severed head on a metal plate on the floor. Recruits to the assassins were brought in. 'Tell them what thou hast seen,' ordered Hasan. The disciple then described all the delights of Paradise he had seen. Hasan then said, 'You have seen the head of a man who died that you knew. I have reanimated him to speak with his own tongue to you.' Later the disciple was actually killed and decapitated and his head stuck where the faithful would see it. This staged illusion, plus murder, created a miracle in the mind of the faithful and increased their belief in the power of martyrdom.

Hasan's elite killers were known as *Fida'is*, or 'Devoted Ones', also 'Men of Sacrifice' or 'Destroying Angels'. These were blind fanatics who, armed with dagger and poison, struck at caliphs, emirs and viziers and even the Christian Crusaders.

Of course it wasn't just the use of hashish that flipped an adept around, '*Assesseen*' in Arabic also signifies guardians and some commentaries have considered this to be the true origin of the word; 'guardians of the secrets' [Arkon Daraul, *Secret Societies*]

Every member of this Ismaili sect was rigorously taught mathematics, philosophy, astrology, alchemy and, of course, given thorough teaching of the Holy Koran, including the esoteric doctrines of Islam. The Ismaili believed that creation began with the intellectual world, moved then to the person's soul and finally united at death with the rest of creation. Hasan taught that the human soul was imprisoned in the body to carry out the teacher's orders, re-joining the universal soul at death. Emphasis was placed on the concept of Paradise, within which resided gardens of pleasure which were the reward of every true follower who died for the Islamic cause as set down by the master. This belief made the murderous suicidal missions mystical, and easier for the martyrs to accept, believing that they would then enter the Kingdom of Paradise.

Hasan bin Sabbah's power and the fanatical devotion of his *Fida'is* came from the transcendental dualistic nature of an absolute god who possessed both total creative and destructive power. And the Imam himself demanded absolute faith and obedience because he was an absolute teacher. Adepts were recruited with the promise that they were to receive hidden power and timeless wisdom both in life and death, and might become as important as their teachers. The adepts had to pass through nine degrees of initiation. These included having the students doubt all teachings they had been previously taught and to rely totally on their new teacher/teachers, Imams, who would impart secret knowledge of the real truth after they would swear a vow of total obedience.

The Imam was the only one who really understood the true inner meanings of Islam, not just the outer trappings of Islamic faith. The adepts learned the secrets of the Seven Imams and Seven Prophetic Periods, as well as the concept that Muhammad was not the last of the prophets and that the Koran, which only the Imams could interpret correctly for them, was not Allah's final revelation to man. They were taught the laws of Islam dealing with prayer, alms and fasting and that pilgrimage, or hajj, was for the common and unenlightened to keep them under control; that they could be abandoned by the accolytes because the prophets would show them the true dualistic nature called the Pre-existent and the Subsequent, which had no name and could not be predicted or worshipped.

Once the adepts reached the final ninth stage of initiation they could abandon dogmatic Islam because now they were free, true philosophers who could adopt any system or systems of beliefs that would serve them in their spiritual quest. The ninth degree brought the revelation of the secret that there was no such thing as belief: 'All that mattered was action. And the only possessor of the reasons for carrying out any action was the chief of the sect'.[2]

Hasan bin Sabbah was born around 1034 at Qumm, located about 240 kilometres (150 miles) south of modern-day Tehran, but spent his childhood in Rayy, which is a suburb of the city today. His father, Hasan bin Aly bin Mohammed bin Ja'far bin Husayn bin Sabbah al-Hamari, an immigrant from Yemen, who was also a prominent leader of the Ashari faith, took a keen interest in Hasan's education and home-schooled him from the age of seven to seventeen. Hasan excelled in the prevailing subjects of mathematics, philosophy and languages. Following this, he went to law school and, under the tutelage of Imam Mowaffak, was joined by two other students who would go on to achieve considerable eminence: the great poet-astrologer Omar Khayy'am and Nizam-al-Mulk, who would become the vizier to Sultan Alp Arslan.

Nizam-al-Mulk recalls in his testament that students were so sure that fame and fortune were in their destiny that they made a solemn vow that whoever attained this first would in turn share equally with the other two. The years passed and Nizam was the first to achieve this by ascending to the elevated position of vizier. Omar returned first and asked for a quiet place to pursue his studies and devote his life to science and the arts. The relieved Nizam immediately granted this request and gave him a house in Naishapur and a pension by which to live. Hasan was more ambitious: although offered an Islamic province to govern, he refused, believing he was destined for a post in the King's court, as he envied the post of vizier.

Hasan bin Sabbah was naturally inclined towards hard work and, possessing extraordinary intelligence, gained favour quickly. Soon Nizam-al-Mulk became worried about his own position in the court and started plotting against Hasan and poisoning the ears of the Sultan against him. The Sultan ordered the arrest of Hasan. And had Hasan not endeared himself to the Sultan he would have probably been executed and met his end there, but he was allowed to escape.

Hasan bin Sabbah fled to Rayy. Before he became an important influence in Islam, Iran was the centre of the Shiite offshoot, differing from the Sunni or orthodox Muslims. There were many interpretations of the Holy Koran, and each little sect had its own version of 'the truth'. The Shiite were a breakaway sect from the orthodox Sunni, and the Ismaili were a breakaway sect from the Shiite. When the sixth Imam died his oldest son, Ismail, was passed over and the younger Musa was appointed as Imam. The Ismaili were Muslims who believed that Ismail was the true Imam.

It was during this time when Hasan was 35 or 36, in about 1071, that a strong religious impulse led him to examine the many branches of Islam. He finally converted to the Ismaili sect, although he was hesitant at first (the Ismaili being generally regarded as heretics and outcasts). After suffering a serious illness, he made his decision. Afraid that he would die before learning 'the True Path to Islam' he swore allegiance to Fatimid Caliph in 1072.

Hasan bin Sabbah was drawn to the Ismaili by their intellectual force and religious fervour. He began preaching and spreading the Ismaili faith and this almost assuredly is what forced his ousting from Rayy in 1074, when Hasan bin Sabbah headed for Cairo, a city built by the Ismaili to serve as their capital. This journey took several years, with Sabbah finally reaching Egypt in 1078–9.

Impressing the Caliph, he became an ardent supporter of Nizam, the Caliph's eldest son. But Hasan's revolutionary temperament got him into trouble, and he was arrested and sentenced to prison. No sooner had he entered the prison at Dumyat than a minaret collapsed, an accident that was interpreted as a holy omen, and as a result Hasan bin Sabbah was believed to be a divinely protected person. The Caliph released Hasan, exiling him from Cairo and giving him many valuable gifts, which he later used for setting up his 'paradise'. Hasan was then put on a ship sailing from Alexandria and in 1081 landed in Isfahan in northwest Africa.

During this journey another interesting situation arose. The ship was seized by a terrible storm and everyone on board – captain, crew and passengers – was terrified that they were going to perish. Everyone but Hasan fell down on their knees and began praying. Hasan calmly stood on deck and explained that he could not die until he had fulfilled his destiny. He said, 'The storm is my doing: how can I pray that it abate? I have indicated the pleasure of the Almighty. If we sink I shall not die, for I am immortal. If you want to be saved believe in me, and I shall subdue the winds.'

At first no one believed him, but, as the ship seemed on the verge of capsizing and sinking, some desperate passengers came to him and swore eternal allegiance. Hasan bin Sabbah's devout self-belief enabled him to remain calm until the violent storm subsided, upon which Hasan instantly took credit for saving everyone from certain death. The ship then sailed on to the sea coast of Syria, where Hasan disembarked along with two of the ship's passengers, who became his first real disciples. Thus was the start of Hasan's fulfilling his own prophetic words. During a tirade upon his exile from the King's court he declared, 'If I had two, just two, devotees who would stand by me, then I could cause the downfall of that Turk and that peasant!' – Sultan Malik Shaw and his old friend, Vizier Nizam-al-Mulk.

At this point Hasan became a wandering missionary, or *dais*, first going to Baghdad and then into the Persian countryside, converting people to his cause. Once he made a disciple he used that disciple to proselytise and create more disciples, building his pyramid scheme of power. His ever-widening circles rippled out and became the breeding ground for his army of *Fida'is*, or self-sacrificers, who were taken from his most promising and loyal followers. And so was created a secret society based on the secret teachings of the Egyptian Ismaili.

* * *

Alamut is located north of modern-day Tehran, on the south side of the Alborz mountain range, approximately halfway between Tehran and the Caspian Sea. There are two stories concerning Hasan bin Sabbah's appropriation of Alamut. One reveals his use of deception, and both show his strategic skills. One of Hasan's lieutenants, Hussein Kahini, found the fortress of Alamut, which was under the governance of Ali Mahdi, and realised this would make a fantastic headquarters for their society. It was set in the remote and forbidding Alborz Mountains but was close enough to the important cities of Kazwin and Rayy. The formidable castle was first built in AD 861.

Coveting it, Hasan bin Sabbah developed a plan, sending his preachers into the castle. He converted some of its inhabitants and then had more of his men infiltrate the castle. Hasan had them enter in disguise and before Governor Ali Mahdi realised it he was overwhelmed and had to surrender the castle. Hasan then paid him 3,000 gold dinars for the castle. Another version of the legend states that Hasan bin Sabbah asked Ali Mahdi to be granted all the land that could be covered by the hide of an ox. He then proceeded to cut the skin into a very fine strip long enough to encompass the castle of Alamut, thus gaining ownership. Whatever the case, the year was 1090, Hasan bin Sabbah was 56 and Alamut was secured.

Now having possession of the fortress, Hasan bin Sabbah attacked the Emir's troops. And because the ruling Turks were hated by the local people he was able to convert the locals and gain more soldiers with everyone obeying his authority alone. Then, village by village, castle by castle, he rippled out through the countryside, taking over more forts through the use of any tactic he could devise: infiltration, direct attacks, forays, poison, stabbings, bribery, whatever would accomplish his goal.

In 1092 Hasan plotted the death of his greatest enemy, Vizier Nizam-al-Mulk. One of Hasan's adepts, Bu Tahir Arrani, volunteered. Disguising himself as a Sufi holy man, Bu Tahir Arrani was allowed to approach Nizam-al-Mulk, then stabbed Nizam to death during Ramadan. Nizam's guards then killed the assassin. Hasan said, 'The killing of this devil is the beginning of bliss.'

Next, Emperor Malik Shah, who had sent troops against Hasan, died of a suspected poisoning. Then one of Nizam's sons, Fakhri, was stabbed to death by a beggar seeking for alms, who conned him by saying, 'The true Muslims are no more and there are none left to take the hand of the afflicted.' When Fakhri took the beggar's hand he was rewarded with a dagger through the heart. Another one of Nizam's sons, Ahmed, tried to lay siege to Alamut, but was unsuccessful, and he too was later attacked by an assassin, although he survived the stabbing. Many more political enemies were assassinated, and even rival religious leaders were attacked. One was stabbed while he was praying in a mosque while his bodyguard was standing immediately behind him.

One opponent woke up with a knife stuck next to his head and decided to make peace with the Assassins when he received a message from Hasan saying, 'That dagger just as easily could have been stuck in your heart.' In Syria in 1103, Janah Al Danalauh, the Emir of Homs, was murdered as he prayed in the mosque. In 1106 Khalaf, the ruler of the citadel at Afamiya, was murdered. When a group of Assassins brought the horse, shield and armour of a Crusader enemy to Khalaf, he let them enter his fortress, where they patiently waited, and watched for their moment to strike, dispatching Khalaf to the next world.

But not every attack was a certain victory. One sultan, Muhammad Tapar, seized an Assassin fort located at Isfahan and had the Assassin leaders there flayed alive. In 1118 the Sultan besieged Alamut and it seemed that the Eagle's Nest was finally ready to fall, when, in a drastic turn of events, the Sultan died. The Sultan's army, having been dealt a mortal blow to their morale, returned home. Hasan and the Ismaili Assassins were saved.

Then, in May 1124, Hasan bin Sabbah, the Old Man of The Mountain, sole ruler of Alamut, the grand master who had not left his mountain fortress in over thirty years; Hasan, who from his high castle commanded fanatical obedience and had sent out his Assassins, the masters of disguise and murder, who would sacrifice their very lives to do his bidding, finally died at the age of ninety.

This was not the end for the Assassins. Hasan had appointed Kiya Bozorg-Ummid (the Great Hope) as his successor. He reigned for fourteen years, expanding into Syria, and it was the stories from the Syrian branch, who fought against the Crusaders, that were brought back to Europe, which placed the word 'assassin' into language and legend.

In 1192 the Syrian Grand Master Sinan sent two of his killers disguised as monks into the camp of the Christian knight Conrad of Montferrat and he was stabbed to death. After this murder the Assassins began to figure in every historical chronicle of the Third

Crusade. Saladin, the great Egyptian enemy of the Crusaders, had threatened Sinan. The Grand Master sent a messenger back to him. Saladin had the messenger thoroughly searched. Then the messenger turned to the two guards watching over the Egyptian Sultan and said, 'If I were to order you to kill Saladin, would you do it?' The guards drew their swords. The messenger made his point, then the three bowed and left. Saladin decided to establish friendly relations with the Assassins.

Henry Count of Champagne reported that an Assassin Grand Master gave him a demonstration of the complete obedience of his adepts. As Henry was watching, two white-robed men came and stood on the ramparts of the castle. The Grand Master then made a signal. Instantly they threw up their hands and hurled themselves to their death below.

The master asked Henry, 'Could you command the same?' This might have been a staged piece of macabre theatre, to frighten their enemies, which would fit the Assassins' style. But the Fida'is were certainly prepared to sacrifice their lives, and demonstrations like this enabled them to sow the seeds of fear and spread their myth, not only in the Middle East but all through Europe.

But in 1256 the Assassins could not stop the conquering Mongol hordes led by Hulagu Khan, who, like the deadly desert wind, swept away everything before them. And the last Grand Master of the Assassins, Rukin-ad-Din, surrendered to the Mongols at Maymun-Diz and he and 12,000 men were put to death in a very gruesome manner. There had been more than sixty castles and the Mongols totally dismantled every Ismaili fortification. All their scientific instruments were destroyed, their libraries burned and everything of value ransacked. No trace was left and the Assassins became but a fairy tale riding on the desert wind.

Has the Assassin legend, with its history of devoted martyr killers with heaven as their reward, reached down through time? Did it influence Ayatollah Khomeini when, during the Iran–Iraq War, from which there were a million casualties, he declared, 'War can be as holy as prayer when it is fought for the sake of defending Islam'? Did it influence the Iranians as they employed the 'Basij human wave' attack led by thousands of boy-soldier volunteers who cleared the minefields by walking right over them and drawing enemy fire while rushing with rocket launchers and hand grenades, fighting Saddam Hussein's dug-in Iraqi army? Does it influence the Palestinian suicide bombers or gunmen whose tactics of assassination are their only military tools in their struggle against Israel because conventional military resources are lacking?

It is interesting to note that Osama bin Laden's father, Muhammad, under the bin Laden Corporation, refurbished and rebuilt the two holy mosques in Mecca and Medina. He and Osama were both deeply religiously affected by the opportunity of coming in contact with and being responsible for the reconstruction of Islam's holiest sites. The al-Qaeda organisation definitely drew inspiration from the Assassins in mirroring the structure of the cell system of organisation, which sets up compact action groups in a network but isolates the individual cells from each other for their own protection in case of capture. These cells are controlled from a central command through a chain of blind links so that they are extremely difficult to trace back to the central command. Osama even seems to mimic Hasan bin

Sabbah in that Osama was the hidden man in his hidden fortress in Afghanistan, waging his own holy war against the infidels, using his own martyrs in his interpretation of Jihad. He sent sleeper agents such as Mohammad Atta, Mohammad Jaweed, Ayub ali Khan, Marwan al Shehhri and fifteen others, to be trained at flight schools, melt into the US, be quiet neighbours, collect the data needed, lie in wait till the moment to strike was perfect, and then, with deadly accuracy, execute their orders with military precision, catching the intelligence agencies with their pants down.

Wherever you may be, death will overtake you, though you should be in raised-up towers. [Koran IV: 80]

Both the World Trade Center and the Pentagon were specifically singled out for destruction because they represented the economic and military power of the United States. The first attack in 1993 – using a whole truckload of explosives and engineered by Ramzi Youssef and Sheik Omar Abdul Rahman – fell short of its intended goal, whereas the second attack succeeded when the nineteen terrorists with knowledge, teamwork and armed only with box cutters hijacked four planes, turning them into human-guided flying bombs holding 20,000 gallons of jet fuel burning at 2,000 degrees Celsius as they crashed. The terrorist pilots martyred and cremated themselves in an imagined blaze of glory. The concept of jihad, sometimes thought of as the unofficial sixth pillar of Islam, literally means 'striving'. Militant Islamists use it to describe 'a holy war against the enemies of Islam'. In a book entitled *America and the Third World War* Osama bin Laden calls for a 'Global

Jihad' against the United States: 'There must be a global uprising against the existing world order to fight for the right to live as Muslims – rights which are being trampled by westernisation. There can be no compromise or coexistence with western civilization.' Mysticism, militancy and the quest for perpetual jihad have become the rallying cry of the latest generation of Muslim leaders.

Pakistani Brigadier SK Malik in his 1979 book *The Quranic Concept of War* said: 'The Quranic way of war is infinitely supreme to and more effective than any other form of warfare because: In Islam a war is fought for the cause of Allah and therefore all means and forms are justified and righteous'. Terrorism, Malik argued,

is the quintessence of the Islamic strategy for war . . . Terror struck into the hearts of the enemies is not only a means, it is the end in itself. Once a condition of terror into the opponent's heart is obtained hardly anything is left to be achieved. It is the point where the means and the end meet and merge. Terror is not a means of imposing decision upon the enemy, it is the decision we wish to impose upon him.

In the book *Terrorism is the Solution*, Mustafa Kamil writes:

Terrorism is the means for calling on the oppressed to terrorize the tyrants. Terrorism is the sole viable effective means for stopping the enslavement of mankind, the unfair killing of the oppressed on earth, the corruption of man and land, and the proliferation of destructive weapons that are used by tyrants.

Added to this is the fanatical idea that the Koran contains all the truth needed in order to guide the believer in this world and let him enter Paradise, and that jihad will last to the Day of Judgment. This creates eternal targets in a war in which the whole world is the battlefront in which Islamic terrorists will die in order to kill, putting them beyond all reprisals.

What difference does it make whether you are being bombed from 10,000 feet with a daisycutter or smart bomb, or whether a cruise missile or a 767 is crashing into where you are standing, if you are the collateral damage on the receiving end? Is there a historical co-evolution of terrorism, with the macro-terrorism of the developed countries' military/industrial complexes against the micro-terrorism of the less developed nations, using whatever weapons and tactics they can employ, many of which are being supplied by the developed nations? The superpowers have developed a strategy of taking advantage of struggles for independence and any other disputes in order to keep an escalating arms industry operating. As Tom Gervasi in *Arsenal of Democracy* elegantly stated:

> In order to arm ourselves we really have to arm the world. We have to have longer production runs of equipment so that we can buy what we need, for our Air Force, Army, or Navy. We've got to produce much more armaments to get it down to the price we'd like to pay. The manufacturers really have you blackmailed in that he sets the price. Then we find ourselves unable to buy enough if we don't sell even more to someone else. So there's a great internal need to find a market abroad.

It doesn't really matter if this market changes from friend to foe or back again, because without this shell game continuing the next generation of military equipment cannot be developed. Perhaps it was not a slip of the tongue when President George Bush Jr called the War on Terror a 'crusade'. If one looks at history one will see that the First Crusade in 1096 was called for by Pope Urban II in order to recover the Holy Land from its Islamic rulers, and any Crusaders who died were considered martyrs and assured by the Roman Catholic Church their place in heaven.

The Assassins combined the techniques of guerrilla warfare with unique fundamentalist religious beliefs. Nearly one millennium later, Islamic fundamentalists such as al-Qaeda are believed to have attempted to purchase special chemical/biological agents. Osama bin Laden is reported to have spent over $30 million in an effort to get a nuclear suitcase bomb from the former Soviet Union and nuclear material from Pakistan, with possible help from some members of the Inter Service Intelligence Service of Pakistan. With nuclear proliferation the world is faced with states whose governments increasingly espouse forms of religious fundamentalism leading to the emergence of the Zionist, Islamic and Hindu nuclear states alongside the already existing communist, former-communist and capitalist Christian nuclear powers. In a world that Hasan bin Sabbah would probably recognise, God explodes in mysterious ways.

NOTES
1. Note that all spellings are in their most common Anglicised form.
2. Arkon Daraul, *A History of Secret Societies*, New York: Pocket Books, 1969.

BIBLIOGRAPHY

AJ Arberry, *The Koran Interpreted*, New York: Macmillan Company, 1955.

Yossef Bodansky, *Bin Laden: The Man Who Declared War on America*, New York: Random House, Inc., 1999, 2001.

Edward Burman, *The Assassins: Holy Killers of Islam*, Northamptonshire: Crucible Books/Aquarian Press, 1987.

Arkon Daraul, *A History of Secret Societies*, New York: Pocket Books, 1969.

Cyril Glasse, *Concise Encyclopedia of Islam*, London: HarperCollins, 1991.

Tom Gervasi, *Arsenal of Democracy III: America's War Machine*, New York: Grove Press, 1984.

HAR Gubb, and JH Kramers, *Shorter Encyclopedia of Islam*, New York: Cornell University Press, 1953.

Albert A Hopkins, *Magic Stage Illusions, Special Effects and Trick Photography*, New York: Dover Publications, Inc., 1976.

Dilip Hiro, *The Longest War: The Iran-Iraq Military Conflict*, New York: Routledge, Chapman and Hall Inc., 1991.

Bernard Lewis, *The Assassins*, London: Octagon Books, 1980.

Baqer. Moin, *Khomeini, Life of the Ayatollah*, New York: Thomas Dunne Books, 1999.

David Munro, *The Four Horsemen: The Flames of War in the Third World*, New Jersey: Lyle Stuart Inc., 1987.

JM Roberts, *The Penguin History of Europe*, Harmondsworth: Penguin Books, 1996.

Professor Keith Simpson, *The Mysteries of Life and Death, An Illustrated Investigation into the Incredible World of Death*, London: Salamander Books Ltd, 1979.

Freya Stark, *The Valleys of the Assassins and Other Persian Tales*, London: John Murray Pub., 1934.

Colin Wilson, *The Mammoth Book of the History of Murder*, New York: Carroll and Graf Pub. Inc., 2000.

3. CUT 'EM OFF

THE SKOPTSY

MICHAEL SPANN

On 26 March 1997, the Heaven's Gate sect joined an infamous list of religious groups whose members had committed mass suicide in the name of their faith. But what shocked the public even more than the 39 deaths was the fact that most of the male members of the sect had been castrated. In terms of castration, however, the Heaven's Gate sect will always be small fry compared with the Skoptsy, an ecstatic Russian castration cult that had, at the height of its popularity in the mid-1800s, 100,000 to 200,000 members spread across Russia, the Balkans and Romania.

In fact, the strange and terrible saga that is religious history is filled with examples of genital mutilation practised as a religious ritual across a variety of cultures.[1] It can even be argued that every day countless people, including many children, are subjected to the mutilation of their genitalia as Jews, Christians and Muslims, and others circumcise both male and female according to their beliefs.

In AD 208, one of the foremost leaders and teachers of the early Christian church, Origen of Alexandria, took the words of Matthew 19:12 ('and there be eunuchs, which have made themselves eunuchs for the kingdom of heaven's sake') literally and castrated himself in order to help in his religious instruction of females. In AD 250, Valesius the scholar founded the first Christian community of castrates. And there are 72 eunuchs in the list of saints . . . Further afield, various groups of Aborigines in the central Australian desert are known to practise sub-incision (where the urethra is sliced from the glans to the scrotum on the underside of the penis) as one of the highest levels of their initiatory rites. In India, the infamous sect of eunuchs, the *hijara*, are castrated; reports say that some are kidnapped and forcibly castrated, in an attempt to get closer to their goddess, Behuchara.[2] Another goddess cult still practised in India worships Radha, the consort of Krishna. Like the *hijara*, this all-male sect wear saris and make-up as they attempt to become the goddess Radha and, ultimately, achieve a mystical sexual union with Krishna. The initiation into this sect is particularly painful as new initiates have their testicles crushed between two rocks.

Even further back in history, one of the favourite deities of the Phoenician populace was Eshmun, the beautiful God of Spring, who castrated himself in order to avoid the advances of the Mother Goddess, Astronae. Following this tack of a lust-filled Mother Goddess leading to castration, it is worth exploring two other ancient sects that can be compared to the Skoptsy in the sense that they combined ecstatic religious fervour and castration as central components of their religion.

In Syria the temple of Astarte at Hierapolis, with its castrated priests, was one of the most popular in the East. At the beginning of spring, pilgrims from as far afield as Babylonia and Arabia flocked to the temple to watch the bloody proceedings.

> flutes played, the drums beat, and the eunuch
> priests slashed themselves with knives, the
> religious excitement gradually spread like a wave

among the crowd of onlookers . . . man after man,
his veins throbbing with the music, his eyes
fascinated by the streaming blood, flung his
garments from him . . . and seizing one of the
swords which stood ready for the purpose,
castrated himself on the spot.[3]

The bloodied genitalia would then be thrown into a
residence as the ecstatic initiate ran madly through the
streets. The household that was honoured in this way
would be required to outfit the castrated initiate with
female clothes and jewellery, which would be worn for
the rest of his life.

In Phrygia (modern-day Turkey) the cult of Attis
made castration essential for its priesthood.[4] Attis was
believed to have been a shepherd of unnatural beauty
and, because of this, was lusted after by Cybele, the
Mother of the Gods. As befits an ancient fertility cult
that was 'exported' to both Greece and Rome, there are
various versions as to what happened between Cybele
and Attis. One particularly savage yet slightly confusing
version is that Cybele was a wild hermaphrodite called
Agdistis. Because of Cybele/Agdistis's lewd behaviour
and irregular anatomy, the gods were fearful of this wild
creature and sought to bring it back to the field.

Drinking from a spring that the gods had sneakily
added wine to, Cybele/Agdistis became drunk and
passed out. While he/she was in a stupor, a cord made
of bristles was slipped around Cybele/Agdistis's male
genitalia with the other end around his/her foot. Upon
awakening, Cybele/Agdistis began to prance around but
in doing so ripped off his/her male genitalia. A tree
sprouted in the place of the fallen 'unmentionables', and
the daughter of the River God, Sangario, picked a piece

of fruit from the tree and put it on her breast. Miraculously, Attis was conceived! A few years later, Attis was to marry a young princess when, lo and behold, Cybele/Agdistis showed up at the ceremony and drove the wedding party mad. In the frenzy Attis castrated himself, as did the father of the bride.

The cult of Attis was introduced into Rome in 204 BC and, not surprisingly, proved to be very popular with the castrated priests of the sect, the Gallae, very common on the streets of Rome. Every year, the sect engaged in a festival that featured, on 24 March, the Day of Blood. On this day, novices in the sect acted out the fate of Attis and castrated themselves. Then, with their senses swept away by the pain, music and dancing, they threw their mangled virility against the image of Cybele that hung in the temple.

As history shows, there has never been a shortage of people willing to 'cut 'em off' in their quest for salvation and transcendence.

The Skoptsy came into existence in Russia in the eighteenth century – a product of a major schism in the Russian Orthodox Church. In an attempt to update ecclesiastical ritual and liturgy, the Orthodox Church imposed a number of reforms. These seemingly trivial reforms – e.g. making the sign of the cross with three instead of two fingers – angered many devout Russians, who took these reforms as a sign that the Antichrist was coming. Quite simply, many felt that any deviation from the strict adherence to the 'old ways' would put their immortal souls in danger, and so they refused the reforms. The group that clung obstinately to the 'old ways' and refused the reforms became known as the 'Old Believers'.

In Tsarist Russia, any rebellion against the Orthodox Church was an act of rebellion against the State, and the

Church acted accordingly, persecuting and punishing the 'rebels' harshly. Hundreds of thousands of peasants fled into the inhospitable Russian wilderness to set up communities. Those who couldn't or wouldn't flee chose martyrdom. Whole villages barricaded themselves away and starved to death or self-immolated rather than accept the reforms. The intensity of the Old Believers' conviction is demonstrated by the fact that twenty thousand Old Believers burned themselves alive in the first five years after the implementation of the reforms.

This rebellion about the question of true faith, combined with the fact that a huge number of people had no central governing body such as the Orthodox Church to guide them for the first time in their lives, meant that the wilds of Russia became a fertile breeding ground for sects. There was an explosion of peasant sects quite unlike anything seen before or since. And with the peasants' mixture of paganism, folklore, orthodoxy, mysticism and delusion there were seemingly no limits one could bring to the Christian faith. The range of sects a peasant could choose from was staggering – everything from worshipping a hole in the roof to participating in orgies. These new sects themselves were highly unstable, fragmenting and exploding off each other like a mutating virus. One of the sects that grew from this fertile environment and rose to prominence was the Khlysty sect. Loosely translated this can mean either 'the People of God' or 'Christ Believers'.

The Khlysty is still the best known of the Russian peasant sects, achieving its historical notoriety for three things. First, their name is said to be a distorted form of the verb, 'to flagellate'. But there is no documentation to substantiate the claim that flagellation was a central part of their doctrine. Secondly, it was widely believed that the Khlysty engaged in bloody child sacrifice. It was reported by Melnikov in 1869 that a young woman would be venerated as the Mother of God and impregnated by the leader of the particular Khlysty 'ship' (the Khlysty called their groups 'ships' and they were said to sail across the 'sea of sin'). After she had been impregnated, her left breast would be removed as part of a *radenie* (an ecstatic prayer session) and eaten communally. If a daughter was born, it would be brought up as her mother's successor but if it was a boy-child it was considered to be a 'little Christ'. On the sixth day after its birth this 'little Christ', in an imitation of Jesus being killed on the cross, was ritually murdered by having a spear thrust into the left side of his tiny body. The spilled blood was shared communally and the body was crushed and dried, then made into a powder and used in the communion bread. But, as with the rumours of flagellation, there is no witness documentation that such ritual murders took place.[5] Thirdly, some of the more extreme Khlysty 'ships' engaged in orgies and licentious sex. 'If sinners might comfort themselves with the pleasures of the flesh, surely we the just and the righteous are the more to be forgiven for doing what we do out of necessity, one believer told an official enquiry into the sect.[6] Indeed the 'mad monk' Rasputin was said to have formed some of his religosexual philosophies after coming into contact with wandering Khlysty preachers.[7]

The Khlysty were a mystical ascetic sect who had as the centrepiece of their faith the belief in the 'Holy Spirit'. They renounced sex, marriage, profanity, alcohol, family ties, tobacco and theft – 'if you steal a penny; in the other world this penny will be put on the top of your head and when it melts from the hellish fire you will be in pain.' To achieve their aims they held ecstatic prayer sessions that featured hypnotic chanting and singing and crazed whirling dances. The purpose of these *radenie* was for the believer to achieve a mystical union with the 'Holy Spirit'.

> As they turned they behaved strangely and outrageously, some shook, bent over, fell down like lunatics, others stamped their feet, squatted down and danced or cried out wildly and spoke in unknown tongues believing that the Holy Spirit had come upon them.[8]

The founder of the Khlysty was Danila Phillopov, an army deserter and peasant from Kostroma. Phillopov founded the sect after Lord Sabaoth visited him on a fiery chariot. Lord Sabaoth stayed on earth incarnate in the body of the peasant. Phillopov proclaimed himself as the 'Living God' and denounced all other religions. Phillopov adjudged that he had a son, 'Christ', who endlessly incarnated in the bodies of believers. The first 'Christ' was Ivan Suslov, who set about converting peasants. As the sect grew in size and power it came to the attention of the authorities. Suslov was captured and tortured, but refused to renounce his beliefs. Tsar Mikhailovich ordered Suslov to be crucified on the Kremlin wall, near the Saviour's Gate.

According to legend, Suslov resurrected and appeared in front of some of his disciples in a village near Moscow. Hearing of this, the authorities captured him again. Not willing to be made to look foolish for a second time the authorities flayed Suslov alive *then* nailed him to the Kremlin wall. Miraculously, a piece of cloth that a female disciple covered his disfigured corpse with changed into his skin and he was resurrected again!

Able to resurrect but not able to keep clear of the authorities, he was soon captured again but was given his freedom as the Tsaress Kiriilova had a prophecy that her child, 'Peter the Great', would be born safely only if all the prisoners were freed. Suslov was liberated and continued to preach until 1718, when he ascended to heaven, aged one hundred. As there was always a 'Christ' on earth, others followed Suslov. The 'Living God' Phillopov ascended to heaven after a particularly vigorous prayer session in 1700.

In a perfect example of sects fragmenting off each other, the Skoptsy grew out of the Khlysty, taking all the beliefs of the older sect with them. Even so, the ritual that made them distinctive, that of castration, was entirely their own idea.

The Skoptsy took the ascetic programme of the Khlysty one step further, reasoning that to *truly* shake off the ties of the flesh and ward off damnation it was necessary to undergo a 'baptism with fire', that is, castration. Believing that the original apostles had been castrated, the Skoptsy thought the usual lower form of baptism with water was inferior to the 'baptism with fire' and quoted John the Baptist from Matthew 3:11 accordingly: 'I indeed baptize you with water unto repentance: but he that cometh after me is mightier than I . . . he shall baptize you with the Holy Ghost, and with fire . . .' This higher form of baptism was also essential as the blood that flowed from the castration made the Skoptsy the purified 'sheep' that sat on the right side of Jesus and would inherit the Kingdom of Heaven (Matthew 25:32–34).

To stake further their theological claims for cutting them off, the Skoptsy believed the first parents, Adam and Eve, sinned by having intercourse, thus flooding the world with *lepost*, that is, lust and the pleasures of the flesh. *Lepost* was the Devil's work and only through leaving behind these fleshly pursuits would the faithful receive heavenly glory *because* their flesh would be incorruptible. If not, the 'key to the abyss' – the penis – (the abyss being the vagina) and the 'magnetic stone' of female sexuality would lead the weak straight to the eternal hellfires. As this was the case, the faithful were urged to sit on the 'white horse' and spear the 'furious serpent' that was *lepost*.

The physical operation of the 'baptism with fire' involved two stages. For the male, adult and child, the first stage of the purification/mutilation (depending on your perspective) was the removal of the testicles. To the Skoptsy this was the 'minor seal'. Initially, the 'minor seal' was carried out by burning off the testicles with a red-hot iron. Possibly because of the peasant's familiarity with the mechanics of castration through their dealings with horses and livestock, the Skoptsy soon improved their technique and the scrotum was tied at the base, the skin sliced and the wound either cauterised or had a salve applied to it. Biriukov, a Skopet[9] who renounced his faith and testified against the sect before a judicial enquiry, described the operation he underwent to remove his testicles.

Then seizing a rusty razor, he said: 'Christ is risen!' And with these words my testicles were no longer mine. Though stunned, I did not lose all feeling but watched as blood poured from my veins in two great streams on either side, forming a wide angle. 'All my blood will drain away,' I said. 'No', he said, 'it knows how much to flow.' But the blood kept gushing, collecting in pools. Finally I grew faint, but the teacher stopped my fall. He laid me on the bed, where the pools of blood clotted . . . After the operation I suffered for a long time.[10]

The second stage of purity was the 'major' or 'royal seal', that is, the removal of the penis. This more extreme version of castration was carried out with razors, knives, pieces of bone and axes! Occasionally, the 'major seal' was carried out at the same time as the 'minor seal', with the penis and scrotum being tied together and severed; but, more often than not, the 'major seal' was performed some time after the 'minor seal'. After the penis was removed, a nail would be used to keep the urethra open to permit urination.

For a child, the prospect of the 'major seal' must have been terrifying. Having already endured the 'minor seal' and remembering the excruciating pain involved, the child would have been led crying and trembling into the special room where the ritual purification was to take place. The struggling child's arms were bound behind its back as the faithful chanted prayers and began to sing.

Gerasim Prudkovskii, another Skopet who turned his back on the sect, and published an account of his childhood castration as a 'Voice from the Grave of the Living Dead' in a literary journal, describes the 'major seal'.

a beast grabbed me with its teeth and tore out half my belly . . . the castrator went out and announced that we had 'flown across the burning river' and then tossed a part of my body into the hot stove . . . I lay in the tub, afloat in hot blood. Nausea came and went . . . some excitation deep in the wound caused it suddenly to swell, and I felt strong pressure on the bandage. Then, with a shudder, the swelling shrank and the backed-up blood (you could hear the gurgling) spilled out from under the bandage in warm streams. Feeling the symptom approach and trying to prevent the painful shudder, each time I curled up into a ball, but it was useless: it happened over and over. For an entire week I was lifted each morning from a puddle of blood. The dried spots stuck to my shirt and shook against me like jelly.[11]

Incredibly, most healthy children and adults survived this operation!

Although mutilation of the body or genitals wasn't as common among females as their male counterparts, many women still subjected themselves to a torturous form of ritual purification. As was the case with male children, young girls were forcibly mutilated with an older woman 'snipping' off the genitals and breasts of the girl. Like the males, females endured different stages of purification. The 'minor seal' for the females was the 'excision, removal or cauterising of the nipples'.[12] The royal seal was even more harrowing as the breasts were removed *and* the clitoris, labia minora and the labia majora also taken. Not surprisingly, a woman who had undertaken the 'major seal' enjoyed considerable standing in her 'ship'/community.

But how did such a sect employing such extreme methods come into being? The murky mists of time obscure the exact origins, but there is little doubt that the Skoptsy were formed by renegade Khlysty rebelling against the 'orgiastic' path down which many of their communities were heading. No date can be attached to this occurrence. In an 'official sense' the Skoptsy and their activities first came to light in 1772, when Catherine the Great decreed that the sect be investigated in the central Russian town of Orel. Again, the facts of how this brutal sect came to the attention of the authorities are confusing. Some suggest that a castrated peasant's wife told her local priest, who alerted the authorities, or that a landowner complained to the authorities after discovering thirteen castrated serfs among his workforce.

When the authorities started investigating this strange new sect, they found that the converts had congregated around a peasant, Andrei Ivanov Blokhin. Blokhin was already on the run, because, at the age of fourteen, he'd escaped from the estate where he worked and hit the road, 'hoboing' with a pair of blind beggars and living off the proceeds of what could be begged from markets. During these wanderings, Blokhin came across another serf, Mikhail Nikulin, who as a renegade Khlysty preacher persuaded the twenty-year-old Blokhin not only to give up all the usual suspects of sex, alcohol and meat, but also to castrate. Convinced, Blokhin removed his testicles with a red-hot iron and then persuaded another vagabond, Kondratti, to do the same. After the pair's wounds had healed they followed the time-honoured Russian tradition and hit the road as wandering preachers, transmitting the new message of castration and salvation through songs and prayers. They found instant success in their new calling, castrating as many as 62 other peasants in one village during the first weeks of their journey.

Perhaps because of the apocalyptic mood sweeping central Russia at this time, the authorities acted quickly against the new sect, not wishing to repeat the situation in Moscow, where peasants, concerned about an outbreak of bubonic plague, staged an agitated vigil outside St Barbara's gates to ask for assistance of the icon. The crowd, incensed at being forcibly removed, seized the archbishop and beat him to death. Or the 'trend' where peasants, fearing the time of the Apocalypse was near, buried their families alive, or decapitated their families before committing suicide themselves. Acting on Catherine the Great's edict that it was essential to 'extinguish the first signs of such irrational nonsense', the leaders of the new sect were rounded up and punished by being beaten with knouts (whips) and cudgels before being exiled to the outer reaches of the kingdom. Ironically, this only helped spread the faith. But the charismatic Kondratti,[13] who had become one of the leaders of the new sect, escaped. In the space of three decades, Kondratti took the Skoptsy from a brutal minor sect to a major player that the Russian Holy Synod described as the most dangerous and blasphemous heresy.

On the run from the authorities, Kondratti became the one and only 'Christ' for the sect. For the ever-growing number of faithful he was assumed to be the 'Son of God', who had returned to spread his message of salvation through castration to the world. When the authorities finally ran the 're-embodiment of the Redeemer' to ground in 1775, he was flogged with the knout and exiled to Siberia. This punishment did little to stem the enthusiasm of the converts, who quickly identified Kondratti's punishment with that of the original Jesus.

The Skoptsy's view of their prophet's time on the lam, his capture, flogging and banishment were documented in *The Passion of Kondratti Selivanov*, one of the sect's religious texts.[14] Like most religious books, *Passion* is a fantastic blending of myth, history, delusion and religious imagery. For the authorities wishing to stamp out the increasingly popular sect, *Passion* and Skoptsy theology were 'demented nonsense . . . a vast fairy tale . . . in which Gospel about the true Christ the Savior mixed in garbled form with historical legends . . . until they constituted a fable of fantastic proportions'.[15] But, for the Skoptsy faithful, *Passion* was the truth and served to give credence to the deification of the vagabond serf. In *Passion*, Kondratti assumes the role of 'helmsman' sent by God to steer the 'ships'. Of his time on the run from the authorities he assumes superhuman qualities as he lives without food and talks to animals:

> Wandering from city to city, for I had nowhere to rest my dear little head . . . once for three days I lay without food or drink in a pit of offal. I hid for ten days in a field of rye. Exhausted, I lay down and fell asleep; and when I awoke I saw a wolf was lying beside me and looking at me. But I said to him: 'Go to your place'. He obeyed and left. Then I spent twelve days in the hay, when all I had to keep me was a small jug of water, from which I drank a spoonful a day.[16]

On his capture and flogging: 'his [Kondratti's] little shirt was all soaked in blood, from little head to little toes, all drenched in blood . . . And thereupon my sweet children clothed me in their own dear little white one' (the clean white shirt was a Skoptsy symbol of purity).[17]

But one of the more startling claims made by Kondratti was that he was in fact the murdered Russian Tsar, Peter III![18] Historically, Peter III was murdered on the orders of his wife, Catherine the Great, in 1762. Kondratti and the Skoptsy, though, had an entire other history mapped out about the former Tsar. For them, Peter experienced a mystical vision in 1745, which convinced him that castration was necessary for true salvation. But, while he never consummated his marriage, he didn't act upon his revelation until sixteen years later.[19] In 1761, on the day of his coronation, he severed his penis and threw it on to Catherine's bed.

Hearing of Catherine's plan to murder him, Peter exchanged places with one of his guards (the guard was a Skopet) and escaped dressed as a common soldier. The guard was murdered, martyring himself so his prophet could spread the word. Peter then went to ground and eventually changed his name to Kondratti Selivanov.

The 'real' Kondratti was eventually released from exile in 1796 when Paul I took over as Emperor. Kondratti travelled to Moscow, where he was arrested again and sent to St Petersburg. In St Petersburg, Kondratti met the Emperor and suggested that he should be castrated because if the Emperor kept his 'crown jewels' Kondratti wouldn't recognise the Emperor as his son. The Emperor responded to this request by putting Kondratti in a madhouse.

Even though their prophet was in a madhouse the sect continued to attract adherents, and many members of the upper classes in Moscow and St Petersburg attended ecstatic prayer sessions. The sect also gained prominence among the wealthy merchant classes, some of which castrated their factory workers so they couldn't leave their employment. In fact, the Skoptsy gained a reputation for being ruthless in money matters and many became millionaires. The public perception was that the Skoptsy were willing to exploit their fellow brethren if it meant making a little extra and, as such, they were likened to Jews.

These wealthy Skoptsy lobbied to have Kondratti released from the asylum but it is thought that a castrated Polish courtier in the Russian Imperial Service, Aleski Elenskii, had enough influence to get Kondratti released in 1802. Ironically, Elenskii himself died in an asylum. He was committed after suggesting to Tsar Alexander I (1801–25) that, while the Emperor would still sit on the throne, the *real* power would come from Kondratti and that Russia could achieve world domination through castration.

Kondratti, after being released from the asylum, lived the good life, staying in luxurious mansions provided for him by wealthy Skopets. With their prophet liberated, the Skoptsy believed that they had made some startling converts. Napoleon, for the Skoptsy, was the illegitimate son of Catherine the Great who hadn't died on St Helena, but had been castrated and was lying low in Turkey, waiting to return to Russia on Judgment Day. It was also during this period that the sect continued to grow and could be found throughout Russia, the Balkans and Romania. In 1820, Kondratti was confined once again, this time in a monastery. He died in 1825.

As history shows, when a powerful and charismatic leader dies, more often than not the sect or organisation weakens. This was not the case with the Skoptsy, and the state took further measures to control its influence. For those who castrated themselves, the penalty was a total loss of all civil rights plus permanent exile to Siberia. Exile with hard labour was the punishment for castrating someone or willingly submitting to the operation. Even to preach the faith of the Skoptsy was to risk exile. Females who had undergone the various forms of mutilation were sent to work in Siberian textile mills while children who had been forcibly castrated were inducted into the army as pipers and drummers. Castrates were required to state the fact in their passports and villagers who found Skopets in their midst dressed them in women's clothing and dunce caps and pelted them with dirt and refuse.[20] To counteract these measures the Skoptsy threw a veil of secrecy around the sect. In tactics reminiscent of those employed by the radical Islamic sect, the Assassins, the Skoptsy professed their adherence to an orthodox brand of Christianity and attended church services to give the impression to outsiders that they weren't sectarians.

And, when discovered and interrogated, the Skoptsy told tall tales about how they came to be mutilated. Many former soldiers told of losing their genitalia while fighting in the service of the Fatherland while others told of getting blind drunk and waking up with something amiss. Most women told that their 'injuries' had come through agricultural accidents and that to stop the pain they had, for example, to cut off their breasts. These tales served their purpose, as the laws punished only those who had *willingly* submitted to castration.

Up until the mid-nineteenth century, the sect maintained its numbers as the exiles continued to spread the word. But some of the 'ferocity' of the rituals had been toned down with many of its members foregoing the 'fiery baptism'. Perhaps it was the material comforts enjoyed by many of the Skoptsy that led to this return to 'spiritual castration', but it did lead to a major schism in the sect.

In 1872, Romanian Skoptsy (who enjoyed an existence safe from legal persecution) rebelled against this 'spiritual complacency' (i.e. the lack of castration) that they believed had infected the sect, and formed a group called 'the Society of the Holy Elect'. One of their number, the tailor Kuzma Lisin, experienced a revelation and declared himself to be Kondratti Selivanov in his Second Coming. Lisin and his followers crossed into Russia illegally and began to urge the faithful to leave behind their material comforts and return to the 'old ways'. In the more rural communities, the 'Second Coming' was successful with Skoptsy 'surgeons' working overtime to cope with the demand. However, other wealthier communities were less than impressed with Lisin. Lisin, apparently unconcerned with the harsh penalties against the Skoptsy, preached his message openly. To the wealthy Skoptsy who had built up good relations in their communities this firebrand could only bring trouble. They argued that Lisin was a false prophet because there had been no momentous happenings to announce his arrival. The sky had not been torn asunder and the angels had not danced in the skies. At *radenie*, presided over by Lisin, those who pledged allegiance to the 'Second Coming' were heckled and beaten with sticks. Lisin was eventually betrayed by fellow Skoptsy and exiled.

The Skoptsy continued on into the twentieth century and, in 1905, they were allowed to leave their places of banishment and live where they chose. Even though the glory years of the sect were well past, they continued to be active, and, in 1910, 142 castrates were arrested and deported. The ending of the Imperial reign and the coming of the Bolsheviks put another nail in the coffin of the Skoptsy. In 1929, the largest trial ever involving Skoptsy took place and one hundred and fifty sectarians were exiled with hard labour, guilty of trying to get 'victims' for their 'fanatic predator-God'.[21] The photos that the prosecution used in the trial – of naked Skoptsy displaying their mutilations/

purification – were amazing. The pictures of the females who had cut off their breasts were particularly harrowing as, through the extensive scarring, it was possible to see the surface area affected by the ritual.

By the start of World War Two, the Skoptsy were largely extinguished as a sect large enough to worry the authorities. Even so, Skoptsy could still be found in rural areas, and in 1970 an ethnologist found one hundred Skoptsy living in a community in Crimea. Contemporary reports suggest that there are still Skoptsy 'ships' operating in post-Soviet Russia, Romania and the Balkans. So, when you meet another 'modern primitive' waxing lyrical about the 'spirituality' of their genital piercings, just think of the Skoptsy, cutting 'em off so that they can be saved.

NOTES

1. Possibly circumcision grew out of the necessity for self-mutilation to become more symbolic. As such, in some religions, circumcision may subconsciously represent castration.
2. The *hijara* earn their crust by bestowing blessings and entertaining at weddings and baptisms. Recently, they have even branched out into the debt-collection industry, threatening to reveal their scarred pubic areas if the debt isn't paid.
3. Sir James George Frazer, *The Golden Bough: A Study in Magic and Religion*, London: Macmillan & Co., 1923, p. 350.
4. The cults of Attis, Astarte and Eshmun are so similar that throughout history many have taken the three sects to be one and the same.
5. However, in the highly charged world of the 'peasant sects' it is almost impossible to be abso-

lutely certain of all the rituals and practices of certain sects. First, they were, by definition, heterodox, and, secondly, as 'outlaw' religions, they were shrouded in secrecy.

6. Novoselov in Alex DeJonge, *The Life and Times of Grigorii Rasputin*, New York: Coward, McCann and Geoghegan, 1982, p. 36.

7. Rasputin preached that sin was necessary to overcome sin and the more one sinned the more one suffered. He told the females who flocked to him that he was above sin, so it was no sin to have sex with him, or that sin was the first step towards true salvation. Rasputin was also reported to have come in contact with Skoptsy preachers and got some of his philosophical ideas from them as well. If this is the case, then, in a strange twist of fate, some sources indicate that Bolshevik troops disinterred Rasputin's corpse and cut off his thirteen-inch penis as a trophy, thus castrating the noted libertine, if only in death.

8. Bogolovskii in Alex DeJonge, *The Life and Times of Grigorii Rasputin*, New York: Coward, McCann and Geoghegan, 1982, p. 37.

9. 'Skopet' is the masculine singular term employed by the Skoptsy.

10. Biriukov in Laura Engelstien, *Castration and the Heavenly Kingdom*, New York: Cornell University Press, 1999, p. 78.

11. Prudkovskii in Laura Engelstien, ibid. p. 86.

12. Pelikan in Laura Engelstien, ibid. p. 63.

13. For ease, I use the name Kondratti without a surname, as, while he was on the run the Prophet of the Skoptsy used many surnames: Emelianov, Trifonov, Trofimov, Nikiforov and the surname that he eventually took as his own, Selivanov.

14. The authorship of *Passion* is unknown.
15. Nadezhdin in Laura Engelstien, ibid. p. 39.
16. Unknown in Laura Engelstien, ibid. p. 35.
17. Unknown in Laura Engelstien, ibid.
18. Taking on the identity of Peter III was not solely confined to Kondratti. Pugachev, who led a popular rebellion against landowners and the Empire in 1773–74, also declared himself to be the murdered Russian Tsar.
19. Many historical sources indicate that Peter was impotent and the children who came from his marriage to Catherine didn't come from his loins. Maybe this rumour of impotency was the germ of the idea that connected Peter with castration in the minds of the Skoptsy.
20. Unlike most sects that featured castrates, the male Skoptsy did not wear women's clothes (they dressed for the most part in everyday apparel) and did not aspire to femininity.
21. Nadezhdin in Laura Engelstien, ibid. p. 211.

BIBLIOGRAPHY

Alex DeJonge, *The Life and Times of Grigorii Rasputin*, New York: Coward, McCann and Geoghegan, 1982.

Didier Diers and Xavier Valla, 'La Secte Russe des Castrats', 4th International Symposium on Sexual Mutilation, Lausanne, 1996.

Laura Engelstien, *Castration and the Heavenly Kingdom*, New York: Cornell University Press, 1999.

Sir James George Frazer, *The Golden Bough: A Study in Magic and Religion*, London: Macmillan & Co., 1923.

F Gonzalez-Crussi, *Notes of an Anatomist*, London: Pan Books, 1986.

IA Tulpe and EA Torchinov, 'The Skoptsy Sect in Russia: History, Teaching and Religious Practice', *The International Journal for Transpersonal Studies*: Vol. 19, 2000.

4. ACID FASCISM

ECOLOGICAL TERROR, RACE WAR, DUNE BUGGY, CREEPY CRAWL – CHARLES MANSON, THE FAMILY AND THE SIX SIX SIXTIES

MICHAEL SPANN

On 10 August 1969, the various news services ran hot with the news that 'ritual murders' had taken place the night before at the home of the film director Roman Polanski and his wife, Sharon Tate. In hindsight, these murders and the subsequent killings attributed to Charlie Manson's 'Family' were some of the final nails driven into the dilapidated coffin that was the 1960s. The final nail in that coffin would be driven home on 6 December at Altamont Speedway to the sounds of the Rolling Stones . . .

Charles Manson and his band of acid-munching, apocalyptic, gun-toting, snuff-fixated hippie chicks are the subjects of dozens of books, movies and television programmes. The crimes attributed to the Family, and dark rumours of other unsolved crimes, have reached mythic proportions. Even after the incarceration of Manson and members of the Family, the group – or those allied to it – have rarely left the headlines: in 1975 Lynette 'Squeaky' Fromme pulled a gun on President Gerald Ford, and was sentenced to jail.

In the end the so-called Manson Family escape definition. Their links – whether real or imagined – to various cults, to Hollywood celebrity, to everything from fascism to the Beatles' *White Album*, are a melting pot of sixties-into-seventies sociopolitical and cultural events.

What created the Family, what drove its members, was a combination of fascinations: rebellion, pop culture, religion, sex and drugs. The same fixations still define aspects of our society. The Family continue to escape easy explanation or definition: are they an aberration, or are they located far closer to home? as Manson stated, 'these children that come at you with knives, they are your children'.[1]

Finally, Manson and the Family have emerged as contemporary myth.

Gary Hinman was known around Topanga Canyon as an easy touch if you needed a place to stay for the night and, indeed, some members of the Family crashed on his floor from time to time. Hinman, in the spirit of the sixties was many things: a PhD candidate in sociology, a practitioner of Buddhism and a manufacturer and dealer in mescaline. He has also gone down in history as the first murder victim of the Family.

There are various versions concerning Hinman's murder. One theory is that Charlie Manson wanted Hinman to finance a recording session, as he was becoming increasingly desperate with his inability to make it in the music business. Hinman declined to help Manson to become a musical superstar. Manson, thinking of other ways to get the $20,000 that Hinman supposedly had stashed in his house, ordered Hinman to join his band of dune-buggy-riding doomsayers, thus giving Charlie all of his money and possessions. Hinman wanted no part of this and Manson warned him that it was his last chance. Hinman told the cult leader that he would look after his own karma.

Another version, told to various people at different times, was that Hinman's murder came about because of a 'dope burn' – a drug deal gone wrong. Hinman's killer,

Bobby Beausoleil, corroborated this version from prison in 1980. Beausoleil claims that he went to Hinman's house on the night of 25 July to reclaim $1,000 that he'd paid to Hinman for 1,000 tabs of mescaline. The money belonged to the Straight Satans Motorcycle Club (one of the biker gangs that hung around the Family) and the bikers were livid because the mescaline that they had received was of a very low quality. Fearing for his own safety, Beausoleil wanted his money back.

Various versions exist as to what happened at Hinman's that night. The commonly accepted version was that Hinman refused to give any money and Manson arrived at the residence and cut open Hinman's face and ear with a sword. Then he left. Later, Beausoleil rang up Manson and asked him what he should do, as Hinman was saying that he would go to the police, and tell them about the Family's illegal activities, such as car theft. Allegedly, Manson told Beausoleil to kill Hinman. After a struggle, Beausoleil stabbed Hinman twice in the heart. Beausoleil maintains that Manson never went to the house. After killing Hinman, Bobby, or the girls Mary Brunner and Susan Atkins, wrote POLITICAL PIGGY in blood on the wall and then drew a paw to make it look as if the black militants the Black Panthers had committed the murder. As if opening a valve, this murder would trigger the Tate/LaBianca murders, two of the most infamous in history.

When police entered the Polanski residence on Cielo Drive they found five bodies (three in the grounds and two in the house) and a bloody mess that reminded one of the officers of a 'battlefield'. PIG was written in blood on the front door.

Flashback to the killers arriving at the well-to-do residence at 10050 Cielo Drive. After disabling the residence's telephone lines, Susan Atkins (a.k.a. Sadie Mae Glutz), Tex Watson, Linda Kasabian and Patricia 'Katie' Krenwinkel clambered over the fence surrounding the property. They were armed with ropes and knives, and Tex carried a revolver. As the killers made their way towards the house they spotted a car moving down the driveway, leaving the house. The driver of this car, Steven Parent, was to be the first victim in their 'religious' rampage. Parent was slowing down to activate the exit button on the electronic gate when Tex Watson reached through the open window and rammed his .22 against Parent's head. Despite desperate pleas from Parent, Tex shot him four times in the head then stabbed him.

The bloodletting had commenced.

At Tex's command, the dark-clothed foursome moved on. At the house, Tex cut the lower part of a screen window and crawled inside. Then, he opened the front door to let Katie and Sadie in. Linda had been ordered to keep a lookout at the driveway.

Voityck Frykowski was lying on a couch, zoning on some MDA. Frykowski came to with a start when he saw the 'visitors'. Realising he had no idea who the armed intruders were, he asked what they wanted. Tex Watson replied, 'I am the Devil and I'm here to do the Devil's business . . .'[2]

Sadie tied Frykowski's hands behind his back in a loose knot and went and explored the house to see if there were others present. There were three: the heavily pregnant Sharon Tate, Jay Sebring and Abigail Folger. She collected them and took them into the living room.

Tex ordered all the captives to lie on their stomachs. Sebring protested that Tate was pregnant and went for Tex's weapon. For his trouble he was shot in the armpit and kicked in the face. Because Sadie had tied Frykowski's hands so loosely, Tex ordered her to retie him, and she did so with a towel that she got from a bathroom.

Sadie later recalled the scene: 'Tex proceeded to tie a rope around Sebring's neck then to Sharon Tate's neck, then to Abigail Folger's neck . . . Tex said, "You are all going to die." '³ Sebring's unconscious body was the dead weight attached to the end of the rope. The captives shouted and pleaded and began to struggle valiantly. In keeping with her amateurish attempts to tie Frykowski's hands, Sadie, when ordered to kill him, hesitated, allowing her victim to get his hands free. He pulled her hair and hit her in the head. They fell to the ground in a struggling mass. Getting her arm free, Sadie stabbed wildly before losing her knife. Katie was also having difficulties. Abigail Folger had grabbed her by the hair in a fight for her life. Frykowski, bleeding profusely from the multitude of wounds caused by Sadie's indiscriminate attack, made it to the front door. Tex shot him, then smashed Frykowski in the head so hard with his gun that the handle broke into three pieces. Pandemonium reigned. Abigail Folger broke free and ran for her life. Sebring also began to struggle despite his wounds.

Taking control of the situation, Tex finished off Sebring with his knife, then caught up with Abigail Folger. Folger, seeing the demented look in Tex's eyes, surrendered. He beat her head in with his gun, then stabbed her in the chest and abdomen. Frykowski, showing amazing reserves of strength and courage, rose and staggered into the garden. Watson tackled him to the ground and stabbed at the Pole's already blood-soaked body.

Being witness to the carnage unfolding around her, Sharon Tate was, quite understandably, pleading for her life and that of the unborn child. Sadie recalls, 'I looked at her and said, "Woman, I have no mercy for you." '[4]

Tex returned from the garden and stabbed the actress. Sadie followed suit. For Sadie, the stabbing was an erotic pleasure, the most intense sexual experience that she'd ever encountered. As she licked the blood from her knife she thought of cutting the unborn baby from the corpse and presenting it to her leader, Charlie – 'How proud Charlie would be if I presented him with the baby cut from the womb of a woman'[5] – and cutting out Tate's heart and sharing it with the Family around a bonfire.

Tex continued his dalliance with the Devil by stabbing all the bodies again and again in a savage frenzy. With blood from Sharon Tate's breast, Sadie wrote PIG on the door. They left 102 stab wounds behind them.

Back at Spahn Ranch, Charlie Manson, ever gauging the success of his programming, asked each of his killers if they felt any remorse for their brutal attack. None of them did.

Deciding the murders at the Polanski residence had been 'too messy', Manson decided they should make another raid. This time, he would go along to show them how it should be done. With Manson (a.k.a. the Devil, the Wizard and Jesus Christ all rolled into one) their deeds would be sure to strike fear deeper into the hearts of all the establishment 'piggies'.

Charles Manson, Linda Kasabian, Steve 'Clem' Grogan, Leslie Van Houten, Tex Watson, Patricia Krenwinkel and Sadie crowded into the same 1959 Ford they'd used the previous night. This time they took bayonets and a sword that they had acquired from the Straight Satans Motorcycle Club.

After a long journey they ended up outside the residence of Leno and Rosemary LaBianca at 3301 Waverley Drive. They'd chosen this house because they once had had a group LSD session in the house next door. Charlie, taking control, sneaked into the house to 'reassure' the intended victims. After finding Leno reading the paper and drinking a can of apple beer in his pyjamas on the couch and his wife in the bedroom, Manson tied them back to back and left them in the living room while he went back to the car to issue further orders. He ordered Tex, Patricia and Leslie to go into the house and 'paint a picture more gruesome than anybody has ever seen'.[6]

Susan, Linda, Clem and Charlie drove off, planning to kill more 'piggies'. Nothing came of these plans because Linda backed out at the last moment, saving the life of the intended victim.

The other group, entering the house, saw the bound couple and went into the kitchen to choose their instruments of torture: a ten-inch carving fork and an eight-inch knife. The girls untied Rosemary and led her to the bedroom where they pushed her face down on to the bed and slipped a pillowcase over her head. They also tied a cord from a heavy bedside lamp around her neck. Back in the living room, Tex pushed Leno back on to the couch and ripped open his top. He stabbed him in the stomach before inflicting damage to the throat and colon. A pillowcase covered his head. Hearing her husband's agonised screams, Rosemary LaBianca began to struggle. Leslie subdued her while Patricia stabbed away, severing her spine. The wound total was at 41, before Leslie added another sixteen to her buttocks.

Remembering Charlie's instructions, Tex carved WAR on Leno LaBianca's chest. Patricia followed suit by stabbing the corpse with a carving knife, which she left sticking out of the stomach. Then, as though trying to re-create the Beatles song, 'Piggies', she twanged the knife so that it vibrated like a musical instrument. With the dead man's blood they scrawled DEATH TO THE PIGS on the wall, then in the same red hue added RISE on another part of the wall. On the double-door refrigerator, Patricia meant to write HELTER SKELTER but instead failed her spelling test and wrote HEALTER SKELTER. After fawning over the LaBianca's dogs and getting a bite to eat for themselves, they showered and changed clothes before hitchhiking back to Spahn Ranch.

The last murder positively identified as the work of the Family was that of 'Shorty' Shea, a Spahn Ranch farmhand. After a series of police raids on the ranch and information about the 'dead piggies' slowly seeping from the barren mountains into the outside world, Manson decided that Shea knew too much and had to go.

> Each one had a razor sharp knife and they went to work on him fast . . . carving him up like a piece of meat . . . He didn't do any screaming because he went down fast, though it took them a while to dismember his body. They cut off the arms and the legs, and one of the legs they cut in half, I think, and then they cut his head off.[7]

The Family's official toll stood at nine.

The notoriety of the Family has led some modern commentators to assume that they were a lone cult that sprang from nowhere and that Manson arrived at his 'ideas' independently. In fact, Manson's vision of the world was heavily influenced by Scientology, personal-development programmes, and astrology, and he even talked about the ideas that he had picked up from Black Muslims whom he had met in jail.

The Family was by no means the only 'odd' cult that flourished in California in the mid- to late 1960s. Some of these groups were peaceful and benign, practising obscure forms of Oriental thought, but there were others that dealt with the darker side of human nature. As young 'seekers', some of Manson's followers had come into contact with other groups. Manson himself, while not being a bona fide member of some of the organisations that he has since been linked with, was no doubt aware of them and, at times, paid them visits, looking for converts and handouts. When you look at some of these other cults you can see where a lot of Charlie's skewed logic came from.

Bobby Beausoleil, the convicted killer of Gary Hinman, was a great influence on Manson. Like Manson, Beausoleil was a charismatic figure who was surrounded by a group of doting young women. Even though he and Manson played together in bands and regularly jammed, there was always an undercurrent of tension between them, possibly stemming from the fact that Bobby refused to join the Family and often cut out when he wanted to. Even so, Charlie and Bobby spent a lot of time racing around the desert in the Family's stolen dune buggies while under the influence of potent LSD. Undoubtedly, during these journeys of body and mind, Beausoleil told Manson about his experiences as Lucifer and his time with the Satanist and avant-garde filmmaker, Kenneth Anger.

Anger, a devotee of the 'wickedest man in the world', Aleister Crowley, and one of the most important film directors of modern times, discovered Bobby while presenting a Winter Solstice ritual at a theatre in Haight

Ashbury. In the crowded theatre, Anger, as 'though sight by destiny', picked out Beausoleil and told the young man, 'You are Lucifer'. Thus, Bobby became Lucifer in Anger's masterpiece *Lucifer Rising*.

Anger told Bobby that he would be feared and revered for generations to come and showered gifts on the young man. As John Gilmore states, 'It was the beginning of the metamorphosis of Bobby Beausoleil . . . into the Angel of Disobedience. Into a Devil.'[8]

But, at the start of his introduction to Satan, Beausoleil thought that all the devil worshipping was just a bunch of homosexuals parading around in flamboyant costumes. Then he dropped acid made by the legendary Augustus Stanley Owsley and it all made sense . . .

Anger put Bobby on an all-meat diet and Anger's home became a sorcerer's temple.

As Bobby gobbled more and more acid, 'he was swimming in all the death and destruction . . . I was covered with this cape of blood . . . I had no fear. There was no fear in me as I suffered the most horrible deaths in the world. There was no fear, I know I was the Devil.'[9]

Anger and Beausoleil eventually fell out, with Bobby reportedly stealing a car, some film equipment and some footage from *Lucifer Rising* and splitting. In turn, Anger retaliated by making a locket that featured, on one side, the figure of a toad and on the other the face of Bobby Beausoleil. After Bobby's arrest and conviction he and Anger reconciled and Beausoleil recorded music for a soundtrack for *Lucifer Rising*. In jail, Beausoleil continues to make music.

'The Process: The Church of the Final Judgment' was an apocalyptic cult that has gained a special significance in the history/mythology of Charles Manson. The Process's notoriety stems largely from the fact that many commentators throughout the years have characterised it as a neo-nazi satanic sect, of which Charlie Manson was a fully fledged member. Ed Sanders, in the first edition of *The Family*, took the Process to task, describing them as, 'black caped, black garbed, death worshipping'.[10] The Process took exception to Sanders's view of them as animal-sacrificing blood drinkers and successfully sued Sanders and his publisher. As a result, the book was pulled from the shelves and the offending sections and passages about the Process were removed. As a result, most editions of *The Family* floating around have no mention of the Process in them. In recent times, the Process received even more bad publicity when the author Maury Terry, in his book *The Ultimate Evil*, linked Manson, the Son of Sam killer David Berkowitz and the Process (or one of its splinter groups) to a global satanic network! It seems that, no matter what, the Process and Charlie Manson will be for ever linked.

The Process were by no means a shadowy group. In fact, in the late 1960s around Haight Ashbury, 'Processians' were a common sight as they hawked their religious texts. And they cut quite a sight doing it. With their neatly trimmed long hair and beards, black shirts and trousers, purple capes featuring a red Mendes goat on the back and large crucifixes hanging around their necks, it was easy to understand why people would think they were Satanists. Their B-grade movie imagery was given an exclamation point by the huge German shepherd attack dogs that the Processians led around on chains. Their supposed satanic link was further aided by their message that the end of the world was nigh, and Jehovah, Christ, Satan and Lucifer were one and the same.

The link to Nazism comes mostly from the symbol that featured on most of the Process's literature. This

symbol featured four P's coming together to form a
symbol that resembled a swastika. In fact, it represented
the four gods the Process worshipped, coming together
and unifying into one power, thereby creating inner
peace.

Robert de Grimston and his wife Mary Anne founded
the Process in 1962 while practising Scientology. Realising the limitations of Scientology, they soon formed
their own group with its own theology.

In a nutshell, the Process recognised a single unfathomable god. When the apocalypse comes Jesus and
Satan will come together.

> Christ said: love thine enemy. Christ's enemy was
> Satan and Satan's enemy was Christ. Through love
> enmity is destroyed . . . through love Christ and
> Satan have destroyed their enmity and come
> together for the end. Christ to judge, Satan to
> execute judgment. [11]

The Process achieved a certain degree of popularity,
with 'chapters' in Los Angeles, Paris, London, Hamburg,
Munich, Amsterdam and New Orleans. At the New
Orleans chapter a group vision was experienced that
instructed that a chapter be set up in Haight Ashbury.
It was here that Charlie Manson came across the Process
as their headquarters were only a couple of blocks from
where he as living at the time.

While never being a card-carrying member of the
Process, Manson got a lot of ideas from the Church of
the Final Judgment and it is interesting to see the ones
that he lifted.

Both groups referred to themselves as the Family and
both encouraged bikers to be a part of their vision. They

wanted the outlaw bikers to be 'shock troops' on wheels when the apocalypse rained down. The worship of animals as perfect beings was also central to both groups. Both de Grimston and Manson also believed they were the reincarnation of Jesus Christ.

One of the major ideas that Manson gleaned from the Process was the idea that Jesus and Satan were one and the same and the worship of Satan was necessary in escaping the doomsday notion shared by both groups. After contact with the Process, Manson began ending his philosophical/theological discourses with the phrase, 'As it is'. This was a phrase employed by the Process.

When news of the Manson murders broke, the Family were reported to be a splinter group of the Process. This came about in part from the similarities noted above, but also from both groups' views on killing and murder. Manson drilled into his group that killing was essentially an act of love or understanding. Each person must judge him- or herself, then take the judgment out on the rest of the world. Thus, killing was simply the logical con-clusion to the necessary judgment of love and under-standing. This is an idea that was also espoused by the Process in their literature. Not surprisingly, the Process took a dim view of the Tate/LaBianca murders but admitted Manson had got some of his chops from them.

Manson has obviously got hold of some of our ideas from somewhere and distorted them in a particular way. It is unfortunate. If we had had the opportunity to speak with him, we could have avoided that series of brutal killings.[12]

The Process were so concerned with their links to Manson that Robert de Grimston ordered two of his leading 'priests' to interview Manson in jail just to make sure that he wasn't a member of any of their chapters. He wasn't, but the prosecutor in the Manson case, Vincent Bugliosi, also interviewed them. Bugliosi was sceptical of the Process's insistence that they had nothing to do with the murders and Bugliosi asked Manson if he knew anyone called Robert Moore/de Grimston. Manson denied knowing anyone by the latter name but said, 'You're looking at him, Moore and I are one and the same.'[13] Bugliosi took this to mean that Manson and Moore/de Grimston, and therefore the Process, followed the same philosophies.

But, even as the Process were trying to distance themselves from Manson, they themselves kept drawing Manson into their universe. In 1971 in the 'Death' edition of their newsletter, they printed an article entitled 'Pseudo Profundity in Death', written by Manson, who waxed lyrical that in death he would escape the madness of the world and find paradise in his own self.

Like most of the other cults that flourished in the 1960s, the Process eventually split into a series of groups, all competing against each other. Robert de Grimston is still alive and living in the United States.

The Solar Lodge was another apocalyptic cult that achieved a certain amount of infamy in the late sixties. The Solar Lodge maintained they were an official lodge of the Ordo Templi Orientis, but the OTO regarded the Solar Lodge as a renegade group and never supported it. The Solar Lodge had views similar to those of Manson. This led to their being described as 'a loonytune magical cult specialising in blood drinking, sadosodo sex magic and the hatred of blacks'.[14]

Like Manson, The Solar Lodge proposed that the end of the world would come with a huge race war. The blacks would revolt and lead an uprising, and lots of blood, both black and white, would be spilled. To hasten the Armageddon, the group used to hold special ceremonies where they would try to transmit 'hate vibrations' into the notorious Watts ghetto. They believed these sessions would cause the blacks to begin rioting, much in the same violent manner as the riots that swept through Watts in 1965. The Solar Lodge, like Charlie, also had the notion of beating a tactical retreat into the desert to escape the violent upheavals. For this they constructed 'the Arc' in the Mojave Desert. The Arc was built in the shape of a pyramid, both to collect energy and also because the Solar Lodge had placed it at roughly the same latitude as Cairo. Jean Brayton, the leader of the sect, also had the special gift of deciphering 'hidden' messages in Beatles songs, a gift that she may have passed on to Charlie.

The Solar Lodge was a wealthy organisation, owning service stations, businesses and numerous houses, but it still actively recruited members. Apart from Brayton's offer of 'salvation on credit' by loan-sharking to university students, the major methods of recruitment were the 'profane parties' held by the Lodge. It was at these 'profane parties' that Manson allegedly came across the ideas of the Solar Lodge (although the evidence for this is vague and it has been dismissed by others writing on the period).[15]

As was the custom of the times, the main features of the parties were sex and drugs, both of which were freely available in a variety of forms. As this was the case, the Lodge attracted a strange mix of punters: Hollywood types, bikers, seekers and Charlie and the girls.

Once adopted into the fold of the Lodge, the initiate would begin the rituals. The lower levels were relatively benign but the upper levels reportedly involved 'sacrificing cats, dogs, chickens . . . and consummating acts of sex-magic while animal blood was poured on the fornicators'.[16]

The use of drugs to deprogramme the mind was also part of the group's ethos, with the incredibly powerful and often dangerous plants belladonna, datura and jimson weed being administered. Interestingly, Manson also began to experiment with belladonna. Timothy Leary of 'Turn On, Tune In and Drop Out' fame once remarked that he had never heard of a good belladonna trip. This was true of Manson, who took some in a tea and lapsed into a three-day coma. After coming out of it, Manson wanted to sneak into parties and 'spike' the drinks of the unsuspecting. Then the Family could rob the house as the affected were writhing around the floor in nightmarish convulsions!

The Solar Lodge's forms of psychological and physical punishment were also brutal. A former member of the Solar Lodge, Candace Reos, told police that a member, in order to curb his sexual desires, was 'programmed' to cut his wrists every time he became aroused. When Reos herself fell pregnant she was told to focus her thoughts on hating her baby.

The sect's downfall came in 1969. A child had accidentally started a fire at the sect's main residence, killing some animals. As punishment, the child was beaten with bamboo sticks, then placed in a packing crate. Thankfully, there was a small gap to allow in a little air. As temperatures reached close to 45 degrees Celsius, the boy was left in the box for days. A couple of unsuspecting horse buyers stumbled across the boy and reported it to police. The sect was raided and eleven people were arrested for child abuse. The leader, Jean Brayton, escaped to either Mexico or Argentina.

The downfall of the Solar Lodge occurred at roughly the time the Family started their murderous spree. It was almost as if Charlie couldn't wait for the 'hate vibes' to enflame the ghettoes and wanted to kick-start the Apocalypse.

A sect that was situated close to the Spahn Ranch was the Fountain of the World. Charlie and the Family had close dealings with this group, living at the Fountain's headquarters for a week in 1968. They even helped out the Fountain of the World financially, supposedly donating $2,000.

The Fountain of the World required all the usual things of their initiates: giving material possessions and money to the organisation and cutting all ties with families and so forth. Even though the Fountain of the World trumpeted 'Peace through Love and Service', the sect had a violent and sordid history, which undoubtedly piqued Manson's interest in it.

The Fountain of the World was founded in the early 1950s by a former con man and convicted criminal, Francis Pencovick. Pencovick proclaimed himself the final messiah and preached that the Buddha, Krishna, Jesus and Isaiah were all packed into his frame. As this was the case, he discarded his old name and took the moniker Krishna Venta.

Venta started to spread the word and, like Manson, attracted mainly young women who hung off his every word. Venta assigned these women different colours according to their personalities. This was an idea which Manson later used when he assigned 'colours of the rainbow' to various women in the Family.

The Fountain of the World was situated in a box canyon and its impressive natural setting included subterranean caverns and catacombs. These underground lairs were where the more secret rites of the sect took place. Some of these secret rites involved group sex sessions presided over by Venta.

In 1958, Venta's time in the earthly realm came to an end when he was killed in a mysterious 'accident' at the sect headquarters.

What happened to the final messiah isn't clear but some suggest that a number of his followers failed to heed his philosophy – failed, that is, to worship what Venta represented, not the man himself – and wanted Venta to prove his holy personage. The test they devised for the holy man focused on dynamiting the cavern where Venta and some of his inner circle were holding a rite. Subsequently, Venta and nine others died in the blast.

Another theory of the explosion was that a couple of former members dynamited the cavern in protest at Venta's sleeping with their wives, who had stayed loyal to the former convict.

By the time Manson and the Family encountered the Fountain of the World, the priesthood wore obligatory black robes and, to outsiders at least, practised celibacy. Manson, feeling the first urges of 'messiahood', wanted to take control of the Fountain of the World and, utilising tactics that worked well with the bikers who had attached themselves to the Family, ordered the girls to 'strip and suck' the priests. The priests declined the invitation and Manson was reduced to lifting ideas from the group.

Atop the catacombs at Fountain of the World HQ was a large rock shaped like a human skull. Atop 'Skull Rock', the Fountain of the World had built a cross so their members could strap themselves to it and meditate. Taking this idea a step further, Manson erected his own cross and made his own 'Hill of Martyrdom' near Spahn Ranch. After gobbling acid, Manson was strapped to the cross and members of the Family threw abuse at him or wailed in torment at his crucifixion. One lucky female was also given the role of Mother Mary, who knelt at the foot of the cross. This psychoreligious drama ended with Manson/Christ being pulled off the cross into an acid-fuelled orgy. Soon after his dealings with the Fountain of the World, many of the women in the Family began to say 'amen' after Charlie's philosophical ramblings. Charlie had added another piece to the unfathomable jigsaw puzzle inside his head.

But what was the jigsaw puzzle that Manson presented to those who were prepared to listen? Manson believed that there was going to be a race war that would engulf the world. The Family were extremely paranoid about blacks, believing that the militant group, the Black Panthers, could raid them at any time. One of the theories about the Tate/LaBianca murders was that they were supposed to start the race war, as the black militants would be victimised because of the high-profile killings they had supposedly committed.

When the race war started, Manson and his followers would escape into the desert in their armed psychedelic-coloured dune buggies along a specially built trail. If anyone believed his followers weren't taking Charlie seriously, they needed only to look at the food, water and weapons they had stockpiled in the desert for this journey. The journey would eventually lead them to 'The Devil's Hole'. This intriguingly titled location, named by Manson, was based on a Hopi Indian myth. The Hopi nation believed they had emerged from an underground world to live on earth. Manson believed 'the Hole' existed.

I found a hole in the desert that goes down into a
river . . . and I call it a bottomless pit. So I covered
it up and I hid it. I called it . . . The Devil's Hole.[17]

The 'bottomless pit' mentioned in Chapter 9 of the
Book of Revelations convinced the rest of the Family
that such a place did exist.

When the race war was ending and the earth was a
smouldering collection of ruins, the blacks would
assume control. After a period of time, the blacks would
realise that they couldn't run the whole shebang and
Charlie and his band of merry followers would ascend
from 'the Hole'. The blacks would recognise Charlie as
the true leader and he would lead the world according
to his vision. This is pretty amazing, considering
Manson was a racist and wouldn't even let the music of
Jimi Hendrix (whose band was rounded out by two
white members) be played at the ranch. He backed up
his claims by again producing The Book of Revelations
which prophesised that the 'angel of the bottomless pit'
would emerge from it on horses with breastplates of fire.

From the shaft of the bottomless pit . . . came
locusts on the Earth and they were given the power
of scorpions. They were told not to harm any green
growth on any tree . . . they have as king over them
the angel of the bottomless pit. [Revelations: 9].

The 'locusts' were the Family and the steeds with
breastplates of fire were the psychedelic dune buggies.

But how would Charlie have run the world, or what
would have been the philosophy behind his reign? In
recent times, Manson has given a name to the ideas that
he rammed into his followers' heads: ATWA or Air Trees

Water Animals. As the name suggests, it has an ecological basis.

Manson believes that human beings have placed themselves above nature, thereby separating themselves from it. As such, humans view themselves as the conquerors of nature and have created an imbalance by polluting the planet and wiping out the animals.

Manson allies himself with the animals, particularly the coyote, which he believed he could communicate with. The only chance that the human race has to survive, according to Manson, is to reintroduce animal instincts into the human consciousness.

> I just don't think in goods or bads, just is's. What *it*
> is. Whatever life is, it *is* and bad and good got
> nothing to do with it. A snake eats the baby
> squirrel. Mamma squirrel may say that it's bad, but
> snake's got to eat. The life cycles *are* and only
> humans got the order fucked up. [18]

Manson demonstrated his philosophy to his followers by letting snakes and scorpions crawl all over him. This led some to believe that he had some sort of power over animals. Manson spent weeks in the desert observing how animals could live in such a hostile environment. Followers were forbidden to brush scorpions and spiders off their bodies, and he encouraged members of the Family to squat in front of rattlesnakes and stare into their faces. Under the influence of a potent hallucinogenic such as LSD, this must have been a profound experience, putting the participant deeper under Charlie's 'spell'.

And Charlie's 'spell' continues to bewitch people. In 1999, Christian groups of every possible persuasion flooded into Jerusalem for the millennium celebrations. One of these groups, the Concerned Christians from the USA, was an apocalyptic doomsday cult that was kicked out of Israel for allegedly plotting violence to bring about the Second Coming of Christ. The Concerned Christians allegedly have formed many of their ideas around Manson's life and his role as the divine law-maker or Son of Man. The group refers to Charlie as 'Man Son', thus emphasising his own belief that he is Jesus Christ. A tape found at the house rented by the Concerned Christians in Jerusalem stated, 'The Charles Manson murders connect to the Son of Man judgments, that is the return of Jesus Christ.' The group also believes that the killing of Sharon Tate's foetus was a divine judgment as the foetus represented the Antichrist, or, as the voice on the tape put it, 'The killing of Sharon Tate's baby represents a killing of Rosemary's baby (the Roman Antichrists) by the Lord . . .'[19]

In the documentary, *Charles Manson – Superstar* (Nikolas Schreck, 1989), the idea is put forward that you have made it if the public refer to you only by one name: 'Marilyn' for Marilyn Monroe, 'Mike' for Michael Jordan and 'Keith' for Keith Richards. If this is the case then Charles Manson *is* the only leader of an apocalyptic doomsday cult who *has* made it. Over a quarter of a century after the murders that catapulted him and the Family into the public spotlight, his popularity and infamy haven't diminished. In fact, with the advent of the Internet, his popularity has grown to staggering proportions. He is something different for everyone. Right-wingers regard him in the same light as Adolf Hitler, as a symbol of Caucasian supremacy. To some hardcore ecologists his back-to-nature philosophy makes him a messenger who must be heard. To civil libertarians the fact that he was denied his constitutional right to defend himself at his trail is another case of government meddling. For others he is the ultimate outsider, still giving the finger to the authorities and the world even as he rots in jail. And he is still the ultimate symbol for kids to put on T-shirts if they want to shock their parents.

The psychedelic dune buggies that the Family tore around the desert in left a trail of images: murder, mind control, hallucinogenic drugs, Satanism, witchcraft, Black Panthers, sexuality, rock 'n' roll and biker gangs – images that are as strange and compelling now as they were then.

No matter how you look at it or how you view him, in our society, Charlie Manson *is* an icon, a star. Or, as John Gilmore memorably puts it,

> Others have killed but the chemical ingredients to make them *stars* just weren't on the menu . . . we've mutated to the point where twelve-year-old junkies and mass killers grinning from headlines is just our American way of life. We are mutants perhaps – and these sociological stars are our knights who ride ahead – lowering the lance of annihilation. Charlie doesn't even see himself as real anymore. He sees himself as a spirit – *the* guru of annihilation.[20]

So what is Charlie Manson? Misunderstood prophet or drug-fucked lunatic? You make up your own mind.

NOTES

1. Charles Manson, 'I Am The Beast: The Trial Testimony of Charles Manson, November 19, 1970, A

Transcript' in Simon Dwyer, ed, *Rapid Eye* #1, London: Creation Books, 1995, p. 215.

2. Quoted in John Gilmore and Ron Kenner, *Manson: The Unholy Trial of Charlie and The Family*, Los Angeles: Amok Books, 2000, p. 52.
3. Ibid. p. 53.
4. Ibid. p. 19.
5. Ibid. p. 111.
6. John Gilmore and Ron Kenner, ibid. p. 124.
7. Foster, quoted in ibid. p. 134.
8. John Gilmore and Ron Kenner, ibid. p. 47.
9. Beausoleil, quoted in John Gilmore, ibid. p. 49.
10. Ed Sanders, *The Family: The Story of Charles Manson's Dune Buggy Attack Battalion*, Herts: Panther Books, 1973, p. 85.
11. De Grimston quoted in RN Taylor, 'The Process: A Personal Reminiscence', in *Apocalypse Culture*, Portland: Feral House, 1990, p. 165.
12. WS Bainbridge, *Satan's Power*, Berkeley: University of California Press, 1978, p. 162.
13. V Bugliosi, *Helter Skelter: The True Story of the Manson Murders*, New York: Bantam Books, 1974, p. 636.
14. Ed Sanders, *The Family*, op. cit. p. 63.
15. See, for example, Gary Valentine Lachman, *Turn Off Your Mind: The Mystic Sixties and the Dark Age of Aquarius*, London: Sidwick & Jackson, 2001.
16. Ed Sanders, op. cit. p. 129.
17. Ibid. p. 99.
18. Access Manson website.
19. Salt Lake Tribune, 9 January 1999. See also the Center for Studies on New Religions' website: http://www.cesnur.org/testi/Concerned.htm.
20. John Gilmore and Ron Kenner, *Manson*, op. cit. p. 4.

BIBLIOGRAPHY

WS Bainbridge, *Satan's Power*, Berkeley: University of California Press, 1978.

V Bugliosi, *Helter Skelter: The True Story of the Manson Murders*, New York: Bantam Books, 1974.

John Gilmore and Ron Kenner, *Manson: The Unholy Trial of Charlie and The Family*, Los Angeles: Amok Books, 2000.

Charles Manson, 'I Am The Beast: The Trial Testimony of Charles Manson, November 19, 1970, A Transcript' in Simon Dwyer, ed, *Rapid Eye* #1, London: Creation Books, 1995.

Ed Sanders, *The Family: The Story of Charles Manson's Dune Buggy Attack Battalion*, Herts: Panther Books, 1973.

RN Taylor, 'The Process: A Personal Reminiscence', in *Apocalypse Culture*, Portland: Feral House, 1990.

M Terry, *The Ultimate Evil: An Investigation into America's Most Dangerous Satanic Cult*, New York: Doubleday Books, 1987.

Nikolas Schreck, *Charles Manson-Superstar*, Video Werewolf, 1989.

INTERNET

http://members.aol.com/KarolMay/manson.html
http://labyrinth13.crimespider.com/Process.htm
http://home.sunrise.ch/prkoenig/manson.htm
http://www.charliemanson.com/beausoleil.htm
http://web.archive.org/web/20010603182156/
    www.atwa.com/atwa.htm

5. JONESTOWN

SUICIDE OR SALVATION?

JOHN HARRISON

How very much I've tried my best to give you a good life. In spite of all that I've tried, a handful of people, with their lies, have made our lives impossible. There's no way to distract ourselves from what's happened today.

— Reverend Jim Jones[1]

Retrospection can be a powerful and emotive tool. When one has the extravagance of time to reflect, one can look back at ostensibly trivial, insignificant moments, momentary thoughts and split-second decisions, and absorb the bigger picture that those actions helped to paint. A prime case in point:

When US Congressman Leo J Ryan picked up the *San Francisco Examiner* on the morning of 13 November 1977, he would have had no suspicion that the article he was about to read would lead him inextricably down the corridor to his violent death exactly twelve months later. He would have been even less aware that his killing would be for ever intertwined with the most appalling mass suicide in modern history.

The article in question, entitled 'Scared Too Long', concerned the death of one Sam Houston's son, Bob, in October 1976. Houston had decided to speak out about his son's death because he was convinced that the reason Bob had died – thrown under the wheels of a train by either himself or persons unknown – was because he had announced his decision to leave a religious congregation called the People's Temple the day before. Houston was also concerned that his two granddaughters, sent to New York for a vacation, had wound up instead in a place run by the Temple, dubbed 'Jonestown', in the South American country of Guyana, and never returned.

His concern aroused, Ryan began to investigate the activities of the People's Temple. What he soon found didn't paint a particularly flattering portrait. There were indications of massive social-security fraud, overseas bank accounts siphoning millions of dollars from the pockets of Temple worshippers and, most disturbing of all, claims from concerned relatives that some of the people of Jonestown were being held against their will, their human rights violated on an almost daily basis. Even darker were the whispers that the Jonestown community had on several occasions conducted rehearsals for a planned mass suicide.

In September 1978 – after reading a sworn affidavit of Debbie Blakey, a Jonestown defector who reiterated the mass-suicide intent – Ryan met with State Department officials to discuss the possibility of his making a trip to Jonestown. The request was made official on 4 October. Permission was quickly granted and Ryan's visit was scheduled for the week of 12–18 November. The official party, or 'Codel' (Congressional Delegation), would include Ryan, his personal assistant Jackie Speier and James Schollaert, staff consultant for the House Foreign Affairs Committee. Accompanying them would be nine media reporters and cameramen, and eighteen representatives from a delegation of concerned relatives.

In the days leading up to the visit, Ryan had contacted the leader and founder of the People's Temple – the Reverend Jim Jones – and announced his intention to visit Jonestown in order to check up on the health and welfare of American citizens living there. Under threat of having access to his US funds cut off, Jones had little choice but to grant permission, but his response to the news was bitter to say the least. Accusing Ryan of conducting a 'witch hunt' against him and his people, Jones allowed the visit only after he had been given assurances that the party would not be biased, that Mark Lane – serving as legal counsel for the People's Temple – would have to be present at all times and that no media representatives would be brought into Jonestown.

Touching down at Georgetown Airport in Guyana shortly before midnight on 14 November, the party slammed into an instant brick wall. A *San Francisco Chronicle* reporter, Ron Javers, was detained at the airport for not having an entry visa, and several members of the concerned-relatives delegation were forced to sleep on the floor of the Pegasus Hotel in Georgetown, despite the fact that reservations had been made and confirmed for them. It also became quickly obvious that Guyana officials were not planning to go out of their way to help the party.

Over the next two days, Ryan met with embassy officials and set up a meeting between Ambassador Burke and the relatives. An attempt to speak with a representative of the People's Temple at their head-quarters in Georgetown was thwarted when Burke and the family members were refused entry. Ryan himself was also continuing to be frustrated, with his scheduled flight to Jonestown repeatedly being postponed by Mark Lane.

By Friday morning, with negotiations still making no headway, Ryan – a tough veteran of many dangerous missions – decided enough was enough, and announced to Lane that he was flying out to Jonestown at 2.30 p.m.

that day, with or without his OK. The plane took off as scheduled. On board were Ryan, Speier, the deputy chief of mission Richard Dwyer, all nine media representatives, four representatives of the concerned-relatives delegation, Mark Lane and Charles Garry (another Jonestown legal voice), and Neville Annibourne, a representative of Guyana's government.

With the light aircraft buzzing its way over the steaming, humid jungles of Guyana en route to Jonestown, Leo Ryan would no doubt have been wondering exactly what kind of man would be waiting for him upon touchdown at the other end.

THE MESSIAH IN DARK GLASSES

James Warren Jones was born in Lynn, Indiana, in 1931. His father was an alcoholic Klansman with a deep but distorted sense of religion, his mother a self-proclaimed mystic. The seeds seem to have been sown for James Jones from birth. With his parents out trying to make a living during the Depression, young Jones was left free to develop his own interests, and create his own analysis of the world.

Jones's religious leanings emerged at an early age. He presided over funeral services for dead animals, before stumbling across a Pentecostal congregation known as the Gospel Tabernacle, which existed on the fringes and consisted primarily of people who had moved to the area from Tennessee and Kentucky. The people of Lynn dubbed the members of the Gospel Tabernacle 'holy-rollers' and 'tongues people'.

By 1947, Jones's ties with the Gospel Tabernacle were so strong that he took to preaching on street corners, delivering fervent sermons of the fire-and-brimstone variety that were to later become his hallmark. It was also during this time that Jones's sympathies for the poor and oppressed began to emerge, with the teenager frequently venturing into black neighbourhoods to spread the word. Although he denounced the 'sinful' behaviour of other boys his age, he would frequently fly into a rage whenever they hurled criticism his way, at one point going so far as to take a few (off-target) shots at a boy with his father's gun.

As Jones entered high school, an increasing allegiance to socialism had already begun to cultivate within him, and his speeches started to reflect a growing concern for government policies and social injustice, particularly among minority races. Not long after his graduation (with honours), Jones married Marceline, a student nurse whom he'd met at the hospital where Jones worked part-time to support his studies. Happy days for the couple weren't long-lasting, with Jones emerging as a domineering and insecure husband, his budding paranoia fuelled by jealousy and fears of rejection by Marceline. Indications of the crisis Jones was undergoing during this period can be gleaned from his growing lack of faith, his newfound proclamation that there was no God, and his threats to commit suicide if Marceline continued to worship.

Jones's faith began to return in 1952, when he discovered that the Methodist church that Marceline attended was an outspoken champion for the rights of minorities and the poverty-stricken. It was an ethic that appealed to Jones, and later that year he accepted a position as a student pastor at the Somerset Methodist Church in Indianapolis. Although the church was situated in a lower-middle-class white neighbourhood, Jones would frequently venture into the poor black areas of town, inviting people to attend his church.

After an attempt to adopt Marceline's twelve-year-old cousin ended in an outburst of spiteful anger from Jones, the pastor defected from the Somerset Methodist Church, rapidly building a loyal following by preaching at Pentecostal meetings and other churches (where he would often claim to be a miracle worker possessed of healing powers), and by the late 1950s had dubbed his burgeoning congregation the 'People's Temple'. To back up its name, he established soup kitchens and provided shelter for the homeless. Marceline gave birth to their son, and the pair also adopted a Korean and an African-American child. Needless to say, Jones's view on equality and calls for the integration of all races did not go down too well in the still racially divided America of the mid-1950s. Local newspapers carried stories on threats made to Jones's life (although no convictions ever seemed to be made, and it appears Jones himself may have sparked many of these stories as a means of gaining publicity).

As his followers grew in number, Jones began the process of communalising his congregation. He began referring to passages in the Bible that spoke of people sacrificing their possessions, and used his 'visions' of a nuclear attack on the Midwest as the pretext for uprooting his congregation and transporting them to safer climes (i.e. further away from the influence of family and friends). It was during the following two-year jaunt – in which he travelled the world in search of possible hiding spots for his followers – that Jones first visited Guyana.

By the time Jones and 140 of his followers migrated to Mendocino County in California (the decision to move there was based on a proclamation in *Esquire* that the area would be safe from fallout in the event of a nuclear attack), Marceline decided she had put up with enough of his extramarital encounters with female members of his flock. His son Stephen had also grown to despise his father's hypocritical nature, and once made an attempt to kill himself by downing some of the Quaaludes that Jones had now become dependant upon.

The collapse in his home life also impacted on Jones's extended family and, by the late 1960s, his congregation had dwindled to well below a hundred members. As he had done earlier, Jones demonstrated his ability to bounce back from near-ruin by successfully gaining an affiliation, this time with the Disciples of Christ, a congregation that boasted a huge membership of nearly 2 million. But Jones's allegiance with the Disciples of Christ was one merely forged for his own self-gain. He preached socialism, and used his position as a member of a legitimised church to gain tax exemptions. He also began to cultivate an exotic, charismatic image: wearing slick, well-cut polyester suits, his thick black hair clipped in a trendy mod hairdo, and more often than not preaching to his children with his dark eyes hidden behind a fashionable pair of metal-rimmed sunglasses, he looked every inch the cool, 1970s Lothario – one could easily picture him as a producer of low-budget exploitation or porno films.

Jones also cunningly used his membership in the Disciples of Christ to boost the ranks of his own depleted following. By tirelessly promoting his church through charity works, radio broadcasts and the publication of his own nationwide newsletter, Jones, using his preferred, shortened first name of Jim, was soon preaching to congregations of over two and half thousand, with his influence spreading to major West Coast cities such as San Francisco and Los Angeles.

THE BIRTH OF JONESTOWN

In 1974, Jim Jones began construction on his vision of Heaven: a 300-acre allotment in Guyana, situated 140 miles from Georgetown. Jones modestly christened his private fantasyland 'Jonestown'.

While construction of Jonestown was forging ahead (several of his senior followers had already moved there to oversee its development), Jones returned to the US to continue his recruitment drive in earnest. Jones's reputation as a healer was achieved with the help of his loyal staff members, who would sift through the garbage of temple members to extract information Jones could later use to feign clairvoyance at his meetings. Jones's strict screening policy for potential Temple members – political conservatism was not favoured, while antiestablishment leanings were – ensured that the majority of his followers were a mix of demoralised African-Americans and lower-middle-class, radical whites.

According to Jones, socialism was the manifestation of God. His miracles, healing of the sick and nurturing of the poor were all proof that he was Christ incarnate. Jones considered himself a social revolutionary. Temple members were easily coerced into pooling their incomes and turning their property over to the People's Temple to be sold (most of these funds ended up in overseas bank accounts). In return for this sacrifice, the congregation received room, board, meals and a two-dollar-a-week allowance.

One of the most intriguing layers of Jones's persona was his decidedly distorted views on sexuality and fidelity. He advocated sexual freedom within marriages, yet also preached on the need for celibacy. His female followers – including some not of legal age – were expected to cater to his every carnal whim, yet any member of his congregation caught having sex without his prior permission was publicly humiliated by Jones (at Jonestown, he would make them perform public sex acts with Temple members of his choosing). Jones claimed that sex was a 'revolutionary act', not to be indulged in for pleasure, and a Jonestown doctor who supported his claims that nonrevolutionary sex caused cancer was rewarded with a succession of teenage girls.

While he favoured young female flesh, Jones was not averse to taking same-sex partners, if it meant increasing his own power (by sleeping with both members of a married couple, Jones would weaken the bond between them, while strengthening their allegiance to the Temple and himself in the process). In 1973 he was arrested in MacArthur Park, a notorious meeting place for San Francisco's homosexual population, and booked for lewd conduct. Jones also later justified his sodomising of a male as being the only true way of making the man face up to his homosexuality.

As Jones's psychological grip on his congregation tightened, rumours and negative publicity began to seep into the press. Jones tried to curtail this as much as he could, with journalists being woken in the middle of the night by angry telephone calls, and letters threatening that physical harm would be delivered to their doorstep. Some Temple members were found jobs within major newspapers, where they could warn Jones of any upcoming negative stories about him. Jones would immediately begin threats of legal action should the story see print.

As with the leaders of many religious cults, it wasn't the opinions of the outside world that stung Jones the hardest: it was the perceived treachery of his members. He considered himself the father of his followers (and encouraged them to address him as such), and he reserved the right to exert a father's strict hand over them. Threats of grave punishment were meted out to anyone who considered defection from the Temple. Jones had by now surrounded himself with a small army of devoted henchmen, who delighted in handing out severe beatings to anyone who dared criticise Jones or question his actions.

It seems obvious that the desire to wield absolute power over his followers was the factor that led Jim Jones to move his entire congregation to Jonestown. Convinced he would be out of reach of US intervention, and with his followers seemingly free from the meddling influence of fretful relatives, Jones was able to maintain a commanding, militarian control over his community. Isolated and so far from home, their visas confiscated, members of his temple would no longer find it easy to abandon him. Jonestown residents lived in cramped quarters, were fed meagre rations of often spoiled food, and forced to work sixteen to eighteen hours of labour per day, toiling away in the fields of the Jonestown 'Agricultural Project'.

Yet, as desperately as he might have tried to keep his own little Utopian dream under control, Jones's world was rapidly spiralling towards catastrophe. Beginning on New Year's Day, 1976, Jones had led his followers on several rehearsals for a 'revolutionary suicide', commanding them to drink a concoction which he claimed was fatal poison, but was in fact a harmless soft drink. Any followers who became hysterical or refused to drink were brought into line by the mock shooting of a member who tried to run away. When Jones would later reveal to his congregation that the 'poison' was innocuous, they thanked him for testing them.

But the test runs for these 'white nights' (as they were dubbed) convinced Jones that he could persuade his followers to do anything, and with Congressman Leo Ryan winging his way towards him, it seemed that the time for practice was quickly coming to an end . . .

We win, we win when we go down, they don't have nobody else to hate. They've got nobody else to hate. Many will destroy themselves. I'm speaking here not as the administrator but as a prophet today.

THE HAPPIEST PLACE ON EARTH?

Touching down at the Port Kaituma airstrip, Ryan's plane was met by Corporal Rudder, regional officer for the Northwest district of Guyana. Negotiations as to who would be allowed to visit Jonestown then ensued between Ryan and Jonestown representatives who had accompanied Rudder to the airport. Jones had delivered specific instructions that only his lawyer, Mark Lane, be allowed to exit the plane. Eventually, it was agreed that all but one member of the party would be allowed access to Jonestown. Gordon Lindsay, a news consultant for the NBC network, was denied entry because of a critical article that he had written on the People's Temple.

Upon arrival at Jonestown, the delegation was greeted with a well-rehearsed charade. Dinner was served, and a musical revue performed to entertain the visitors. Jones himself seemed friendly but wary, never quite able to relax. At first, the ruse seemed to work, with Ryan himself being fooled into believing the majority of people at Jonestown felt the retreat was 'the best thing that has ever happened to them' (a comment that Ryan made to the congregation, and that was greeted with rapturous applause).

By the time night began to fall, however, things started to fall apart rapidly. As Ryan and Jackie Speier enquired of the wellbeing of people whose names had been given to them by relatives back in the US, a note was slipped to the NBC reporter Don Harris from a Temple member, Monica Bagby, indicating that she and her friend Vern Gosney were desperate to leave Jonestown. Richard Dwyer received a similar message from another Temple member. As midnight approached, Jones banished all of the media and family representatives from the compound, refusing to let them stay the night. Only Ryan, Speier, Richard Dwyer and Neville Annibourne were allowed to remain, along with Lane and Garry.

Ironically, it may have been his decision not to allow everyone to stay that hastened Jones's demise. For, while Ryan and the others were no doubt getting a restless, disturbed sleep, the media representatives, who had been shuffled back to Port Kaituma, were approached by a number of local Guyanese (including a police official), who related horror stories of alleged beatings at Jonestown, and the presence of a 'torture hole', an old well into which children who had displeased Jones were thrown in the middle of the night, after being terrified with tales of a monster who dwelled at the bottom (Jones would have one of his henchmen – unseen in the darkness – grab at the child's feet as he was being lowered, kicking and screaming, into the well). Other, older, children were said to have been tied up naked and had electric shocks administered to their genitalia. Several Guyanese officials had attempted to investigate the reports, but were continually denied entry to the compound.

The media and relatives were returned to Jonestown at 11 a.m. the following day – several hours later than planned. Upon their arrival, they discovered that a number of people had expressed their desire to Ryan to leave Guyana and return to the United States. When Ryan confronted Jones with the letter that had been slipped to Harris the previous evening, Jones became increasingly agitated and on edge. His eyes black, soulless inkwells, his speech disjointed and slurred, he blamed the letter on a singular troublemaker within the group, then pleaded for him and his 'family' to be left alone in peace:

> People play games, friend. They lie . . . what can I do about liars? Leave us. I just beg you, please leave us. We won't bother nobody. Anybody who wants to get out of here can get out of here. We have no problem about getting out of here . . . they come and go all the time. I don't know what kind of game . . . people like . . . who, who . . . people like publicity. Some people do . . . I don't.

With the delegation preparing to leave for their flight back to the United States – accompanied by fifteen brave defectors from the camp – Jones became increasingly concerned about the way the visit was likely to be reported by the media. A rather chilling piece of news-camera footage taken just as the party was departing shows Jones leaning over and clearly whispering something into the ear of one of his generals. It seems safe to say that the words Jim Jones whispered at that point were the ones that sealed the fate of Congressman Leo Ryan, along with that of the entire Jonestown community.

Initially, Ryan had intended to stay on at Jonestown to conduct further investigations, but was attacked by a People's Temple member, Don Sly, with a knife. He was not hurt, but decided that staying behind alone would not be a wise move. The party arrived back at the Port Kaituma airstrip at 4.30 p.m., where they waited for around 45 minutes for their two planes to arrive (the US Embassy request for an additional plane to transport the defecting Jonestown members had caused the delay).

Before long, one of the planes – a small, six-seater Cessna – was loaded and ready to go. As it taxied down the runway ready for take-off, all hell broke loose as one of the defectors on board, Larry Layton – in actuality a staunch Jones supporter and one of his senior generals – produced a gun and began to open fire on the other passengers. Two people were killed, including Monica Bagby.

As this happened, Ryan's party was preparing to board the second plane, a twin-engine Otter. Ryan had walked over to shake the pilot's hand through the window when the firing broke out aboard the Cessna. The party, thrown into chaos and confusion, probably failed even to notice the tractor and trailer that pulled up by the edge of the airstrip. Crouched down in the trailer were several of Jones's armed guards. Moving quickly, they emerged from the trailer and opened fire on the party, killing Leo Ryan, three media representatives and one of the Jonestown defectors, in a hail of gunfire that lasted five minutes (the surprise attack was captured on a TV camera, pointed towards the tractor and left running on the ground as its operator Robert Brown lay dying). Jackie Speier was seriously wounded, along with five others. Although the Otter had been damaged by gunfire and was unable to take off, the

Cessna was able to get itself airborne, the pilot radioing the emergency to the tower controllers at Georgetown Airport, who in turn notified Guyanese officials. The gunmen fled from the Port Kaituma airstrip soon after, leaving the terrified survivors huddling together for protection.

KOOL-AID: A REFRESHINGLY FATAL DRINK

According to most sources and reports, the mass suicide began at almost the same time as the shootings at the airstrip were taking place. Jones gathered his followers together and, in a tone that sounded more like a prediction than a simple statement of fact, told them that someone was going to shoot Ryan's plane out of the sky:

> Right then, what's going to happen in a few
> minutes is that one of the people on that plane is
> gonna, is gonna shoot the pilot, I know that. I
> didn't plan it but I know it's gonna happen. They're
> gonna shoot that pilot and down comes that plane
> into the jungle and we had better not have any of
> our children left when it's over 'cause they'll
> [inaudible] on us.

According to Jones, the consequences of this action would be dire. The unseen, mysterious 'enemy' of the People's Temple would soon descend upon Jonestown, annihilating both the compound and its inhabitants. This mythical invasion was something that Jones had lived in fear of for many years, and his response to it had been well planned and rehearsed in advance. The 'revolutionary suicide', as Jones liked to call it, was about to be acted out for one final time.

We'll set an example for others . . . one thousand people who've said we don't like the way the world is. Take our life from us. We laid it down. We got tired. We didn't commit suicide, we committed an act or revolutionary suicide protesting the conditions of an inhumane world . . .

The Kool-Aid (a popular American cordial that Jonestown kept in plentiful supply) was laced with Valium and cyanide, and brought to the assembly hall in two big steel buckets, where it was dispensed in small paper cups. The first to die were the babies and small children, over two hundred of them, who had the poison squirted down their throats with a syringe. Then it was the adults' turn to swallow the fatal concoction – many blindly did so even after watching their children die horribly.

A tape recording made of Jones's suicide plea reveals spots of resistance from several of the followers, but their moment of lucidity came far too late. Many had the cyanide poured down their throat; others who tried to hide were tracked down and shot dead by armed guards. In all, 913 of the 1,110 people believed to have been in Jonestown at the time were either pushed or jumped willingly into death that afternoon; the rest managed to escape into the jungle. Among the dead was Jim Jones himself, who had died not from poison but from a single gunshot wound to the head. To this day, there is still confusion as to whether Jones pulled the trigger himself, or was shot by persons unknown.

Within hours, word of the mass suicide had reached the eyes and ears of a stunned and horrified world. News footage of the seemingly endless parade of bodies scattered across the Jonestown complex, many lying arm-in-arm, created a nightmarish image which brought forth visions of Dante's *Inferno*. Jim Jones, the man who believed he was Christ, had created his own black mark in history – along with Adolf Hitler, Charles Manson and Lee Harvey Oswald, he would be remembered by the masses as one of the most vile figures of the twentieth century.

The People's Temple died at precisely the same moment as Jim Jones. Their former headquarters in San Francisco was eventually demolished by the Loma Prieta earthquake of 1989. Larry Layton, who survived the Jonestown suicides, became the only person charged with any of the airstrip killings (he was eventually set free when the jury could not decide on a verdict).

AFTERMATH

Nearly a quarter of a century after the fact, the question for many remains the same: how was Jim Jones able to wield so much influence and power over his followers as to drag nearly one thousand of them into the abyss with him? Does responsibility for the tragedy fall solely on the shoulders of Jones, or do his followers need to be accountable for their eventual actions?

There is no doubt that Jim Jones was an abusive, deluded individual. Yet, unlike the majority of cult leaders whose preachings led down a road of violent death (Manson, David Koresh), Jones did accomplish many positive things during his early years as leader of the People's Temple. He supported racial integration at a time when it was extremely unpopular (and potentially fatal) to do so, earning the wrath of many senior church officials in the process. At the People's Temple, black and white were not only free, but encouraged, to worship together. Jones and his congregation worked to feed the poor, shelter the homeless, and help ex-convicts and drug addicts to re-enter society. Jones offered up a sympathetic hand to the downtrodden, the abused, the ignored and the hated. Perhaps, in turn, they felt that they owed him the gift of their ultimate sacrifice.

> I want to go – I want to see you go through. They can take me, and they can do whatever they want to do. I want to see you go. I don't wanna see you go through this hell no more. No more, no more, no more.

CONSPIRACY?

While most people readily accepted the events as described in the media as gospel, conspiracy theories did circulate among the underground. The most popular of these – and the one that continues to flourish on the dozens of websites devoted to Jones – revolves around the alleged connections between Jim Jones, Jonestown and the CIA. What the connection is varies widely, depending on whose version of events you care to listen to. Some believe Jones himself was a CIA agent, and Jonestown an enormous mind-control experiment that went haywire and had to be terminated. Among the wide variety of drugs claimed to be found in abundance at Jonestown were: Quaaludes, Valium, morphine, Demerol, Thorazine (an aggressive tranquilliser), sodium pentathol (used as a truth serum), chloral hydrate (a hypnotic chemical agent) and thallium (which distorts thinking), along with the cyanide used in the suicides.

Others believe the CIA seized the moment as the perfect opportunity to assassinate Leo Ryan. Ryan had long been a harsh critic of the CIA, and had authored the Hughes–Ryan Amendment, which if passed would have required the CIA to report all of its planned covert operations to Congress for approval before they actually commenced. One can easily see why the CIA would not wish to have this amendment passed – and indeed it was quashed not long after Ryan's death – but it does seem a bit of a stretch to consider they would have orchestrated the deaths of nearly a thousand people in order to cover up the killing of just one man (in 1980, the House Permanent Select Committee on Intelligence announced that there was 'no evidence' of CIA involvement at Jonestown). Still, the theories, and the doubts, continue in the minds of many to this day . . .

The suicide cults also continue to flourish, gladly laying down their lives for seemingly senseless causes that mystify the rest of the world. The suicide in 1997 of 39 members of the Heaven's Gate cult – who were convinced by their leader Marshall Applewhite that they were destined for an eternal journey aboard a spaceship that was travelling within the fiery tail of the Hale-Bop comet – being one of the most recent cult suicides to generate an enormous amount of media attention and public curiosity (and, perhaps significantly, the first cult suicide where the Internet was perceived as one of the influential factors).

But it seems highly unlikely that any cult leader will ever get as many of his followers to jump into the deep, dark void of death as Reverend Jim Jones did on 8 November 1978.

NOTES

1. All Jim Jones, quotes are taken from the transcription of his last speech, made available both in printed format and on vinyl LP.

BIBLIOGRAPHY

Jim Jones, *The Jonestown Massacre: The Transcript of Reverend Jim Jones' Last Speech, Guyana 1978*, Karl Eden introduction, Brighton: Temple Press Limited, 1993.

ME Knerr, *Suicide in Guyana*. Cammery: Horwitz, 1978.

Murder Casebook #78, *High Priests of Death*, London: Marshall Cavendish, 1991.

Kenneth Wooden, *The Children of Jonestown*, New York: McGraw-Hill, 1981.

DISCOGRAPHY

Jim Jones, *Christian Crusades – Messages for the Total Man*, US.

LP released in the mid-1970s, featuring a selection of Jones's speeches. Was rereleased in the late-1990s as a CD picture disc (featuring a photo of Jones's bloated corpse on the disc).

Jim Jones, *He's Able – People's Temple Choir*, UK.

CD featuring music recorded in the 1970s by the People's Temple Choir, along with Jones's suicide speech. CD cover features photos of the dead at Guyana.

FILMOGRAPHY

Guyana – Crime of the Century (1980, original title *Guyana, el Crimen del Siglo*):

Extremely trashy re-enactment of the Jonestown story from the Mexican-born writer/director Rene Cardona Jr (whose previous works include the *Jaws* knock-off *Tintorera* and the true-life cannibal drama *Survive*). A Spanish–Mexican co-production, *Guyana – Crime of the Century* casts Stuart Whitman in a very energetic and impressive performance as the Reverend James Johnson (one wonders why the name had to be changed – surely not to protect the innocent?). In the US, the film was re-edited, had the narration of a supposed survivor of the tragedy added, and was released as *Guyana: Cult of the Damned*. Slumming co-stars in this film include Bradford Dillman, Yvonne DeCarlo, Joseph Cotten and Gene Barry.

Guyana Tragedy – The Story of Jim Jones (1980):

A gripping, two-part TV movie, with Powers Booth giving an Emmy-winning performance as Jim Jones. Rare for a TV production, this presents a faithful version of the events leading up to the suicides, and due to its 192 minute running time is able to take its time with some genuine character building. Co-stars include Ned Beatty (as Leo Ryan), Irene Cara, Veronica Cartwright, Rosalind Cash, Brad Douriff, Diane Ladd, Randy Quaid, Meg Foster and Diana Scarwind. Directed by William A Graham, it is available on video in the US as a two-tape box set.

6. FAMILY TIES

THE STRANGE HISTORY OF THE LORBER SOCIETY

MIKITA BROTTMAN

In the afternoon of 20 December 1970, on the peaceful
Spanish island of Tenerife, police were called to a
building on Jesus of Nazareth Street in the town of Santa
Cruz after neighbours reported hearing strange noises
from one of the nearby apartments. Apparently, shouts
and screams had been heard, partially drowned out by
loud organ music and the singing of hymns. By the time
the police arrived, however, the bizarre noises had
stopped and the apartment was silent. After beating
loudly on the door and getting no reply, the police made
the decision to break into the apartment.

Nobody could possibly have been prepared, that
December afternoon, for the dreadful scene that lay
inside the apartment on Jesus of Nazareth Street. There
was blood everywhere, all over the walls, the furniture,
the floor and even dripping from the ceiling. In the
living room, the freshly killed bodies of three females
were lying on the floor. One was a middle-aged woman
and the others were both young girls. All had apparently
been bludgeoned to death, since their skulls were
bashed in and their faces smashed beyond recognition.
The blood-coated weapon lay on the floor nearby – a
heavy wooden coat hanger. Even more horrifying, the
bodies of the women had all been mutilated, their
breasts and sex organs carved out with a knife and
nailed to the walls of the apartment like a set of
grotesque hunting trophies. The body of the older

woman had suffered the most abuse – her heart had been torn out of her chest and impaled on a wooden stake in the middle of the room. The whole scene was reminiscent of some horrifying primitive ceremony, some ghastly ritual sacrifice. Police reported that 'every inch of the apartment was dripping with blood'.

Meanwhile, a few streets away, a young German girl, Sabine Alexander, was folding linen in the house of a local doctor, where she worked as a housekeeper. When the doorbell rang, she went to answer it as usual. Outside stood her father, Harald, and her brother, Frank, both solemn-faced and covered in blood. 'We wanted you to know', said her father, 'that Frank and I have just killed your mother and your sisters.'

JAKOB LORBER

To understand the origins of this bizarre and horrible crime, we need to turn to nineteenth-century Slovenia, birthplace of the prophet and mystic Jakob Lorber. Lorber was born on 22 July 1800 in Kanischka, a small village in the wine-growing area along the River Drau. His family were simple farmers, and Jakob went to teacher-training college and initially began work as a village teacher. After further training, however, he was unable to secure a post in a secondary school, and decided to change the direction of his career and make use of his musical talent.

Those who consider themselves to be prophets or emissaries of God are often very ordinary people. According to the German mystic Jakob Boehme, 'to exclude from the very beginning any claim for personal merit, the Lord sometimes makes use of very insignificant people when revealing His mysteries, so it shall be all the more clearly evident that they are from His hand only.'

A mystic in the same tradition as Boehme, Lorber played the violin as a soloist in concerts, and also reported on opera and concert performances for provincial newspapers. To enhance his technique, he took lessons from the famous violin virtuoso Paganini, which clearly enhanced his reputation, and at the height of his career gave a concert at La Scala Opera House in Milan. He was close to the circle around Franz Schubert, and in 1840 was offered the position of assistant musical director of the Trieste Theatre – an opportunity he declined, having by this time received his calling from God.

On 15 March 1840, Jakob Lorber heard a voice in the area of his heart that said, 'Jakob, get up, take your pencil and write.' Lorber obeyed the command, and for the next 24 years wrote down what was dictated to him by this voice, which identified itself as Jesus Christ. His writings comprise 24 long volumes, plus several other shorter articles. This work includes an almost daily report of the three-year ministry of Jesus, including the crucifixion, plus information about the history of mankind, a description of the universe and all it contains, a report on life in the hereafter plus abundant information about planetary systems, elementary particles, galactic structures, and more – the manuscript equivalent to 10,000 pages of print.

When Lorber told his friends about the Inner Voice, and that he had been given the mission of recording a revelation from the supernatural world, they became worried that he was developing a mental illness. Friends began to visit him daily, watching as he wrote for several hours at a stretch. Others were suspicious, believing the words to have been dictated by someone else, or copied from scientific books. Lorber was unable to understand many of the things he was told by the Inner Voice, but he was confident that everything he wrote would be seen to have meaning, and that later generations would be startled by the truth of his predictions. Only a few pages of the manuscript were actually published in Lorber's lifetime, and without reference to his name. But the Inner Voice told Lorber that there would come a time when everything he had written would be published and made known to all mankind.

After he began taking down the words of the Inner Voice, Lorber decided on a life of independence and retirement, with few material luxuries. From that time on, his outside work was limited to giving music lessons to children in Graz, and his only diversion was meeting his friends to talk in the evenings. He never married, lived alone in a single room, and never really came into the public eye. During the final years of his life, his physical condition deteriorated steadily and his financial position became so precarious that his friends had to take care of his most urgent needs, and Lorber had to dictate the prophecies he received to other people to write down. Jakob Lorber died in 1864.

THE NEW REVELATION
Jakob Lorber's 10,000-page manuscript was known as *The New Revelation*. In this work, Lorber provides a mystic revelation encompassing elucidation and supplementation of the gospels as well as a number of prophecies relating to disasters that were supposed to befall the whole of mankind before the end of the twentieth century. Lorber makes it clear that mankind faces a turning point in time and that terrible disasters are going to befall the inhabitants of the earth. The disclosures also contain an urgent warning for modern

man to abandon the path of theoretical and practical materialism before a worldwide catastrophe occurs.

The tenor of the work and its content seem to indicate that the seed of Lorber's prophecies would come to bear full fruit at the turn of the millennium. His followers claim that *The New Revelation* contains many true facts about later discoveries in astronomy, atomic physics and anthropology, about which Lorber could not possibly have known. According to Lorber Society adherents, *The New Revelation* contains 'amazingly accurate' statements concerning atoms and elementary particles and palaeontological details relating to early and prehistoric man.

Lorber's endtime prophecies are of apocalyptic proportions and involve worldwide terror and dismay. In the twentieth century, technology, according to Lorber, would become an evil spirit, placed in the service of demonic powers to destroy the environment. The Last Days started with the two World Wars, and the terrorism of Hitler and Stalin also form part of the events predicted by Lorber as bringing great tribulation. 'One nation shall rise against another and fight it with weapons of fire,' claims Lorber of the endtimes. 'Tremendous scarcities will develop, starvation, many dreadful diseases, epidemics and plagues among men, animals and plants. Great storms will also arise, earthquakes . . .' And at the end of time, as Lorber cryptically puts it, 'the world will become utterly leaky'.

Several volumes of *The New Revelation* contain detailed descriptions of the destiny of dead souls and of conditions in the next world. 'Things are quite different in the spirit world than on this earth,' Lorber tells us, reassuringly. He goes on to explain that hell was created not by God but by evil men, 'wholly worldly men, who believe in no God and yet enjoy life in health to a great age and in the end die a quick and painless death'. According to Lorber, such sinners have already received their rewards in life, and should not expect any pleasure in the hereafter. 'In the society of such souls,' he explains, 'outer darkness will prevail, and' – predictably, perhaps – 'there will be much wailing and gnashing of teeth among them.'

Lorber's followers also like to draw attention to those sections of *The New Revelation* where the prophet discusses the 'adversary from the air' and 'lights in the heavens'. These disclosures are considered to refer to the existence of UFOs, mainly in connection to another passage in *The New Revelation* which appears to suggest that extraterrestrial people will come and intervene in the lives of earthlings. 'Now the time is coming when I shall open a view of the earth to the inhabitants of the greater planets,' writes Lorber, 'and make clear to them the standpoint of those who set to look for Me and came to this earth. Then they shall grow greatly excited, and this excitement will extend from Venus to Urka. Then it shall come about that "the forces of heaven are shaken", and a tremendous call shall go out from all sides to the inhabitants of this earth.' Others interpret this disclosure to the effect that the inhabitants of other heavenly bodies will give men spiritual help.

Lorber Society adherents claim that about a million copies of *The New Revelation* have been sold since it was first published. The manuscripts show no corrections or revisions, and are currently held at the Lorber Publishing House in Wuerttemberg, Germany, which has also published later editions of the text.

HARALD ALEXANDER

Like most prophets, Jakob Lorber has attracted a number of followers over the years, most of them devout and sincere. When Lorber died in 1864, he passed on his knowledge to one of the most devoted of these followers, a wheelwright named Greg Riehle. When Riehle died he, in turn, passed on his knowledge – and the portable organ that accompanied the group's worship sessions – to his constant companion, Harald Alexander. Unfortunately, this was not a wise decision: Alexander may have been a devoted follower of Jakob Lorber, but, when Riehle bequeathed him the sacred manuscripts and Lorber's portable organ, Harald Alexander began to develop delusions of grandeur, which eventually progressed into a genuine messianic complex.

In 1945, Harald Alexander moved to Hamburg, taking Lorber's sacred portable organ and manuscript with him and installing them in the apartment where he lived with his wife, Dagmar. Since there were no other followers of Jakob Lorber in Hamburg, and thus no one to recognise Harald Alexander's role as officially sanctioned spiritual leader, he resorted to establishing his own small sect of the Lorber Society at home. And, like all death cults, Harald Alexander's own version of the Lorber Society was a bizarre perversion and distortion of the religious tradition from which it emerged.

Dagmar Alexander, who fully supported her husband's self-bestowed religious authority, eventually gave birth to four children. First came a daughter, Marina; next came twin girls, Petra and Sabine; and finally came a long-awaited son, who was named Frank. To Harald Alexander, his son was the next in line to inherit Lorber's sacred knowledge; Frank was also – at least, according to his father – a genuine seer in the tradition of Swedenborg, Boehme and Jakob Lorber himself. As a result, Harald decreed that every single one of Frank's demands and wishes had to be followed, and decided that he should be referred to as the Prophet of God.

Those who followed the teachings of Jakob Lorber believed in total withdrawal from society, and complete self-sacrifice, coupled with a belief that all nonmembers of the group were owned by Satan. Lorber's *The New Revelation* has a lot to say about devils, which apparently, at least according to Jakob Lorber, populate the world – an aspect of the text that seems to have been taken particularly seriously by Harald Alexander. 'There are personal devils right here, still walking in the flesh,' writes Lorber, 'who are also now and forever endeavouring to have an evil influence on this world . . . through certain secret whisperings and enticements. They are only too well aware of the different weaknesses and potential weaknesses in men, take hold of these and fan them into burning passions.'

Consequently, when young Frank reached his teens and began to have sexual thoughts, things got rather difficult for the Alexander family. According to Lorber's doctrine, all the women outside the family were considered to be sinful and dirty whores who were owned by Satan, and therefore highly inappropriate sexual partners for Frank, the Prophet of God. This was a problem of course: Frank's sexual desires had to be fulfilled, but they had to be fulfilled by the holy, devout kind of women who were worthy of the Prophet of God. There was only one way out of the dilemma – to keep things in the family. So Harald introduced Frank to the delights of sexual congress with his wife, Dagmar – Frank's mother. And, when Frank grew tired of having only one single sexual partner, Harald offered him the body of his older sister, Marina. Finally, Harald Alexander himself joined his wife, son and daughter in the bedroom, indulging in regular four-in-a-bed sessions involving the older members of the family.

This precarious and unorthodox situation seemed to work, at least for a while. Problems arose, however, when the two younger Alexander girls, twins Petra and Sabine – who were not involved in their family's incestuous orgies – began to make comments to their friends at school about the strange things that were going on at home. At least one of these friends passed on the information to their parents, who didn't waste any time informing the police. Rather than wait for charges to be filed against him, Harald Alexander gathered together his family, his sacred manuscripts and his holy organ, and left the country.

JESUS OF NAZARETH STREET

In the early months of 1970, the Alexander family settled into an apartment in Jesus of Nazareth Street in Santa Cruz, capital of balmy Tenerife in the Spanish Canary Islands. Now a busy tourist resort, Tenerife in 1970 was sparsely populated, peaceful and serene – a suitable place for the Alexander family's unusual form of worship to continue undisturbed.

Interestingly, however, for a small island, Tenerife has an unusual number of cult connections. The founder of Scientology, L. Ron Hubbard, lived there for a while, and in January 1998 nineteen people were arrested in Santa Cruz after planning to take part in a mass suicide in anticipation of the end of the world. The followers of the group, led by a German psychologist named Heide Fittkau-Garthe, apparently believed a spaceship would come and pick up their bodies from the ridge of a volcano. The sect, whose name was not released, has been linked to the Order of the Solar Temple, whose followers have carried out mass suicides in Canada, France and Switzerland.

In Tenerife, the Alexander family continued their unusual lifestyle pretty much as before, with Frank and his sisters supporting their parents through a succession of dreary clerking and domestic jobs. In the evening, the family would gather together to read the works of Jakob Lorber and sing hymns, accompanied by Harald Alexander on Lorber's sacred portable organ. And then, one December morning, just eleven months after the Alexander family had moved to Tenerife, Frank Alexander decided that the 'hour of the killing' had come.

THE 'HOUR OF THE KILLING'
20 December 1970 began as a normal day for the Alexander family. It was a warm, crisp winter's day and the streets of Santa Cruz were decorated for the holiday season. Sabine, the only member of the family to be working that last week before Christmas, went off as usual to her job as housekeeper in the home of a local doctor and his family. The rest of the family were at home, reading and praying quietly. And then at some point in the afternoon, apparently at random and out of the blue, Frank – the Prophet of God – announced to his father that 'the hour of killing' had come.

Consequently, Harald Alexander sat down at Jakob Lorber's portable organ and began to play a series of hymns, while Frank instructed his mother and the two of his sisters who were home at the time – Petra and Marina – to kneel down in front of him on the floor, which they did without question. The women bowed their heads submissively and waited for further instructions from the Prophet.

But there were no further instructions: this, as Frank later put it, was 'The Time of the Cleansing'. There were no weapons in the house, and so Frank picked up a large, heavy coat hanger and began to beat his mother and sisters over the head until they were bludgeoned unconscious – a process that must have been exceedingly difficult and taken a very long time. The women began to scream in horror and pain, but made no attempt to defend themselves against the shocking onslaught.

Once the women were dead – or no longer conscious, at least – Frank Alexander took over on the organ while his father set about hacking up the bodies of his family. Apparently, he ripped apart the women's bodies while singing hymns to the Lord, hacking out their breasts and vaginal areas and nailing them to the walls of the apartment. Next, he carved his wife's heart out of her body and impaled it on a wooden stake in the middle of the floor. Finally, still covered in blood and gore, Frank and Harald Alexander left the apartment and walked over to the house where Sabine was working to tell her what the Prophet of God had done. Meanwhile, frantic neighbours had called the police, who were about to discover the aftermath of one of the bloodiest and most deranged acts they had ever seen.

'THE TIME OF THE CLEANSING'

Could there have been any reasonable motive for such an apparently insane crime? Jakob Lorber's endtime prophesies are of apocalyptic proportions and involve worldwide terror and dismay. Had Frank Alexander perhaps decided to take the Apocalypse into his own hands? Was this what Lorber meant when he predicted that 'the world would become utterly leaky'? Perhaps there is also a clue to motivation in Frank Alexander's cryptic description of the killings as 'The Time of the

Cleansing'. Had the women of the family betrayed him somehow, or refused to go along with his sexual demands? Had one of them had sexual relations outside the family? Could it be that – according to Frank Alexander – Dagmar, Marina and Petra Alexander had revealed themselves to be the kind of 'devils in disguise' that Lorber had warned about?

To the rational mind, however, there could be no justification for such a horrible, brutal series of murders. Unsurprisingly, after openly admitting their guilt to the police, Harald and Frank Alexander were found unfit to stand trial by reason of insanity, and both were sent to a psychiatric institution. Sabine Alexander apparently begged the judge to be allowed to go with them, feeling the need to suffer along with her father and brother, despite her innocence. But her appeal was denied, and she was sent instead to a convent – outside which, in appropriate fairy-tale fashion, she has never since set foot.

BIBLIOGRAPHY
Brian Lane, *Forces From Beyond*, London: Morrow/Avon, 1997.

Brian Lane, *The Encyclopedia of Occult and Supernatural Murder*, London: Brockhampton Press, 1997.

Jakob Lorber, *The New Revelation* (trans. Violet Ozols), Lorber Verlag Bietigheim, 2000.

7. WACO AND THE FINE ART OF KILLING

JOHN HARRISON

For many of those who sat bolted to their television sets during the months of March and April 1993, there was never any question of the outcome. The sweeping fire that suddenly raged through the compound, incinerating those inside who weren't already dead, merely confirmed the world's belief that a religious cult, when backed into a corner and threatened, will always choose self-destruction over enslavement.

In the strange milieu of religious cults, the raid, siege and subsequent destruction of the Branch Davidians at Waco, Texas, was exceptional for two distinct reasons: it was played out in almost real time on television stations across the globe, and it was the first mass destruction of a cult in which the authorities were present before, during and after the fact.

These two points are irrevocably entwined with what eventuated at Waco. Were it not for the raid on the Branch Davidian headquarters at Mount Carmel on the morning of 28 February 1993 – carried out by the Bureau of Alcohol, Tobacco and Firearms (ATF) – we can only speculate as to what path David Koresh would have eventually led his ferociously devoted band of followers down. While many believe that Koresh had long been plotting an eventual course of self-destruction that was merely rushed along by the ATF raid, there are others who view Waco as the perfect example of America's deep-rooted fear of and paranoia towards religious cults, a cult systematically and deliberately destroyed for nothing more than being a cult, and as such a symbol of something that is inherently evil, and defiles the beliefs of 'normal' religions.

Of course, whose side of the story one believes depends largely on one's interpretations of the actions, motivations and words of David Koresh – Jesus Christ, rock-'n'-roll preacher with divine vision, or sociopathic paedophile who used the Bible as a convenient cover for his crimes?

A SHORT HISTORY OF THE SON OF GOD

David Koresh was born Vernon Wayne Howell in Houston, Texas, in 1959 to a fourteen-year-old girl named Bonnie Clark. Like Christ, Vernon was the son of a carpenter, twenty-year-old Bobby Howell.

While talking with FBI agents during the Waco siege, Vernon Howell described his childhood as lonely. A high school dropout, he had two passions as a teenager: music and the Bible. At twenty, Howell joined his mother's church, the Seventh Day Adventists, but was expelled for purportedly bringing a negative influence on some of the younger members.

It was this expulsion that drew Howell into the arms of the Branch Davidians in 1981. Founded in the mid-1950s by Ben Roden (although the seeds of the Davidians can be traced back as far as 1831, when William Miller, an atheist turned Baptist preacher, began studying the prophesies of the Bible), the Branch Davidians were a splinter group of the Seventh Day Adventists, whose teachings focused on the Book of Revelations. Offshoots of the Seventh Day Adventists had established a headquarters on the outskirts of Waco, Texas. It was here that the Davidians solidified their base, and it was here that Howell first arrived to work as a handyman and quickly decided it was his destiny to take over and lead the sect.

Dishevelled in appearance, but possessed of an undeniable charisma and the ability to talk almost anybody into submission, Howell initiated his long-term plans by having an affair with Lois Roden, the near seventy-year-old leader of the Davidians, who had taken power after the death of her husband Ben in 1978. The pair travelled to Israel together, but the relationship – initiated through Howell's interpretation of Isaiah, Chapter 8, as a commandment for the pair to cohabit – sparked an intense hatred between Howell and Roden's son George, who also claimed the power of prophesy and saw himself as the future leader of the Davidians, not the skinny, black-jeans-clad, myopic seducer of his mother.

When Lois died of cancer in 1986, the power struggle between Howell and George Roden escalated, with Howell and his small group of devoted followers eventually being driven from Mount Carmel at gunpoint. After retreating to eastern Texas to lick his wounds, Howell returned to Mount Carmel with seven of his male flock in 1987, armed to the teeth with five .223-calibre semiautomatic assault rifles, two .22-calibre rifles, two 12-gauge shotguns and nearly 400 rounds of ammunition.

During the resultant firefight (sparked over a challenge to see who could resurrect the corpse of Anna Hughes, a Davidian dead for over twenty years and buried on the Mount Carmel property), George Roden was shot in the chest and hands, and put on trial for attempted murder. He was eventually acquitted, but soon landed back in jail for splitting a man's head open with an axe. A mistrial was declared in Howell's case, and he quickly seized upon the opportunity to make his triumphant return to Mount Carmel as the new Messiah.

To go along with his new status, Howell legally changed his name to David Koresh. (*Koresh* was the Hebrew translation of Persia's King Cyrus, who allowed the Jews being held captive in Babylon to return to Israel. Koresh named his firstborn son Cyrus.) Koresh's new first name arose from his belief that he was now head of the biblical House of David. (Koresh's legal document mentioned none of this, citing 'publicity and business purposes' as the reason for his name change.)

Like Charles Manson, Koresh harboured dreams of rock-'n'-roll stardom, spending tens of thousands of dollars on musical equipment, and even forming his own tentative band named Messiah (a business card for the band which he had made up during this time credited Koresh with 'Guitar, Vocals'. The band logo on the card featured a knife slicing through the band name, with what looks to be the Star of David on top of the 'i'). At Mount Carmel, Koresh would treat his assembled followers to mini-concerts, wailing away on his electric guitar while belting out self-penned tunes like 'Mad Man in Waco', written not as an introspective self-portrait but rather about the shootout with George Roden, and featuring versus such as:

In the light of the darkness,
Risking our lives for the Lord.
Helping the women and children,
To their houses restore.

Koresh was convinced that he was the 'Lamb of God', who would break the Seven Seals, thereby bringing about the Apocalypse and the Second Coming of Christ, as prophesised in the Book of Revelations. These prophecies are extremely bloodthirsty and violent. As the Lamb breaks each of the Seals, the Book of Revelations prophesises:

1. A rider on a white horse will come forth to conquer.
2. A rider on a red horse will take away peace so men may slaughter.
3. A rider on a black horse will appear holding a pair of scales.
4. A rider of a pale horse named death will appear, with power to kill by sword, famine, pestilence and wild beasts.

    (A former Davidian, David Block, told ATF agents that he 'left the cult group because Koresh would always remind them that if they were to have a confrontation with the local or federal authorities, that the group should be ready to fight and resist'. And Branch Davidian Kathryn Schroeder claims that Koresh 'told his followers that soon they would have to go into the world, turn their weapons on individual members of the public, and kill those who did not say they were believers. As he explained to his followers, "you can't die for God if you can't kill for God".')

5. Those slaughtered for God's word are told to rest a little longer, until all brothers in Christ's service are put to death.

    (When the ATF raided Mount Carmel and killed six Branch Davidians, Koresh and his followers were convinced that they had to wait a little longer, and then they too would be put to death, fulfilling the Fifth Seal.)

6. After a violent earthquake, the great day of wrath comes.

   (During the siege at Waco, Koresh made several references to an earthquake opening up and swallowing the agents surrounding the Davidians.)

7. 'When the Lamb broke open the seventh seal, there was silence in heaven for about half an hour.'

THE BRIDES OF CHRIST

Like many cult leaders, Koresh possessed a roaring sex drive, and a predilection for young girls that would prove to play a major part in his undoing.

When Marc Breault, who spent years as Koresh's right-hand man, recruiting agent and one of his few trusted confidants, began to doubt the word of his leader, it was seeing Koresh's taste for underage girls that finally persuaded him not only to flee from Mount Carmel, but also to ensure Koresh and his sexual deviances were exposed. This was easier said than done, with US authorities dismissing or simply ignoring Breault's warnings and presentations of evidence. Often, he was accused of bad-mouthing Koresh because he wanted to establish and lead his own cult (no indication has ever arisen of his trying to do so). When it became clear that Breault was not going to get any help from his own country, he turned to the Australian media for help (when Breault fled from the Davidians, he returned to Melbourne to be with his Australian wife, Elizabeth – also a former cult member).

Koresh had had a long-standing connection to Australia, visiting the country several times during the mid- to late 1980s on recruiting drives. On one such occasion, he had met and seduced a thirteen-year-old named Aisha Gyarfas, who returned to Mount Carmel with Koresh, where she bore two of his children (she would eventually perish in the Waco inferno).

Sniffing out a story that was not only ripe for sensationalism, but hit close to home as well, the Australian media were only too glad to help Marc Breault accomplish his mission. In January 1992, the Australian *A Current Affair* television programme (not affiliated to its American namesake) sent a reporter, Martin King, to Waco to interview Koresh and expose the cult leader's illegal (and immoral) activities.

According to King, who would go on to co-author the book *Preacher of Death* with Marc Breault (see Bibliography), Koresh agreed to the interview only when given the impression that a young female reporter was being sent to meet him, and was none too pleased to discover he had been misled. But his ego could not resist the lure of the media spotlight, and King and his cameras were allowed inside the Waco compound, garnering an exclusive interview, which, exactly twelve months later, would be seen on news broadcasts around the world.

In the *Current Affair* piece, King confronts Koresh about the rumours of weapons being stockpiled by the Davidians:

Koresh: You know what the public thinks about guns. In this country right now the legislation is to ban all guns, and it makes nobody's business if we have a gun or not in this place. Guns are the right of Americans to have. So you know I want you to understand that bringing up guns – ya'll don't have guns in Australia, your government says your people are not supposed to have them. Our government says we can.

King: So you keep guns?

Koresh: Yeah, we got a gun here and a gun there. Most of the guns were sold. A lot of people say: 'He's got guns, that makes him bad, that makes him a cult.' It's just a raw deal in this touchy subject we're dealing with.

King also questioned Koresh on the claims that he was a polygamist who claimed every woman he slept with (including the partners of Davidian members) to be one of his 'wives':

King: She [Robyn Bunds, former cult member] says you've got seventeen wives.

Koresh: 'Seventeen wives'?

King: Seventeen women you've slept with who then became your wives.

Koresh: And how does she know all that? Why is it that these individuals are making all these accusations?

King: I don't know, you tell me.

Koresh: The truth is, there is a doctrine, there is a truth, they don't want me to be the Son of God, and they need to attack me on the Seven Seals and not according to 'sticks and stones can break my bones', but there are Seven Seals, and the one that can reveal the Seven Seals is the one that is going to set people free.

King: I'm not testing your faith in the Bible: I'm testing your morality.

Koresh: Yeah . . . I'm not a saint but I know something that no one else knows and I want to share it. Free.

King: How do you describe these allegations?

Koresh: Like I said before, there are Seven Seals.

King: Is it bullshit?

Koresh: What they're saying? If you want to use that terminology, yes, they're bull dung, OK?

Finally, King asks Koresh about Gyarfas:

King: Did you do that?
Koresh: No, I did not.
King: Were you there [the Australian home of a former Davidian, Bruce Gent] with the thirteen-year-old girl?
Koresh: I was there with a lot of people – thirteen, ah, what's he talking about – Aisha? Was it, ah Nicki, let's see . . .
King: I think the girl's name was Aisha.
Koresh: Was the parents there? Her parents were there.
King: Did you do it?
Koresh: No, I didn't do it!

In 1995, another former Davidian, Kiri Jewell, described how Koresh used the sect as a cover for rape. The teenager revealed she was five when her mother (who died at Waco) took her to join the Davidians at Mount Carmel. According to Jewell, he was obsessed with the biblical Apocalypse and sex. 'David was planning to lead the group to Israel to retake Jerusalem. He taught that there would be a big battle between the forces of the world and his people.'

Kiri claims to have slept with Koresh and her mother in one bed, and had her first sexual encounter with the cult leader at a motel in Waco when she was ten. 'He kissed me. I just sat there, but he then laid me down,' she said. After committing the sex act, Koresh told Jewell to take a shower and then read from the Bible. 'He sat on the bed and read the Song of Solomon.' Jewell said that Koresh used Biblical quotations to explain himself and his actions. He told her that 'King David from the Bible would sleep with young virgins to keep him warm'. [1]

THE OVERTURE

In May 1992 the United Parcel Service informed the McLennan County Sheriff's Department that the Branch Davidians were receiving 'suspicious' deliveries, including shipments of firearms worth more than $10,000, inert grenade casings and a substantial quantity of black powder.

The Sheriff's Department contacted the ATF, who assigned Special Agent Davy Aguilera to investigate. It was also around this time that the *Waco Tribune-Herald* began researching an article about the Branch Davidians' stockpiling of arms (fuelled by reports from several ex-members who had contacted the paper).

By December, the ATF began interviewing disgruntled former members (including Marc Breault) and set up an undercover house across the street from the Mount Carmel Center. Although Koresh and the Branch Davidians were apparently aware throughout the investigation that some agency was monitoring them, the ATF went forward with plans for a full-scale paramilitary raid on Mount Carmel.

On 25 February ATF Special Agent Davy Aguilera, with the assistance of two US attorneys, Bill Johnston and John Phinizy, produced a 'Probable Cause Affidavit in Support of Search Warrant'. On the basis of that affidavit, Magistrate Judge Dennis S Green signed a search warrant for illegal weapons and explosives at Mount Carmel and an arrest warrant for David Koresh. The ATF's Director Higgins convinced officials that, because of the impending *Waco Herald-Tribune* series on the Branch Davidians, 28 February might be the last opportunity to catch the cult members unprepared. Higgins also told officials that raid planners had assured him that the raid would be called off if the element of surprise was lost. What they did not tell him was that they were expecting a shootout.

On Saturday, 27 February 1993, the *Waco Herald-Tribune* ran the first instalment of their series 'The Sinful Messiah'. The following day – despite their knowledge that the Branch Davidians had been forewarned – 76 armed ATF agents descended upon Mount Carmel.

THE SIEGE: A TIMELINE TO DISASTER

SUNDAY, 28 FEBRUARY

At approximately 9.30 a.m., agents of the Bureau of Alcohol, Tobacco and Firearms attempt to execute arrest-and-search warrants against David Koresh and the Branch Davidian compound. Gunfire erupts, during which four ATF agents are killed and sixteen wounded. An unknown number of Davidians are killed and injured.

Within hours, the FBI are brought in to resolve the standoff, with Jeff Jamar being appointed on-site commander, and Byron Sage as chief negotiator. Koresh, who claims to have been shot in the hip and left wrist, is interviewed via telephone by CNN and is allowed to broadcast his religious teachings on the Dallas radio station KRLD.

Michael Schroeder, a Branch Davidian, is killed while he tries to return to the main building, and Texas Rangers are barred by the FBI from continuing their investigation.

MONDAY, 1 MARCH

Negotiations with Koresh continue, and, over the course of the day, ten children are sent out from the compound. FBI agents in armoured vehicles deploy to the compound's perimeter. Koresh tells negotiators that suicide is not being considered, but becomes extremely distressed when the armoured vehicles move closer to the compound, and again when his phone line is cut except for outgoing calls to the negotiators.

The US President, Bill Clinton, approves the FBI director William Sessions's decision to employ a 'waiting strategy'.

TUESDAY, 2 MARCH
Koresh records a one-hour audiotape of his religious teachings, promising to surrender upon the tape's national broadcast. Although the tape is broadcast over the Christian Broadcasting Network that afternoon, Koresh reneges on his deal to surrender, telling negotiators that God has spoken to him and has told him to wait.

Clinton agrees to deploy military vehicles to the area for 'safety purposes'.

WEDNESDAY, 3 MARCH
To try to appease Koresh, the FBI intervenes to have murder charges dropped against two Davidians – both elderly women – who had left the compound on 2 March.

Koresh delivers sermons that focus on the Seven Seals and interpret God's intentions about the end of the world, and says the FBI should 'look at some of the pictures of the little ones that ended up perishing'.[2]

FRIDAY, 5 MARCH
Nine-year-old Heather Jones walks from the compound with a note from her mother pinned to her jacket. The note states that, once the children are out, the adults will die. Koresh denies they are contemplating suicide.

The Davidians are said to have twelve months' supply of food.

SATURDAY, 6 MARCH
In an early-morning conversation, Steve Schneider (one of Koresh's most senior right-hand men) makes suggestions that federal agents might burn the compound down in order to destroy evidence.

SUNDAY, 7 MARCH
The FBI refuses to deliver milk to the compound unless more of the children are released. Koresh claims that the only children left in the compound are his own, and will not be released.

MONDAY, 8 MARCH
The FBI delivers six gallons of milk to the compound. A videotape of the children in the compound is sent out by the Davidians. Negotiators fear that, if the tape is released to the media, Koresh will gain sympathy from the public.

TUESDAY, 9 MARCH
Electricity to the compound is cut off at 2.15 a.m., then later restored when Koresh says he will not talk further until it is done. Hostage Rescue Team (HRT) members claim to see firing ports being cut in plywood placed in the compound windows.

FRIDAY, 12 MARCH
Janet Reno is sworn in as Attorney General as Schneider claims no mass suicide will occur.

All power inside the compound is cut off, this time for good, as Jamar wants the Davidians 'to experience the same wet and cold night as the tactical personnel outside'.[3] The Davidians cite the power shut-off as a 'huge, huge setback',[4] causing them to change their minds about coming out.

SATURDAY, 13 MARCH
Schneider complains that people inside the compound are cold and freezing. The FBI informs Koresh that his mother has retained attorneys Richard DeGuerin and Jack Zimmerman to represent him.

SUNDAY, 14 MARCH
At nightfall, the FBI illuminate the compound with bright lights in order 'to disrupt sleep, to put additional pressure on those inside and to increase the safety of the HRT'.[5]

MONDAY, 15 MARCH
The FBI continues to insist on a peaceful resolution to the siege, but refuses to listen to any more of what it dubs 'Bible babble'.

THURSDAY, 18 MARCH
The FBI broadcasts a message to those in the compound over a loudspeaker, saying they will be treated fairly if they come out.

Koresh claims to be ready to come out, but only two Davidians – Brad Branch and Kevin Whitecliff – emerge from of the compound.

SATURDAY, 20 MARCH
Branch Davidian Rita Riddle emerges from the compound.

SUNDAY, 21 MARCH

Two more women, Victorine Hollingsworth and Annetta Richards, leave the compound just after midday. They are soon followed by Gladys Ottman, Sheila Martin, James Lawton and Ofelia Santoya.

In the evening, the FBI begins playing extremely loud music, including Tibetan chants and the Stevie Ray Cyrus song 'Achy Breaky Heart', over the loudspeaker system. Koresh responds with, 'Because of the loud music, nobody is coming out.'[6]

MONDAY, 22 MARCH

Negotiators suggest the introduction of tear gas as a nonlethal alternative means for clearing the compound.

The FBI delivers a new offer to Koresh, which would allow him still to preach and communicate while in jail, provided all Davidians begin leaving the compound from 10.00 a.m. the following day.

TUESDAY, 23 MARCH

At 10.05 a.m., Livingstone Fagan leaves the compound.

Assistant US Attorney William Johnson of Waco writes a letter to Janet Reno, complaining about the FBI's handling of the crime scene.

At night, the FBI shines floodlights on the compound and plays over the loudspeaker tapes of previous negotiations and messages from those Davidians who have exited the compound.

WEDNESDAY, 24 MARCH

FBI plays Tibetan chants and Christmas music during the early hours of the morning. Angered by the music, Schneider refuses to talk further. The FBI brands Koresh a coward and a liar at its press briefing.

THURSDAY, 25 MARCH
The FBI issues an ultimatum: at least ten to twenty people must leave the compound by 4 p.m., or some action will be taken. No one emerges. At 4 p.m. armoured vehicles move into the compound, where they remove motorcycles and go-karts belonging to the Davidians.

FRIDAY, 26 MARCH
Lights, music and helicopter activity occur throughout the night. FBI issues another ultimatum, and armoured vehicles began clearing the front side of the compound.

SUNDAY, 28 MARCH
Another FBI ultimatum. Koresh says that he has no intention to die, and is waiting for the word from God. A videotape is sent out from the compound that shows the nineteen children still inside, looking scared and tired.

MONDAY, 29 MARCH
Koresh and DeGuerin spend two hours talking face to face at the door of the compound. No progress is made.

WEDNESDAY, 31 MARCH
Mark Richard, the Deputy Assistant Attorney General representing Reno, holds meetings in Waco and San Antonio, to try to sort out the infighting between Waco officials.

THURSDAY, 1 APRIL
After Richard reports his findings to Reno, she assigns Ray Jahn as lead prosecutor and co-ordinator in the case. The Davidians tell DeGuerin that they will leave on

either 2 or 10 April, depending on their Passover observance.

MONDAY, 5 APRIL
The Davidians observe Passover.

TUESDAY, 6 APRIL
The FBI continues broadcasting music throughout the night.

WEDNESDAY, 7 APRIL
Koresh refuses to confirm an exit date. HRT commander Richard Rogers proposes a tear-gas plan.

FRIDAY, 9 APRIL
Experts who have been analysing letters that Koresh has been sending to the FBI conclude that he is possibly a psychotic who has no intention of leaving voluntarily. The FBI seeks Reno's approval to deploy tear gas.

SATURDAY, 10 APRIL
HRT members begin surrounding the compound with concertina wire.

EASTER SUNDAY, 11 APRIL
Negotiations still go nowhere. Three more Davidians prepare to leave the compound, but eventually decide against it.

MONDAY, 12 APRIL
FBI officials present the tear-gas plan to Reno for approval. She initially wants to wait a while longer, but is finally convinced that some action is needed.

The tear-gas plan is presented to Reno 'not as an all-out assault but as a tactic whereby gas will be inserted in stages, initially into only one small area of the compound. The goal was to allow the exit through uncontaminated portions of the compound.'[7] Reno also asks about whether it would be possible to cut off the water supply to the compound.

WEDNESDAY, 14 APRIL

Koresh delivers a message stating that he will not surrender until he has written a manuscript explaining the Seven Seals.

Two military experts and the Army's Dr Harry Salem brief Reno on the possible effects of tear gas on children. Reno asks the FBI to gather information about the compound's water supply, and an estimate of how long the Davidians could hold out. FBI calculates the Davidians have enough provisions to last a year.

Reno meets with Delta Force commanders to review the tear-gas plan.

FRIDAY, 16 APRIL

Koresh tells negotiators that he has completed the manuscript on the First Seal. Reno requests a report 'describing the situation inside the compound, the progress of negotiations, and the merits'[8] of the tear-gas plan.

SATURDAY, 17 APRIL

Reno approves the tear-gas plan but gives the material presented to her 'only a cursory review, leaving tactical decisions to those at Waco'.[9]

SUNDAY, 18 APRIL
Clinton is briefed by Reno on the tear-gas plan. The President concurs, but adds, 'It is your decision.'[10]

Armoured vehicles sweep a number of vehicles, including Koresh's Chevrolet Camero, away from the front of the compound. The FBI warns the Davidians to stay out of the compound tower. In one window, a sign saying FLAMES AWAIT is reportedly held up.

MONDAY, 19 APRIL – THE FINAL DAY
Sage telephones the Davidians at 5.59 a.m., advising them of an imminent tear-gas assault. A message is sent over the loudspeaker, informing the Davidians that they are under arrest and should surrender. No one emerges.

Five minutes later, two FBI combat engineering vehicles (CEVs) start inserting gas into the compound through spray nozzles attached to a boom. As the Davidians start shooting, the FBI deploys Bradley vehicles to fire ferret rounds through the windows.

At 7.00 a.m., Reno and senior advisers meet in the FBI situation room. The FBI calls for more gas from outside Waco, and 48 more ferret rounds arrive from Houston. With the supply of ferret rounds dwindling by 9.30 a.m., one CEV begins enlarging the opening in the middle-front of the compound, so the occupants can escape. Another CEV without a gas-delivery system breaches the rear side of the building, in order to create an opening near the gymnasium.

In Washington, Reno tells Clinton that everything seems to be going well, before leaving for a judicial conference in Baltimore. The CEV without a gas-delivery system breaches the back side of the compound, concentrating on the back right corner near the warehouse-gymnasium.

The last ferret rounds are delivered at 11.40 a.m., five minutes before a wall on the right rear side of the compound collapses.

At 12.07 p.m., an HRT observer reports seeing 'a male starting a fire'[11] in the front of the building. Sage calls on Koresh to lead the Davidians out to safety. Nine Davidians are arrested as they flee the burning compound.

At 12.25 p.m., gunfire is heard emanating from the compound, leading FBI agents to believe that the Davidians are either killing themselves or each other.

With the raging fire now spreading rapidly through the complex (helped along by openings created by the CEVs, which produce violent wind tunnels), Ranch Apocalypse (as Koresh has dubbed Mount Carmel) is engulfed by an enormous fireball and razed to the ground. Seventy-four men, women and children (including twelve under the age of five) die in the blaze. Despite initial fears that Koresh may have escaped death – and the authorities – through an underground tunnel, his body is found near the kitchen area of the compound and officially identified using dental records on 2 May. Like many of the Davidians, Koresh has died from a gunshot wound to the head.

MASS SUICIDE PLANNED?

According to Marc Breault, Koresh originally planned a mass suicide for Easter, 1992. In *Preacher of Death*, he states that members began selling off their remaining assets and calling their families to say goodbye. Koresh responded to these rumours by telling the *Waco Tribune-Herald*, 'I'm not ready to die. It's all lies. Every year we've gathered for Passover. Every year. Look, the place is being built up. We're spending lots of money. A lot of people are putting time and effort in. I've got the

water-well man coming in. I mean, two weeks in a row
we're supposed to be committing suicide. I wish they'd
get their story straight.'

This statement certainly contradicts claims by Kiri
Jewell, who reported that she had been trained by
Koresh and his advisers 'to commit suicide in several
different ways, including placing the barrel of a hand-
gun in my mouth and pulling the trigger'. Another
former member, Dana Okimoto, alleged that 'Koresh's
biggest fear was someone would take his wives away and
that he felt that rather than letting someone take his
wife, the wife should kill herself and if she could not do
so one of the "Mighty Men" [as Koresh dubbed his
henchmen] should do it, since this was one of their
duties.'

RENO: MISTAKEN OR MISLED?
Though Attorney General Janet Reno had approved the
tank attack, largely on the grounds that the FBI had told
her the cult's children were being physically abused, she
later said she had 'misunderstood', and in May 1995
called her actions 'a mistake'. In November 2000, she
told the children of a Brooklyn community centre that
'I'll never know what the right thing to do was', adding
that people have to 'live with their judgments ... I've
tried to do what is right.'[12]

A 1995 report obtained by the *Dallas Morning News*
says that Peter Smerick, a retired FBI agent, blamed FBI
headquarters for convincing Reno that using tear gas
was the only way to end the standoff peacefully. He said
that he and one of the FBI's top negotiators had by then
'concluded that the best strategy would have been to
convert the Branch Davidian compound into a prison
and simply announce to Koresh that he was in the

custody of the United States. This idea was not endorsed, however.'

Smerick based his allegation that Reno was misled on the fact that his five Waco profiling memos were not in the briefing book that FBI leaders gave her when they began lobbying her to approve using tear gas. Said memos warned that using force against the Branch Davidians would intensify a 'bunker mentality' in which 'they would rather die than surrender'. In addition, Smerick's memos also cautioned that the sect considered Mount Carmel to be 'sacred ground' and would 'fight back to the death' if the authorities tried to take it. 'The bottom line is that we can always resort to tactical pressure, but it should be the absolute last option we should consider.'[13]

LEGACY

Almost a decade on from Waco, David Koresh has attained near mythical status among many Americans, who see his death as a government conspiracy (a 1993 review of the tear-gas assault exonerated both the FBI and the Justice Department).

Timothy McVeigh, convicted of (and recently executed for) the Oklahoma bombing, timed the attack on the Alfred P Murrah Building so that it coincided with the second anniversary of the Waco fire. McVeigh revealed that he had visited Waco, where a militia group has erected a memorial to Koresh.

The legacy and influence of David Koresh also lives on in the minds of many of his remaining followers, who eagerly await his return. The remnants of the Davidian community now call themselves the Students of the Seven Seals, and are led by Clive Doyle, an Australian who survived the siege but lost his eighteen-year-old daughter Shari.

'We're waiting for his return. Until then, we're basically treading water,' claims Doyle, whose twenty-odd-member congregation comprises mostly fellow Waco survivors, along with a few new recruits drawn by the publicity that has surrounded the movement since the siege.

'There are some survivors who have chosen the easy way out, and who say that was all in the past, but most of the survivors are hanging on for the truth,' says Doyle. 'The doctrine is the same, but we're in a holding pattern because David's not here.'[14]

David Koresh, talking to his Bible-study class during one of his epic sermons (captured in 1992 by the *A Current Affair* film crew):

Koresh: When a man comes again, what's he gonna bring?
Class: The Book.
David Koresh: Those who want to learn – are they gonna live?
Class: Yes.
Koresh: Looks like someone's gonna get a butt-whipping in the near future, aren't they?

How terrifying it must be to live in the shadows of a man who you truly believe is the Son of God.

NOTES
1. 'Girl, 14, tells of sex abuse' by Hugh Davies, *Waco Leader*, 21 July 1995.
2. Justice Department: *Report to the Deputy Attorney General on the Events at Waco, Texas, February 28 to April 19, 1993*, compiled by Assistant DA Richard Scruggs, pp. 38–41.

3. Ibid. p. 142.
4. *Evaluation of the Handling of the Branch Davidian Stand-off in Waco, Texas, February 28 to April 19, 1993*, by Edward SG Dennis Jr, a Philadelphia lawyer and former assistant attorney general in the Criminal Division of the Justice Department, p.14.
5. Justice Department, ibid. p. 69.
6. Ibid. pp. 76–9.
7. *Evaluation*, op. cit. pp. 25–6.
8. Justice Department, op. cit. p. 271.
9. Ibid. p. 273.
10. Ibid. pp. 108–9.
11. Ibid. pp. 285–92.
12. 'Reno Expresses Waco Doubts' by Dan Mangan, *New York Post*, 21 November 2000.
13. All Smerick quotes from 'FBI misled Reno to get tear-gas OK, ex-agent alleged' by Lee Hancock, *The Dallas Morning News*, 6 March 2000.
14. 'Branch Davidians await return of leader Koresh' by Jan Cienski, *National Post*, 24 June 2000.

BIBLIOGRAPHY

Brad Baily and Bob Darden, *Mad Man In Waco: The Complete Story of the Davidian Cult, David Koresh and the Waco Massacre*, Waco: WRS Publishers, 1993.

David Hardy and Rex Kimbal, *This is Not an Assault: Penetrating the Web of Official Lies Regarding the Waco Incident*, US, 2001.

Martin King & Marc Breault, *Preacher of Death*, Ringwood: Signet, 1993.

Tim Madigan, *See No Evil: Blind Devotion and Bloodshed in David Koresh's Holy War*, Fort Worth: The Summit Group, 1993.

Dick J Reavis, *The Ashes of Waco: An Investigation*, Syracuse: Syracuse University Press, 1993.

FILMOGRAPHY

A Current Affair (April, 1992): The Australian journalist Martin King journeys to Waco and garners an exclusive interview with Koresh. It is the first major media piece on Koresh and the Branch Davidians, and the footage obtained by King and his crew provides an invaluable insight into the Davidian cult, in particular the scenes of Koresh delivering one of his epic, resistance-breaking Bible studies, and of the rock-'n'-roll messiah entertaining his flock with a blast of feedback-drenched electric guitar.

In the Line of Duty: Ambush in Waco (1993): American studios simply couldn't wait to cash in on Waco, rushing this TV movie into production before the siege had even finished. As a result, the film ends with the BAFT raid. Bad even by US television standards. Timothy Daly won the coveted role of David Koresh. It was directed by Dick Lowry, who helmed a series of *In the Line of Duty* telemovies in the early 1990s.

Waco: The Inside Story (1995): 60-minute *Frontline* special screened on the PBS network in the US.

Waco: Rules of Engagement (1997): William Gazecki's Academy Award-nominated documentary is a riveting and uncompromising piece of work, which would convincingly make anyone reassess their views on who actually started the fire at Waco – David Koresh, or the government? The film's power comes from the way in which it manipulates the viewer though selective evidence and footage, much as the authorities and mainstream media manipulate us into their own way of thinking. The question we're left with is: who is right? In 1999, Michael McNulty, one of the producers of *Rules of Engagement*, directed his own documentary on the subject, entitled *Waco: A New Revelation*.

8. APOCALYPSE OM

THE DOOMSDAY GAS SQUADS OF AUM SHINRIKYO

ANDREW LEAVOLD

Tokyo, 1995. In a darkened room the gathered watch the blinking television in awe. On the screen, a chubby man with a beard, long flowing hair and a perpetual squint is seated in the lotus position, then levitates into the air like Ali Baba on an invisible carpet. In a display of dazzling effects that would make the *Dr Who* team flushed with embarrassment, the chubby bearded man passes through walls, floats above his followers, and sails through blue-screen cities with the greatest of ease. The palpable sense of awe now fills the room.

Godzilla and Mothra may have the monopoly in Japan on special effects, but Shoko Asahara, the chubby floating guru, has something else up his kaftan. He is the 'Lamb of God', according to his army of followers, the reincarnation of Christ and Buddha and possessed by Shiva, the Hindu god of destruction. He has thousands of the faithful ready to do his bidding, and over a billion US dollars at his disposal. He is also about to launch his first strike in the final holy battle of Armageddon.

In Tokyo's most crowded subway station on a crowded weekday morning ten members of Asahara's inner circle punctured plastic bags full of sarin, a nerve gas developed by Nazi scientists during World War Two, and left before the chaos erupted. For most Japanese, 22 March 1995 will be etched in their memories as the day modern Japan lost its feeling of security and innocence. For Asahara and his Aum followers, it was the start of World War Three. Apocalypse, Aum style.

Asahara now sits in a Tokyo prison cell waiting for his trial to begin. His Aum religion (renamed Aleph) continues to exist, albeit in a more benign form, and continues to draw in new followers seeking the truth in its amalgam of Buddhism, Christianity and Asahara's own divine revelations. Asahara himself is becoming a martyr to Japan's increasingly marginalised youth – a Charles Manson figure with visions of death and destruction of the status quo, a charismatic countenance which conceals a much larger 'truth', railing against the stern paternal society he and his followers wish to bring down.

Like Manson, Asahara believed (and most probably still believes) society was ready to be torn apart by violent upheaval: Manson's was a race war, Asahara's version was an assault on Japan by a shadowy World Government of Jews and Freemasons. Both stockpiled weapons for the coming conflagration. Both had an army ready to emerge victorious at the end of the struggle. But, whereas Manson led a small ragtag band of college dropouts and social misfits in a desert commune, Asahara presided over a small empire. His vision of a dark and violent future drew in scientists, financial wizards, politicians and intellectuals, all happily signing over their small fortunes to Aum. Come the Apocalypse, they would be seated next to the Lamb of God ruling over the Chosen Ones.

Aum is just one of thousands of splinter religions in Japan. Shintoism is the largest formal religion at 100 million adherents, with its main sect, Jinja Honcho, claiming more than 70 million members. Buddhism runs a close second with more than 90 million adherents; Christianity is the poor cousin with just over a million. As Japan's population is just over 120 million, it appears that most Japanese claim allegiance to more than one religion. In fact, all but a small percentage of the Japanese population are atheists. Many blame the American Occupation after World War Two for devaluing the traditional Shinto belief, and promoting rampant materialism and individualism. It is this spiritual vacuum in Japanese society, in which people more or less pay lip service to their one or more gods, that forces seekers of the 'truth' into the margins of religion.

Aum also emerged at a time of great upheaval in Japanese society. The so-called 'bubble economy' of the late 1980s had just burst; millions of small-time investors had made fortunes on stock and land speculations, only to lose them in the Tokyo stock market crash of 1990. The inevitable recession lasted several years and seriously shook confidence in Japan's previously unshakable economy. 'The extraordinary profits made in the 1980s made it a unique time in Japan's business history,' said a Baring Securities analyst, Nobuyoshi Kobayashi, in late 1990. 'What we are seeing now is those fortunes being wiped away – the get-rich-quick culture being smothered at birth.'[1]

The early 1990s saw a rise in the number of violent crimes reported in Japan: the tabloid newspaper *Sunday Mainichi* called Japan the 'murder archipelago', and its featured essay by the playwright Tetsu Yamazaki attributed the crime wave following the Tokyo crash to the 'collapse of individual dreams'.[2] In 1994 alone, a series of bizarre murders rocked Japan. A pretty hairdresser called Mayumi Iwasaki, aged thirty, was cut into pieces and strewn like a trail of breadcrumbs along

Japan's highways. Her head was never found, so police could identify the body only when enough parts had been assembled. A 53-year-old man killed his parents and dumped them in rubbish bags in the forest. The motive: they turned down his requests for money. The wife of a philandering policeman murdered the lover, burned the body and deposited the remains in front of a supermarket. This was not the crime-free Japan people remembered. People were succumbing to the 'American disease'.[3] One man believed he would free Japan of the disease for ever.

Chizuo Matsumoto was born the fourth son of a poor family in a small town on the southern island of Kyushu on 2 March 1955. As a young child he suffered from glaucoma, reportedly (but never proven) leaving one eye useless and only 30 per cent vision in the other. In public he read at a crawl with a magnifying glass, but was filmed playing a game of catch with some disciples. Whatever affliction he was cursed with, he was able to use his near-blindness to his own advantage from an early age. Unable to follow his father into the family mat-weaving business, he left home for a prefectural school for the blind, where he led students by the hand to the local shop in return for payment. At school he began a life-long obsession with robots, death rays and machines of mass destruction.

In the early 1970s, the blind were expected to train as masseurs or acupuncturists. Matsumoto had greater ambitions in politics and tried to enter Tokyo University in 1973, failed, and entered the world of faith healers, fortune-tellers, mystics and madmen. Using his new gifts of acupuncture, herbalism and the occult, he opened a shop in Tokyo and changed his name to the less common Shoko Asahara. People flocked to see the charismatic healer. His appeal was simple: he listened to people, smiled, joked, and his plumpness was considered by women to be 'cuddly'. Japanese men on the whole displayed none of these qualities, preferring to keep a cold and aloof exterior.

In 1982 Asahara lost his licence and closed his shop following an investigation into one of his bogus orange-peel medications. At the time he declared, 'I believe that the future lies in religion',[4] and left for India. He reportedly discovered enlightenment somewhere in the Himalayas in 1984, aged 29. He returned to Japan, rented a room and founded a yoga meditation circle of around half a dozen followers. He called them the New Society of Aum, after the Sanskrit mantra ('Om') for the major Hindu gods of Brahma, Vishnu and Shiva. He later changed the name to Aum Shinrikyo, or the True Teachings of Aum. The Japanese occult magazine *Twilight Zone* snapped a photo of him in 1985 floating in midair while meditating, and this proved to be his breakthrough.

One of Aum's earliest marshals was a business whiz and in 1989 formed Aum into a religious corporation recognised by the Tokyo Metropolitan Government. This meant tax exemptions or reductions for any of its business concerns. Within eighteen months Aum was receiving gifts from some of its members in excess of half a million dollars each, which financed their growing empire of computer shops, noodle bars, health clubs and even a telephone dating agency. Set-up costs were low and labour was cheap and plentiful, mostly from the growing number of Japanese youth who were unhappy with their perception of modern cultural slavery – work, obedience, mortgage, marriage, death – and were waiting for a new guru to lead them down a path to a new consciousness.

What happened to Japan in the late 1980s was basically Woodstock-era America revisited: a cultural explosion among Japan's youth, turned on by newly rediscovered Eastern mysticism and a 'do your own thing' mentality, aided by music, meditation and mind-expanding drugs (manufactured by Aum, of course). They headed for Aum's communes in droves. Followers clad in dazzling white robes stood at subway exits distributing handouts for free yoga sessions. Inside, impressionable minds were shown TV footage of the guru floating, and animated footage of him flying over Tokyo and passing through walls.

Once in the grip of Aum, however, they were forbidden to leave and were told they would burn in a Buddhist version of hell if they tried. Initiates were subjected to unbearable tortures of the body – hung upside down, immersed in scalding hot baths – to make their minds more malleable to Asahara's vision of 'enlightenment'. Those who escaped were kidnapped by Aum members and in some cases tortured and killed. Ex-members on trial for the sarin gas attacks tell of following Aum orders unconditionally – they honestly believed Asahara would order their demise.

Unlike many New Age cults, many Aum members were not naïve wide-eyed youth: they held university degrees in business, religion, science and technology. Yet, despite their qualifications, all craved spiritual fulfilment. Shinnosuke Sakamoto visited Aum as a possible subject for his anthropology doctorate at Toyko University. After spending over twelve hours alone in a cramped cell, he later told of the experience: 'I felt as if I had ascended to a higher stage . . . A bright light fell from above and entered me.'[5] After the subway attacks he remained unrepentant.

Once Aum believed a convert had reached a suitable level of 'spiritual enlightenment' (particularly those with money or scientific credentials), they were invited to be ordained. This meant taking a vow of chastity, renouncing all worldly ties and possessions – savings, real estate, even their signatures on phone and credit cards. By 1995 Aum had spread to other countries such as America, Australia and Russia, where it boasted thirty thousand members alone. In total, it is estimated Aum had around fifty thousand members, with massive financial resources.

In 1989 six families appeared on national TV and accused Aum of stealing their children. The high-profile media campaign surprisingly worked to Aum's advantage – Aum representatives were portrayed as young, intelligent and good-looking, and the kids were merely doing their own thing. Aum received a flood of new recruits. The parents formed 'Concerned Parents of Aum Children' and recruited a young hotshot lawyer, Tsutsumi Sakamoto, to represent them. Sakamoto compiled a comprehensive dossier on Aum's religious and business practices, intending to bring a lawsuit against the cult to return both the children and the coerced 'donations'. After Tokyo TV broadcast a scathing interview with Sakamoto, he was visited by an Aum delegation. Sakamoto was furious. Rather than issue an apology, he declared he would fight even harder to bring Aum to justice.

On 4 November 1989, Sakamoto, his wife and year-old son disappeared. Their shallow graves were discovered in late 1995. According to a former Aum member, a six-man Aum assassination squad broke into the lawyer's apartment before dawn, strangled Sakamoto and his wife and smothered the sleeping baby. They wrapped their bodies in futons and buried them in the mountains. An Aum member, Tomomasa Nakagawa, went on trial in 1995 and pleaded guilty to the murders, claiming he was acting under threat of death by Asahara. The murder was also added to Asahara's crimes, over which he maintains his innocence to this day.

In addition to the blindingly obvious motive, police found an Aum lapel badge on the floor of Sakamoto's apartment. They did not question Aum, or issue a search warrant to raid the organisation's premises. It's said that the group was neither a communist nor a right-wing nationalist group, so it slipped under everyone's radar. Many claim the police were fearful of Article 20 in Japan's postwar Constitution, which prohibited state involvement in 'religious activity'. The law did not prohibit religious interference in Japanese politics, and, with its first victory against the forces of oppression under its collective robes, Aum was ready to tackle its next hurdle – the government itself.

Asahara announced that his own political party, 'Shinrito', or 'Truth', would contest the February 1990 elections. Its main spokesman was not Asahara but Fumihiro Joyu, a charming and well-dressed business-man with a master's degree in artificial intelligence. He bowled over the Japanese media and became the darling of young female voters by claiming Aum had given him the strength to stop masturbating. Asahara also appeared on news shows denying Aum's involvement in Sakamoto's disappearance, and said a rival sect had planted the Aum badge on the dead lawyer's floor.

Despite its glowing media image, 'Truth' failed miser-ably at the polls; even Asahara attracted just over 1,700 votes in his own district of 500,000 – fewer than the total number of Aum followers in the district. In protest,

Asahara led a thousand of his closest initiates to a small island off Okinawa (later revealed to be a dry run for a mass evacuation from the mainland in the event of a nuclear attack), and the media followed, wanting to know if they intended to commit suicide. Many communities resisted the onslaught of Aum, refusing the sale of land to the cult. Aum would countersue, and in some cases received millions from communities to leave them well alone.

Asahara realised his path to political power was blocked. Until the 1990 elections, he believed the Japanese people would welcome him as the saviour of mankind, the reincarnation of both Christ and Buddha. Asahara now began to blame outside influences for their failure at the polls. He expounded his apocalyptic visions of Armageddon, drawing on biblical prophecies and those of Nostradamus, and on a notorious document known as *The Protocols of the Elders of Zion*, a forged document from Czarist Russia in the early twentieth century, purporting to be the blueprint for Jews and Freemasons to destroy Western Christian civilisation. The enemy had become clearer: the New World Order and specifically the United States, identified in the Book of Revelation as 'The Beast', which they maintained was ruled by a satanic cabal of Jews and Freemasons (referred to in some conspiracist circles as 'the Illuminati'). This cabal included the Rockefellers, the Kennedys and the British royal family. The New World Order was seen to be the culmination of hundreds of years of Illuminati plans to create a one-world government, currency and religion based on the Freemason principles of pure free-trade capitalism and the renegade branch of Christianity known as Gnosticism (branded by orthodox Christians, and particularly the Catholic Church, as the work of Satan).

In the official Aum magazine *Vajrayana Sacca* dated January 1995, Asahara wrote:

> On behalf of the earth's 5.5 billion people,
> *Vajrayana Sacca* hereby formally declares war on
> the 'world shadow government' that murders
> untold numbers of people and, while hiding
> behind sonorous phrases and high sounding
> principles, plans to brainwash and control the rest.
> Japanese awake! The enemy's plot has long since
> torn our lives to shreds.[6]

Asahara identified a 'black aristocracy' of Japanese businessmen who had sold out the country to the Illuminati, and who had contributed to Aum's failure in the election. He also branded many ordinary Japanese people as 'Jewish Japanese'[7] – those city dwellers, businessmen and public servants who embraced materialism, and the unwilling future participants in Aum's terrorist war.

In its earliest form, Aum drew mostly on Buddhism and its Four Noble Truths: (1) all human life is suffering; (2) suffering comes from desire, which leads to endless rebirth, and so to more suffering; (3) by eliminating desire, we can end suffering; and (4) enlightenment, the end of suffering, can be achieved by following the Eightfold Noble Path, which, though not in Aum's case, means finding the middle way between excessive self-indulgence and over severe self-punishment. The Four Noble Truths, rightly understood, led the believers to Nirvana – to perfect knowledge and the escape from rebirth and the relentless Wheel of Life.

None of the basic doctrines of Buddhism allow murder; Asahara perverted an obscure term in Tantric Buddhism called *poa*, in which a follower may dispatch an evil-doer and release them from their bad karma, thereby increasing the follower's spiritual merit. *Poa*, or 'sending to Shiva', was the excuse Asahara used for the subsequent assassinations and subway attacks. It is also the reason why many Aum adherents were unaware of any wrongdoing. As for stockpiling weapons, a taboo in Buddhist teachings, Asahara used Revelations and its apocalyptic vision of the end of mankind. With enough firepower at its disposal, he reasoned, Aum would still be standing.

Asahara unveiled Aum's version of Armageddon to his followers in his 1992 book *Declaring Myself The Christ*. He urged followers to heed the Last Judgment that was upon them – using a Nostradamus prophecy that war with the Mongols was due in July 1999. Mt Fuji would erupt, Tokyo would be attacked by the Illuminati with gas and nuclear weapons and the world would end. A small percentage of mankind would survive, but only if Aum had 30,000 disciples to spread the word of salvation.

Aum published two more books expounding Asahara's bleak vision of the future. In *Shivering Predictions by Shoko Asahara*, he stated:

From now until the year 2000, a series of violent phenomena filled with fear that are too difficult to describe will occur. Japan will turn into wasteland as a result of a nuclear weapons' attack. This will occur from 1996 through January 1998. An alliance centering on the United States will attack Japan. In large cities in Japan, only one-tenth of the population will be able to survive. Nine out of ten people will die.[8]

The next book, *Second Set of Predictions by Shoko Asahara,* continued the apocalyptic verse:

I am certain that in 1997, Armageddon will break out. By 'break out' I mean that war will erupt and that it will not end soon. Violent battles will continue for a couple of years. During that time, the world population will shrink markedly . . . A Third World War will break out. I stake my religious future on this prediction. I am sure it will occur.[9]

With world war looming, Asahara gave the orders to arm his organisation. He began a worldwide search, known only to a small inner circle of confidants, for cheap and basic weapons of mass destruction: chemical, biological and nuclear. They built their headquarters in Kamikuishiki at the base of Mt Fuji, southwest of Tokyo. Land was cheap and plentiful from failed dairy farmers (the area was traditionally a wasteland) who were not interested in the new owners' religious backgrounds. It was an enormous complex of buildings, the largest three storeys high – a meditation hall watched over by a huge polystyrene moulding of Shiva which hid the entrance to the chemical factory and a maze of basements containing gas-analysing machines, gun-making facilities and an industrial-sized microwave oven (reportedly where the remains of at least thirty people were reduced to powder before being scattered to the winds). Five kilometres (three miles) away was the heliport (and Aum's Soviet chopper), and a private 20-foot-high stockade.

In March 1992 Asahara visited Russia seeking the Nobel Prize-winning physicist Nikolay Basov's work on lasers. Three months later Aum Russia was officially recognised as an organised religion, and began broadcasting its message of salvation via Moscow radio to Russia and East Asia. By 1995 Aum claimed to have 90,000 converts (the US Senate's estimate is between 20,000 and 40,000). Kiyhide Hayakawa was Aum's chief weapons buyer and made numerous visits to Russian munitions factories.

In September 1992 Aum bought a factory in Isikawa and ran it into the ground; the factory was then used to make parts for Soviet AK-74 rifles, which were then assembled in their building complex at Kamikuishiki. Aum bought a sheep ranch in Western Australia in September 1993, and Asahara brought 24 Aum scientists with him for a mysterious visit. Customs officials were bewildered by Aum's luggage (containing gas masks, protective clothing and various containers of acid) but, after paying almost 50,000 US dollars in excess baggage and 'dangerous goods' charges, they were allowed to proceed to Banjawarn Station.[10] Federal police made a few phone calls to Tokyo; the group were not granted return visas when they left in October, and the ranch was sold. Prosecutors say the Australian visit was for one or more reasons: scouting the area as a possible post-holocaust refuge, investigating the possibility of mining uranium or gold, and (most likely) testing their new gas weapon sarin, which they had already begun to manufacture at Kamikuishiki. Although they buried a number of sheep carcasses at Banjawarn, there were no traces of sarin in their systems.

Aum continued on their global mission. They mysteriously appeared in Zaïre (now the Democratic Republic of Congo) at the outbreak of the Ebola virus in 1992; in Belgrade Aum scientists studied the work of the famous scientist Nikola Tesla, the discoverer of alternating current, among whose ideas was a 'death ray' that could destroy thousands of planes at once and create shock waves that could split the earth in two. In the United States they purchased sophisticated equipment – computer software for biological-weapon experiments, air filtration systems – which could legally be exported to Japan (as it was a 'friendly' nation). Blueprints for lasers, seismological and nuclear weapons were found at Kamikuishiki after the gas attacks, suggesting Aum was preparing for an intense and protracted campaign against the 'enemy'.

In a March 1994 sermon to his chapter in Kochi, Asahara stated, 'The law in an emergency is to kill one's opponent in a single blow, for instance the way research was conducted on soman and sarin during World War II.'[11] Then, in June 1994, sarin gas drifted through Matsumoto, a small mountain town west of Tokyo, killing seven people and injuring more than six hundred. Aum had tried to purchase a property near the town; the owner peeked behind the front company and refused the sale. Aum was in the process of suing the owner when gas escaped from the back of a truck parked near a guesthouse where the judges were staying. Matsumoto police immediately jumped on their suspect: a former chemical salesman making agricultural fertiliser in his kitchen, who first reported the gas leak. Although he was proven innocent, the police had already leaked the suspect's name to the media. The Aum link was never followed. Asahara appeared on TV accusing US navy pilots of dropping gas on the town. The reality: the truck had been fitted with a remote-controlled gas canister at Aum Headquarters. Sarin proved its effectiveness.

A month later, Aum's neighbours near their Kamikuishiki headquarters contacted police over 'a horrible smell, like burning plastic'.[12] The family living closest to the Aum buildings complained of sore eyes and nausea, and noticed that the leaves on the trees near the compound had turned brown almost overnight. Police took soil samples, later reported in the local newspaper to contain organic phosphorous compounds – the potential residues of sarin. Aum was issued with a warning.

Aum's 1994 Christmas broadcast from Vladivostok declared once again that the end of the world was imminent, and may have possibly begun. At some point during 1994 Asahara amended the date of Armageddon from 1997 to November 1995 – government analysists believe Asahara intended to 'speed up' the oncoming apocalypse. The month coincides with President Clinton's visit, along with seventeen Asian leaders, to the annual Asia-Pacific Economic Co-operation (APEC) meeting in Tokyo between 16 and 19 November. November also appears to be the date for Aum's terrorist campaign against the US mainland. According to the confession of Aum's chief physician Ikuo Hayashi, packages of sarin gas were to be mailed to US targets in early November. Hayashi was later charged with murder following the Tokyo gas attack. The subway station of Kasumigaseki deep in the Tokyo underground, the attack's intended target, was identified in the broadcast as a secret bomb shelter and command centre for the Japanese army. Among Asahara's other Christmas predictions was a major earthquake in the Kobe region once Pluto entered Sagittarius (specifically on 18 January). The earthquake would be the result of an Illuminati microwave particle accelerator or a small nuclear device, and would signal the beginning of World War Three.

The Kobe earthquake of 17 January 1995 killed more than six thousand people. If there was any proof Aum members needed for the Last Battle, this was it. Aum retreated to the mountains, where it believed its followers would be safe from a nuclear cloud over Japan (partly thanks to its new machines, 'Cosmo Cleaners'). Meanwhile, Aum continued its campaign of terror against 'backsliders'. On 28 February cult members were seen bundling the Tokyo notary Kiyoshi Kariya – whose elderly sister was in hiding from the group after they demanded her entire property – into the back of a car. He was driven to Kamikuishiki and injected with a truth serum, but revealed nothing and died of shock. His body was placed in the giant microwave oven and turned into powder.

Spurred on by an increasingly suspicious media, Tokyo police began to investigate Aum's links with Kariya's disappearance, and with the previous year's sarin attack. Without gas masks or protective clothing, they were forced to wait on the army ('Ground Self-Defence Force') to assist with a raid on Aum's mountain headquarters. The date was set for 22 March 1995.

Tokyo at 8 a.m. is the peak of morning rush hour: millions of workers stream in and out of subway stations with military precision. On 20 March, five two-man Aum squads dressed innocuously in business suits and carrying umbrellas and the morning newspaper concealing plastic bags with the deadly sarin gas, boarded crowded subway trains from different locations. Within minutes they converged at Kasumigaseki station, the teeming centre of the subway system handling over four million commuters daily. Witnesses say the men wore surgical masks, but so did many other commuters during the height of hay-fever season. Once the trains pulled into the station the Aum members pierced the newspaper-clad sarin bags with their umbrella tips, took an antidote (atropine), then melted into the crowd and headed for their safe houses.

The first thing commuters noticed was a noxious smell emanating from a damp patch on the outside of the newspaper parcels. Then their eyes started to water and their heads ache. Seconds later a cry spread like a fireball through the station: 'It's gas!' Everyone headed for the three flights of stairs into the clean air above. Some were temporarily blinded, others vomited. Others clawed the air for oxygen. Others lay motionless on the platform.

Asahara had struck a blow against Japan's main nerve – he proved that a major terrorist attack on a busy subway station, the most likely scenario in a large city like New York, was possible. By the time the gas cleared, ten people were dead and more than five hundred were seriously injured. The effect was mostly psychological – had Asahara used full-strength sarin gas, the number killed would have been higher than ten thousand. That is how terrorism works at its most effective: the fear of attack rather than the attack itself. Hospitals reported people checking in up to a week after the attack, believing they were victims of sarin poisoning. Kiyo Arai, a 22-year-old government employee caught at Kodenmacho station, was quoted at the time as saying, 'We're just innocent, ordinary people. It frightens me to think how vulnerable we are.'[13] Much in the same way as America reacted after the 11 September terrorist attack, Japan went into a collective shock. They would watch the unfolding events over the next few months in the way Americans did during the last quarter of 2001 – with a sense of dread, of impending doom. For some – such as Aum – the end of the world had begun. The gas attack was Aum's response to what they believed was the first shot fired in World War Three, the Kobe earthquake.

The police and army raid on Aum began at dawn on 22 March 1995 as planned. More than 2,500 troops broke into the main headquarters at Kamukuishiki, and more than two dozen Aum installations around the country. At Kamukuishiki they were greeted by a young man at the barricades yelling, 'The Aum Supreme Truth has nothing to hide! It is an unjust search, but we will cooperate!'[14] At the main compound police set up a row of canaries in cages, then slowly opened the doors and waited for the canaries to die. They didn't. Police entered the main living quarters and discovered to their horror around fifty cult members in small cubicles clad in nothing but blankets. They claimed to be fasting voluntarily, but were in such an advanced state of malnutrition that the resident doctors were arrested for their neglect.

Then authorities discovered the main warehouse. Clad in protective gear police and army personnel uncovered raw materials and equipment for manufacturing gas weapons, and, most damning of all, the ingredients for making sarin. The ever-present media began to speculate on Aum's capabilities – enough gas to kill four million! Ten million![15] There were numerous arrests, but no Asahara. A pretaped broadcast went out early that morning from Vladivostok calling Aum members to rise up: 'Disciples, the time to awaken and help me is upon you. Let's carry out the salvation plan and face death without regrets.' A second message, presumably intended for Japanese radio, repeated the one line in Asahara's singsong voice: 'I didn't do it. I'm innocent.' Yoshinobu Aoyama, Aum's principal lawyer, released the following statement:

> We practice our religion on the basis of Buddhist doctrines such as no killing, so it is impossible that we are responsible. In my personal view, sarin could not be made by those other than special persons like those in the U.S. military. I speculate that someone in the military and state authorities may have been involved.[16]

He labelled the raids on Aum 'unprecedented religious persecution'.

A month of minor guerrilla attacks followed, including the attempted assassination of Police Commissioner Takaji Kunimatsu, shot three times outside his residence as he left for work. A member of Aum's Construction Ministry, Mitsuo Sunaoshi, was later arrested in connection with the crime. On 15 April more than 20,000 riot police spread through Tokyo after they received information of a possible Aum attack – many Tokyo workers stayed at home that day, and most avoided the subway. Four days later commuters in three subway stations in Yokohama complained of stinging eyes and sore throats. It turned out to be a less powerful and as yet unidentified gas, and no one was arrested. On 23 April Aum's 'science minister' Hideo Murai was killed by a knife-wielding thug live on Japanese TV; it is believed the Yakuza, guilty by association with Aum over the vast quantities of cult-manufactured drugs they trafficked, ordered the hit. Others say the orders came from Asahara.

On 5 May there was a cyanide attack on the busy Shunjuku station in Tokyo: two plastic bags were discovered ablaze in a restroom, one containing powdered sodium cyanide, the other containing 1.5 litres of diluted sulphuric acid. There were no casualties, but, had the two compounds mixed, it is estimated the hydrogen cyanide gas would have killed between 10,000 and 20,000 people. On 12 May an Aum scientist, Masami Tsuchiya, confessed to making sarin gas on orders from Asahara. On 16 May a letter bomb was mailed to the governor of Tokyo which blew off an aide's fingers when he opened the package. Later that day, the guru himself was discovered 'meditating' in a crawl space in one of the Kamikuishiki buildings, clutching nearly $100,000 in cash to his body.

By September most of Aum's hierarchy were in custody. More than four hundred members were indicted on more than two hundred separate charges, including murder, conspiracy, kidnapping, assault, obstruction of justice and theft, as well as petty traffic and licensing offences. Asahara himself was due to stand trial on 26 October 1995, but he fired his lawyer the day before and the trial was postponed. Aum was dissolved as a religious corporation later that year, and the Aum headquarters were confiscated in 1996.

By 1999 a small but influential group of intellectuals and civil libertarians began to question the ongoing persecution of Aum. The religion of Aum itself, they argue, has been tried and found guilty by the Japanese people. 'The neo-fascists in Japan,' said Kenichi Asaho, a professor of journalism at Doshisha University, 'are using the Aum situation as a pretext for increasing their control over Japanese society as a whole and to expedite the creation of a police state.'[17] Playing on the fears of another subway gas attack or worse, the media reported in earnest the upsurge of Aum activities in response to the renewed campaign by the National Police Agency and the Public Security Investigation Agency (PSIA). It timed perfectly with the government's attempts to pass controversial anti-Aum legislation in the National Assembly, a blatant pretext to expand the Anti-Subversive Activities Law to cover all suspect cult groups and political organisations.

However, the more liberal members of the government coalition, the New Komeito, rejected the idea and instead the government is now aiming at drafting new legislation specifically against Aum. Meanwhile Aum purchases of land were blocked, residence registrations were denied so members could not apply for driving licences or send their children to school. Aum properties were subjected constantly to police raids and petty charges laid. 'No Aum' or 'Go to outer space' were outward signs of mass hysteria pointed at a religion more or less in exile. Guilty or not of planning for another strike against the good people of Japan, Aum was still the bogeyman.

In response to the anti-Aum campaigns, the organisation disbanded in September 1999 and changed its name to Aleph. A press release on 1 December 1999 from Tatsuko Muraoka, deputy representative of the religious organisation (formerly Aum Shinrikyo):

Since we announced the suspension of our external
religious activities on September 31st, we, a
religious organisation of the former AUM
Shinrikyo, have been examining our views on the
AUM-related incidents and have so far reached the

following conclusions. After watching our members stand trial, we have reached the conclusion that it is undeniable that some members of our religious group were involved in some of the alleged incidents. Despite the fact that they were involved in the incidents without the knowledge of Chorobu, a group of senior followers, and the rest of the remaining followers, we as once their fellow followers of Aum Shinrikyo feel very sorry for what is being proven in the trials and would like to offer our deepest apologies to the victims and their relatives of the incidents. Also, with a sincere apology, the members of Chorobu, including myself, acknowledge our fault for being unable up until now to form and announce our views and thus have ended up spreading unrest and distrust across the nation. We can just imagine how the feelings might be of the victims who suffered mentally and physically in the incidents. We therefore concluded that not only those who were involved in the incidents but we ourselves who were members of the same religious group at that time should offer heartily as much compensation as possible to the victims and their families. [18]

A later press release dated 18 January 2000 from an Aleph representative, Fumihiro Joyu, grudgingly casts off Asahara.

Concerning the criminal liability of the then representative Asahara, although we cannot say for sure since his trial is still going on, the consensus of the current executives – composed mainly by the elders and the leaders of each department – is that he was likely involved in [text missing]. We could say that the founder Asahara was a genius meditator, but we cannot approve the incidents his organisation caused. While inheriting the superior ascetic practices of Yoga and Buddhism, as well as the meditation method his Yoga talent has left, concerning the incidents, we'd like to make it clear that we deny them.[19]

Asahara was no longer the spiritual leader of the former Aum – the same press release states that 'the fundamental subject of adoration in the new organisation will be the Great God Shiva and the various Buddhas'. However, a police raid on Aum property in July 2001 uncovered a huge number of Asahara video-tapes. Perhaps they were subjects of 'meditation', as Aleph described their former guru.

At the start of the new century, there is the real possibility that Asahara's vision of a One World Government and the start of World War Three will become a reality. The Aleph representative Fumihiro Joyu's view on the terrorist attacks of 11 September were sent to anxious Japanese media:

First of all, I would like to express my deep condolences to the victims . . . The terrorist attacks on the centers of the USA on September 11th astonished us all. Next, I must say, with due reflection on the past, we deny any types of violence. We therefore strongly oppose the terrorist attacks of September 11th.[20]

The press release continues in the same vein, gently castigating the terrorists, and the USA and United

Kingdom for their retaliation against Afghanistan. He concludes, 'I believe that the world needs the third path, which is neither of the path of terrorism nor that of exploitation. That is what we need for the 21st century.'[21] How the organisation formerly known as Aum reacts to the new international political landscape cannot be predicted; perhaps its members will sit on their hands, like so many of their fellow doomsday watchers, and wait for the oncoming Apocalypse.

NOTES

1. Peter Wilson and Matthew Franklin, 'The Fall Of Tokyo', *Courier Mail*, 10 November 1990, p. 29.
2. John Wright, 'Murder On The March: Crime Rocks Safe Japan', *Sunday Mail*, 15 May 1994, p. 66.
3. Ibid.
4. Murray Sayle, 'Nerve Gas and the Four Nobel Truths', *The New Yorker*, 1 April 1996.
5. Ibid.
6. 'Global Proliferation of Weapons of Mass Destruction: A Case Study on the Aum Shinrikyo', Senate Government Affairs Permanent Subcommittee on Investigations, 31st October 1995, Staff Statement (www.fas.org/irp/congress/199582rpt/aum/part03.htm).
7. Ibid.
8. Ibid.
9. Ibid.
10. Murray Sayle, op. cit.
11. David Van Biema, 'Prophet Of Poison', *Time Domestic*, Vol. 145, No. 14, 3 April 1995.
12. Ibid.
13. Ibid.
14. Ibid.

15. Ibid.
16. Ibid.
17. Kenichi Asaho, 'Japan's Imperial-Era Society: From the Anti-AUM Movement to the Elimination of all Heterodoxies', CESNUR Center For Studies on New Religions, http://www.cesnur.org/testi/aum_018. htm
18. From Aleph – formerly Aum – website, www.aleph.com.
19. Ibid.
20. Ibid.
21. Ibid.

9. BURNT OFFERINGS

THE MOVEMENT FOR THE RESTORATION OF THE TEN COMMANDMENTS OF GOD

MIKITA BROTTMAN

On 17 March 2000, hundreds of members of a bizarre endtime cult locked themselves into a small church on a hilly slope in southwestern Uganda, lined the walls with jerricans of gasoline, knelt silently in prayer and, when instructed, lit their candles. The resulting fireball was so hot that the bodies were burned beyond recognition, transformed into lines of ashen skeletons, many still kneeling in prayer. Several looked as if they had died in terror. One man lay on his back, his legs spread-eagled and his arms thrown above his head. The body of a baby – its arm partly missing – lay just outside the main door of the chapel. A huge mass of tangled forms covered the floor of the mud-and-wattle church, burned beyond recognition, even beyond human shape. The death toll remains unknown, but it seems likely that the Movement for the Restoration of the Ten Commandments of God was responsible for one of the worst cult massacres in modern history.

'THE PEARL OF AFRICA'

Over the last hundred years, more than five thousand indigenous churches have arisen in Africa. In Rwanda, the number of separate religious groups has grown from eight to more than three hundred in less than six years, and there may be as many as two thousand separate churches existing in Kenya alone. Most of these sects are based in part on Christianity – both Catholic and Protestant teachings – but many also have apocalyptic or revolutionary leanings, and most deviate from traditional Christian conduct by, for example, adopting animal sacrifices or encouraging charismatic personality cults. Experts suggest that this proliferation of religious cults in Africa may stem from a widespread rejection of mainstream churches, which are often perceived as being too 'Western'. In a way, such cults are akin to a protest movement, a refuge for the many Africans who feel alienated from Christian teachings over which they have no control, and which rarely incorporate native African traditions.

Winston Churchill described Uganda as a paradise, 'the Pearl of Africa', but went on to point out that most paradises are rotten beneath the surface. Uganda is no exception. A barren, impoverished country, in recent years it has been additionally blighted by a number of tragic events. Two decades of chaos followed the fall of the tyrannical Idi Amin in 1979. Famine, the legacy of a long civil war, remnants of primitive superstitions and the rampant spread of AIDS have led thousands to seek refuge in breakaway religious movements, especially those that hold the promise of a better life. The fastest growth has been among the kinds of charismatic ministries that provide easy answers to the country's many hardships.

These kinds of cults often thrive in situations of poverty and despair, where people have no obvious means of support and are easily susceptible to anyone who is able to tap into their insecurity. Charismatic religious cults not only offer instant friendship and a caring family, but also provide uniformity of purpose, a simple lifestyle, and an organised daily agenda in which

cult leaders take the responsibility for all major decisions. Moreover, the pervasiveness of AIDS in Uganda
has bred a kind of fatalism that makes it very easy for
apocalyptic notions to take root. The Movement for the
Restoration of the Ten Commandments of God guaranteed salvation for its followers, and promised to bring
them personally face to face with Jesus in Heaven. First,
however, they had to experience the Apocalypse.

THE PROPHET AND THE PROGRAMMER
The founder of the Movement for the Restoration of the
Ten Commandments was an angelic-looking, dulcet-
voiced ex-prostitute named Credonia Mwerinda. Those
who knew Credonia in her younger days describe her as
violent and mentally unstable, with a lust for money and
a fascination with destruction by fire. In her early
twenties, she torched the household belongings of a local
health official who had apparently jilted her. Her family
sent her away for treatment, and, when she returned, she
claimed to have been 'mentally disturbed'. To make a
living, she scraped together the money to purchase a bar
in Kanungu – a small hillside town in the southwestern
part of Uganda, about 217 miles (350 kilometres) from
the capital, Kampala – where she served up pints of
banana beer, and slept with her customers for cash on
the side. It was reported that she once seduced a motorist
who was passing through, killed him while he slept and
stole his money. When people arrived at the bar the next
morning, they apparently discovered Credonia noncha-
lantly washing blood off the concrete floor.

When all three of Credonia's brothers died under
suspicious circumstances – police now suspect her of
poisoning them – she inherited a small piece of land and
married a man named Eric Mazima, who sold his

property and evicted his second wife to become a partner in Credonia's bar. 'She was never as happy as when she was making money,' said Mazima. Police believe that, over the years, Credonia Mwerinda began to practise the technique of stealthy murder to accumulate further wealth and to silence potential accusers. Family members also claim she had a lifelong need to eliminate anybody who knew her most intimate secrets.

During the early months of 1988, Credonia's bar began to go broke. On 24 August of the same year, she reported experiencing a miraculous, transforming vision of the Virgin Mary on the rock face of a cave just outside Kanungu. This apparently miraculous experience led Credonia to convert to Roman Catholicism, after which her life changed completely – she fasted often, slept without a mattress, never smiled, spent hours writing and praying and blacked out sporadically during conversations to receive 'messages' from the Virgin Mary and Archangel Michael.

According to her ex-husband, Credonia had very little interest in religion before her first vision. 'In the whole time I was with her she never went to church once,' he said. 'But because I could not see the same visions, she left me.' It was apparently during one of these visions that Credonia received instructions to form her own branch of Catholicism, dedicated to the restoration of the Ten Commandments. 'She said she could see the Virgin standing with her back facing out to the world,' claims her ex-husband. 'She said, "The Virgin has turned her back on people because of the terrible sins of the world." I couldn't see the Virgin, I didn't believe it was there, but others believed her and said they could see it, too. Soon they were following her. Soon, more, and then more and more.'

Mwerinda's most important convert was a pious Catholic gentleman named Joseph Kibwetere, the married headmaster of a respectable private boarding school. Born in southwest Uganda in 1932, Kibwetere had taught and served for many years as a successful administrator in Uganda's Catholic school system, despite the fact that he was known to suffer fits of violence, and was prone to dangerous seizures. In the 1960s and 1970s he had been a prominent member of the Roman Catholic-based Democratic Party, but his political career ended abruptly when the rival Ugandan People's Congress won the election in 1980.

Shortly afterwards, Joseph Kibwetere was excommunicated from the Catholic Church for claiming that he could speak directly to God, in effect challenging the leadership of the Pope. In 1984, he announced that Jesus and Mary had visited him and revealed that the Apocalypse would arrive in the year 2000. He consequently began to develop a fascination with visionaries, showing particular interest in an Australian doomsday group led by a self-styled seer named William Kamm, also known as 'Little Pebble'. Kibwetere corresponded with Kamm on the subject of Marian visions, and went to meet him when the Australian visited Kampala. He also devoured books on Our Lady of Fatima and Lourdes, and even drove with his wife to visit a soccer field in Rwanda where holy apparitions were supposed to have occurred.

When Joseph Kibwetere first met Credonia Mwerinda, she told him that not only had she herself had a vision of the Virgin Mary, but that Mary had told her a man named Joseph Kibwetere was going to help her restore the importance of the Ten Commandments. Kibwetere was flattered, struck by his role in the scheme of salvation, and perhaps infatuated with the ex-prostitute's Mary Magdalene-like glamour. He invited her to move into his household, where she lived for three years until his wife threw her out, believing her to be having an affair with her husband. In a rage, Credonia allegedly set fire to Mrs Kibwetere's wardrobe and beat her up.

No longer welcome at home, Joseph Kibwetere moved into Mwerinda's compound with her, and became the nominal leader of the newly formed Movement for the Restoration of the Ten Commandments of God. It appears that the respectable Kibwetere served as the cult's torchbearer; his pious image, popularity, wealth and preaching skills were important factors in winning converts to the movement. Eventually, he became known as 'the Prophet', and Mwerinda as 'the Programmer'. Kibwetere wore a Catholic Bishop's robe and ring, and he alone was allowed to ordain young men into the cult's priesthood. Many of his sermons consisted of criticising Roman Catholic officials for failing to live up to their public teachings. These sermons, delivered in local Catholic churches, brought a steady stream of adherents to the movement, including several priests.

The third member of this unholy trinity was Dominic Kataribabo, a defrocked Roman Catholic priest who studied at Loyola Marymount University in Los Angeles under a Jesuit sponsorship programme aimed at helping to train Third World priests. Granted 'sacramental ministry' by the clergy of the Los Angeles Archdiocese, Kataribabo was awarded a master's degree in religious studies in 1987. His grades were mostly Bs, and his scholarship record at the university was undistinguished. Upon his return to Uganda, Kataribabo was appointed headmaster of the Mbaraba Catholic seminary. He was described by those who knew him as a humble, peaceful man, and so it remains unclear exactly why he was defrocked, but his role in the cult is generally put down to his disappointment at his rejection from the Catholic establishment.

SIN AND SUFFERING: THE CULT'S BELIEF SYSTEM
Mwerinda and Kibwetere, who both already had their own separate groups of followers, made a charismatic pair of evangelists. The cult's first chapel was constructed in the early 1990s on top of Credonia's father's grave in Kanungu, and Kibwetere was appointed as its first Bishop. The sect's belief system revolved around the current sinful state of the world, and the way people had fallen into the habit of ignoring and repudiating the Ten Commandments. Kibwetere claimed to have captured on tape a conversation between the Virgin Mary and Jesus, who were apparently complaining about how evil the world had become. By way of response, the cult preached that material possessions were the root of all sin, banning alcohol, cosmetics, cigarettes and even soap from the compound.

Followers were made to take vows of absolute poverty, chastity and obedience; they were then issued green and white uniforms, instructed to sell their belongings, and, once inside the compound, were not permitted to leave. Their isolation was total, but not uninterrupted – followers could return home to their families for two or three months a year. And there was a break of about six months in 1998 when Joseph Kibwetere was institutionalised in a Kampala mental hospital, receiving treatment for bipolar disorder.

The Movement for the Restoration of the Ten Commandments was essentially a secretive, brutalising cult in which the leadership extorted money and demanded absolute obedience from their followers. Daily life in the compound was arduous. Men and women slept on the floor in separate dormitories, and sex was forbidden, even between married couples. Cult members were woken up at three o'clock every morning for two hours of prayer. They fasted two days a week, and on the other five days were fed virtually nothing, despite working twelve hours a day in the surrounding sugar cane and banana fields. Children sometimes resorted to eating insects to help them survive, for which their parents were severely punished. Illnesses such as scabies were common. Conversation was banned for fear of blocking out the word of God, and so cult members communicated through gestures, sign language, prayer and songs. Clearly, this lack of communication between the cult's followers was an important part of the way the movement's leaders controlled and manipulated their flock.

The Catholic Church was declared an enemy, badly in need of reform. The cult's own rules, followers were told, came from the Virgin Mary, as channelled through Mwerinda. 'Their preaching was good, but taking the money was a problem,' said an ex-cult member, Claudio Sekibibi, adding that he also had some trouble with the prediction that, on a certain date, the world would end for everyone except them. 'They used to say in the New World it would be like the time of Adam and Eve: no clothes, no cultivating, no work,' he said. His wife, who remained in the cult, continued to believe. 'I was telling her all the time, "Jesus went to heaven after death. Mary, his mother, went to heaven after death," ' said Sekibibi. 'Who are you to go to heaven without dying?'

The management structure of the Movement for the Restoration of the Ten Commandments was based on the twelve apostles. Beneath the three heads, Kibwetere, Mwerinda and Kataribabo, were twelve supreme leaders. Then there was a middle tier of leadership – an operational cadre whose job was to carry out the leaders' instructions and demands. This group consisted of six burly men who essentially functioned as the sect's executioners, and who would routinely kill cult members when instructed to do so by their superiors.

Fatigue, hunger and faith led to blind obedience. 'I believed it would save me,' said Catarina Nansana, a 72-year-old woman expelled from the cult when her daughters embarked on a crusade to bring her home. 'I had sores on my feet, my arms, and my legs, but I didn't care. I believed what I was doing was right.' Another former cult member, Mary Kasambi, said, 'Credonia would say, "Today we are going to dig for one week. Today we are not going to eat for three days." Credonia would get a programme from heaven, from the Virgin Mary, and she would transmit it to us. Our job was to obey . . . You didn't ask questions.' The two cult leaders also spent much of their time ingraining into their followers a terrible fear of the Devil. Several former members of the movement have described how Credonia fostered a visceral, overpowering fear of demonic possession. Every object that came into the compound – money, clothes, food and medicine – had to be exorcised with prayer. 'She said the Devil was everywhere,' recalled Mary Kasambi.

At the time, Uganda was beset by an enormous sense of spiritual hunger and despair, and, despite the harsh conditions in the compound and repeated allegations of cruelty to children, the Movement flourished; eventually, eight other branches were established in other areas of Uganda. In a land rife with poverty, conflict, hopelessness and a background of religious belief, people can be easily manipulated – by politicians and businessmen, as well as self-appointed religious leaders. When people have nowhere else to turn, they often start looking for answers in the supernatural; by the late 1990s, the Movement had grown into a thriving community. The main compound in Kanungu contained fifteen wood and stone buildings, including a small primary school, set in plantations of pineapples and bananas beside hilly fields where cows grazed peacefully. Church leaders decided that the group should not plant crops such as cassava, which take a year to mature, because the world might end before the harvest. Instead, they cultivated beans, potatoes and other foods that would be ready in three or four months.

On a 1997 government registration form, Kibwetere claimed the cult had 4,500 followers. Members of the group had little contact with their neighbours, but some local villagers still found them frightening and suspicious. 'As time went on, we started getting more and more scared of them,' said Kisembo Didas, a farmer in Rugazi, the site of one of the movement's rural outposts. 'We thought they were dangerous, a cult of Satan. They used to behave abnormally, suddenly becoming paralysed in the street and then talking nonsense.' However, among Uganda's plethora of religious cults, the Movement – registered officially as a charity with the aim of carrying out observance of the Ten Commandments and preaching the word of Jesus – was considered fairly innocuous. Moreover, in a relatively free society like Uganda, it is very difficult to outlaw religious groups like the Movement. After all, one person's cult is another person's religion.

Significantly, however, police believe that complaints about the cult from concerned relatives were frequently overlooked because Joseph Kibwetere would pay off government officials with bribes and lavish gifts. And there was an even more sinister reason why the cult was allowed to go about its business undisturbed. According to former cult members, relatives who arrived at any of the churches searching for missing loved ones were welcomed to the compound with a cup of poisoned tea, then taken to the cult offices when helpless and thrown into a 'death pit', to be later buried and forgotten under the floorboards, or sometimes in the latrines.

THE FATAL PROPHECY
The manifesto of the Movement for the Restoration of the Ten Commandments of God was a small red book entitled *A Timely Message from Heaven: The End of the Present Times*, which gave details of the prophetic communications that its leading members claimed to have received from the Virgin Mary and other heavenly beings. These disclosures included warnings of millennial Apocalypse and attacks on the official Catholic Church, from whose discontented members the cult drew many of its followers.

Since its inception, the Movement had been preparing for the day when God, finally sickened by the sins of the world, would send flames to destroy it, and take the virtuous to live by his side in heaven. According to cult leaders, this was set to happen on 31 December 1999. Joseph Kibwetere had received a vision from the Holy Virgin informing him that, upon this date, epidemics and whirlwinds would blight the earth. These would be followed by three days of darkness, during which rivers would run red, food would turn to poison, and three-quarters of the world's population would die. And – however unlikely it might have seemed – only those in the cult would be assured of survival.

Authorities revealed that Mwerinda and Kibwetere spent thousands of dollars on radio ads seeking new recruits to their movement. The ads began in early December, announcing that the world would come to an end on 31 December 1999, and that anybody who wanted to go to heaven should join the Movement before the arrival of Armageddon. In his notebook, Kibwetere excitedly announced that the dawn of 'the year one' was near. 'We are all waiting until December 31st,' he wrote on Christmas Morning of 1999. On New Year's Eve, he readied his flock for the end of the world. 'We have to fill all the jerricans with water,' he wrote. 'We have to be clean so that we can prepare ourselves for heaven.'

It remains unclear what happened when the end of the world failed to materialise on 31 December 1999, except that discipline in the cult began to break down. Some claim that Kibwetere and Mwerinda must have come under an enormous amount of pressure from their congregation to repay the money that was turned over to them in preparation for the Apocalypse. Others believe that Kibwetere may have died – several ex-followers say that he hadn't been seen or heard from in months, and his estranged wife Teresa claimed that he died of degenerative disease related to mental illness in October 1999. If this is true, then Mwerinda may have been faced with growing scepticism about her powers and those of the other leaders. Only one fact seems clear: the date of the forthcoming Apocalypse was hastily changed to 17 March 2000.

But many of the cult's followers didn't have to wait so long. Between 1 January and 17 March 2000, it appears that cult leaders began systematically to eliminate their congregation. At some point in January, it was reported that followers in each of the sect's compounds were given a form to fill in, which asked, 'Who among you doesn't believe the world is going to end?' Those who indicated any kind of scepticism about the forthcoming Apocalypse were gradually transported over a period of weeks to one of the cult's five rural outposts, where they were instructed to dig a series of deep pits. Neighbours report hearing no noises from the compounds except the sound of vehicles coming and going at night, and the sound of digging. And when the graves were ready, the killing began.

It appears that these groups of sceptical followers were fed a fast-acting poison with their evening meal, then, once incapacitated, were strangled with fibre ropes made out of banana leaves. Those who tried to escape were stabbed, garrotted or hit over the head by one of the six men who worked as the cult's executioners. The killings, which seem to have been highly organised, were carried out at night, during what locals believed were prayer meetings. The dead bodies were then stripped – their clothes were incinerated – and lowered into pits ten to fifteen feet (3–4.5 metres) deep. One of the most surprising things about the case is that the cult managed to be so efficient in their disposal of the bodies, given their vast numbers and the difficult logistics involved.

A number of mass graves containing 153 bodies were later found at a cult compound in Kalingo, 45 miles (72 kilometres) west of Kanungu. A second series of graves was discovered at Rushojwa, 22 miles (35 kilometres) northeast of Kanungu, containing the bodies of 27 girls, 17 boys and 33 women. Then, at Father Dominic Kataribabo's compound in Rugazi, 50 miles (80 kilometres) north of Kanungu, another 155 bodies were discovered under a newly cemented floor. The mutilated remains of 74 more people were found in the back yard, covered by a patch of sugar cane and a shade, under which the remaining cult members had already begun rearing chickens.

These bodies, many of them women and children, had been hacked, poisoned, strangled or killed by machete, then tightly packed in the earth. The corpses of 26 children were pulled out of this grave, most with ropes tied around their necks; police said they appeared to have been garrotted. At least three were babies. It was almost impossible to distinguish one corpse from another – those exhuming the bodies spoke of having to extricate hipbones from collarbones. It is very unusual for bodies to be buried together in mass graves without coffins in this part of Africa, where proper, organised burials for the dead are considered especially important.

Meanwhile, as the new apocalyptic deadline grew near, Kibwetere wrote letters to all remaining cult members urging them to come to the sect's headquarters in Kanungu to experience the end of the world together. The Prophet claimed in his letters that he had received an important vision from God, and all remaining cult members must come to Kanungu in order to meet Jesus. 'Buy flowers,' Kibwetere wrote in his journal. 'Clean the church, and recruit other members for the special occasion.' At this point, the Prophet still seemed to believe that the end of the world was imminent, but by 3 March he had apparently decided to take matters into his own hands. After a sect member complained that 'the jerricans are all leaking', Kibwetere responded ominously: 'Don't bother with them. Soon everything will be over. We're going to make a big fire and the jerricans will stop leaking.'

A week before the doomsday deadline, followers started arriving in Kanungu from other parts of Uganda in buses and trucks. In the days leading up to 17 March, sect members sold their cattle, sugar and flour to the villagers at half price. Father Dominic was spotted in a local store clutching a rosary and asking for forty litres of sulphuric acid, explaining to the curious shopkeeper that it was to replenish batteries used for power at a remote seminary. And one of the cult's six executioners drove the group's Toyota to the local police station to deposit the title deeds to the land for safekeeping.

To deceive locals into believing that nothing was wrong, followers sent out invitations to a big party to be held at the compound on Saturday, 18 March. On the evening of Thursday, 16 March, the remaining cult members gathered in their dining hall for a feast of roast bull and Coca-Cola – reports claim that the cultists bought up most of the Coke available in southwestern Uganda to drink with their farewell dinner. They also bought up stocks of an insecticide sold in local shops, intended, apparently, to intensify the flames of the inferno. The product's name: Doom.

BLACK FRIDAY

After a night of prayer, the remaining cult followers were served a breakfast of porridge, then ordered to wash, clip their nails, shave their heads and put on their green and white uniforms. Shortly after dawn, Credonia Mwerinda apparently flagged down a bus leaving Kanungu for the Ugandan capital, Kampala. She boarded the vehicle and walked slowly down the aisle, closely studying the face of each passenger, making sure none of her followers were trying to escape. Finding no one on board, she wished the passengers a safe journey and walked slowly back towards the compound.

Here, she summoned all her followers into the chapel, which was lined with 68 jerricans filled with gasoline. A number of flimsy straw prayer mats had also been soaked with gasoline. The doors and windows of the church were then nailed shut from the outside and, when the word was given, the cult members were all instructed to light their candles, igniting the dangerously powerful mixture of gasoline, sulphuric acid and insecticide. It remains unclear whether the followers knew they were about to die at this point, or whether they still believed that the church would be a refuge from the forthcoming Apocalypse.

In a nearby field, a farmer, Pius Kabeireho, was laying bricks and listening to the songs and prayers coming from the simple mud-and-wattle church where the cult held their morning worship. At about ten minutes before ten, a bell began to ring in the chapel. Suddenly, just after 10 a.m., Kabeireho heard an enormous explosion, followed by the screams of children shouting, 'Mother, save me!' Seized by panic, he ran to the nearby police station for help. When he returned, the church was aflame, and Kabeireho gazed on the scene with terror. 'I saw hundreds of charred skeletons pressed together, kneeling, with their hands clasped in prayer,' he said. Everybody inside the building perished in an inferno so intense that skulls exploded. Neighbours who sprinted to the site from a quarter of a mile away found bodies still burning. But no one was left alive.

AFTERSHOCK: THE FINAL DEATH TOLL
At least 530 followers were killed in the inferno at Kanungu. Pathological analysis of the charred bodies indicated that they died of neurotic shock as a result of the fire. Authorities investigating the scene also found

the bodies of the six burly executioners partly dissolved in sulphuric acid in a latrine pit in Credonia Mwerinda's bedroom. Five of these men had been poisoned, and one killed by a blow to the head – evidence that suggests that some of the cultists, including Mwerinda, had survived the massacre. One eyewitness claims to have seen Kibwetere and Mwerinda sneaking out of the compound earlier in the day, carrying small suitcases. Police believe Mwerinda and other cult leaders may have escaped across the frontier into the Eastern Congo, perhaps through a shallow stretch of the Ishaka River. The Eastern Congo is a lawless place, infested with warring factions, including Hutu militiamen who fled to the area after their campaign of genocide in Rwanda. Ugandan police are said to be pursuing international arrest warrants for Joseph Kibwetere, Credonia Mwerinda and Dominic Kataribabo, but a manhunt in the area is out of the question.

In the summer of 2000, a team from Britain's Channel 4 Television began to investigate the case, interviewing surviving ex-members of the cult and other Kanungu residents. Evidence gathered by the team suggests that money and greed were at the centre of Mwerinda's motives for forming the group. The investigators found it difficult to see any other point to the mass killings, and have concluded that Mwerinda probably killed the other cult leaders, then escaped with a select group of followers and family members.

There are rumours that the Movement also had branches in Tanzania and Rwanda, and had plans to move into Kenya, although Roman Catholic Church officials in Kenya said they knew of no such plans. However, the poverty of Uganda means that its police have no access to computer databases. Authorities have speculated that there may be many more graves yet to be found, but the truth is that police simply don't have the resources to look for them. Police say their probe has been hampered by lack of equipment, vehicles and staff. 'We tried, but there isn't much interest, and there is no money,' said Asuman Mugenyi, the national police spokesperson.

Schools, workplaces and churches in Uganda have no crisis counsellors to help deal with problems such as psychotic episodes and post-traumatic disorders on the part of relatives and survivors. The nearest psychiatric centre to any of the affected villages is in Mbarara, a drive of several hours on steep, winding roads that often disintegrate into dirt tracks. Moreover, Ugandan culture tends to discourage exhibitions of grief and trauma, and, in this case, the stigma of association with any member of the Ten Commandments sect means that acquaintances and family members may hold on to their feelings much more tightly. Many people would rather mask their emotions than be interviewed by the police, who are often regarded with suspicion and fear.

A tally in August 2000 put the death toll at 989, which exceeds the 914 members of the Reverend Jim Jones's People's Temple who died in Guyana in 1978. In fact, the two cults had many elements in common. Both were offshoots of Christianity, and both were located in remote regions of poor, tropical countries. Both were also virtually unknown until their leaders – apparently fearing the dissolution of the congregations that worshipped them – decided it was time to launch their own versions of the Apocalypse. Both cults made unusual demands on members, and sought complete obedience and loyalty. Followers were told to give all their belongings to the cult, and families were split apart, with nonbelievers considered to be evil. Children lived separately from their parents and went to special schools. Both cults were characterised by self-sufficiency and a break with the outside world; both promised a utopian lifestyle, but ended up imposing a totalitarian rule within an agrarian setting.

Nobody knows the exact death toll involved in Uganda, but at least 530 followers died in the church inferno, and approximately 459 bodies have been found buried in mass graves at the rural compounds. The actual number of people killed, however, is almost certainly much higher – some say as high as two to three thousand, which seems quite possible, since virtually no members of the large cult have survived. Witnesses said some of the corpses appeared to have been hurriedly reburied before their details were taken, and the true number of victims will never be established.

There is a history of spirit possession in the southwestern part of Uganda, and today ghosts are said to haunt the site of the massacre. 'As dusk approaches, we see figures moving up and down as they used to do before they were killed in the fire. They put on the same green and white uniforms,' said eighteen-year-old Deus Tweyongere, whose aunt and four cousins perished in the inferno. Police still guard the ruins of the burned-out compound, where lizards scramble over the jumble of twisted, corrugated-iron roofing sheets that collapsed inward during the blaze. Officially the investigation into the massacre continues; but the truth is, authorities have little chance of ever tracking down those responsible for this terrible series of atrocities.

BIBLIOGRAPHY
Ian Fisher, 'The Root of All Evil', *Dallas Morning News*, 3 April 2000.

Giles Foden, 'In the Name of Mary', *Guardian*, 21 April 2000.

Joshua Hammer, 'An Apocalyptic Mystery', *Newsweek*, 3 April 2000.

Matthias Mugish, 'Kanungu Dead Poisoned', *The New Vision* (Kampala), 28 July 2000.

Craig Nelson and Tim Sullivan, 'Cult Members Chased Deadly Dream', Associated Press, 8 April 2000.

Lara Santoro, 'Priestess of Death', *Newsweek International*, 6 August 2000.

Author unknown '81 Found in Fifth Grave', Africa News Online, *The New Vision* (Kampala), 31 March 2000.

10. THE WEST END LESBIAN VAMPIRES

SMALL TOWN COMES OF AGE, FILM AT ELEVEN

ANDREW LEAVOLD

Brisbane Australia looks like one of those small country towns that has got too big for its boots. Its population of two million is spread over 100 kilometres (62 miles) of sprawling suburbs. If you ever visit and get the feeling you've missed out on something, don't worry: we locals from the suitably named 'Bris-Vegas' are used to it.

That is why a brutal satanic murder – seen by many as commonplace in major cities – knocked the stuffing out of the community. Mention the name Tracey Wigginton and anyone from Brisbane over the age of 25 shudders. The West End Lesbian Vampire Killer. The big bad world had finally caught up with us.

Not that Brisbane was untainted by senseless murder. There was the eighteen-year-old University of Queensland student who murdered both his parents with an axe in 1988 after reading Dostoyevsky's *Crime and Punishment*. But the Wigginton case was unlike any murder Brisbane had experienced. The body of a middle-aged family man was found near the city with his head brutally hacked almost completely from his shoulders. The true story slowly unfolded of lesbian 'vampire' Wigginton, her group of spellbound followers watching in fascination and repulsion, stabbing a naked Edward Baldock as he knelt by the river and lapping at his blood until sated. Satanism, blood rituals and sacrifice – Tiny Town seemed like a much scarier place than before.

Brisbane in the 1980s was like the poor semi-rural cousin who stares slack-jawed at the 'sirfisticated' Big City ways and mumbles, 'Gee whiz.' The state was scarred from over twenty years of National Party rule by a tiny-minded populist Christian fundamentalist farmer called Johannes Bjelke Petersen. His regime was characterised by cronyism and nepotism, anti-unionism and the use of the police force as a means of social control. He even went as far as gerrymandering, changing the electoral clout of certain areas to favour his own Country Party.[1] Now in retirement after a disastrous 'Joh for Prime Minister' campaign and failing to turn his Kingaroy peanut farm into a theme park called Joh World (despite the pumpkin scones on offer), his presence can still be felt after almost fifteen years out of office.

Queensland is the state that spawned the Confederate Action Party (CAP), a militant group of gun owners and right-wing anarchists with ties to Australian neo-Nazi organisations dedicated to bringing down the Australian government and returning autonomy to self-armed communities. You can find former CAP members in many local councils in the north. Then there is the One Nation Party from the late 1990s, which diluted the CAP platform with some *good ol'* anti-globalism slogans and dragged out the 'fear of the outsider' immigration debate to the Federal Election level. Before the party folded in a mire of campaign fraud in early 2001, One Nation held the balance of power in the Queensland Parliament and was even represented in the Federal Senate. Australia was regarded by the rest of Asia as a nation of bigots and pinheads, thanks to a fish-and-chip shop owner from Ipswich, Brisbane.

While Queensland was known to the rest of the country as 'the Deep North', Brisbane was affectionately known by its subculture in the 1980s as 'Pig City' (after a local punk song) and the name is more than appropriate – whether the Brisbane Task Force were beating heads with batons during the union marches of the 1970s against the conservative Joh regime, or you were getting arrested for vagrancy in the Queen Street Mall for having less than $2 in your pocket. Since the Fitzgerald Enquiry into Police Corruption in 1988 the more overt crimes against decency by the police force have been replaced by a more benign but still sinister presence; I still remember a rock festival in 1996 broken up by riot police on horseback *and* the army, cracking skulls in front of hundreds of horrified kids. The reason? They were waiting for people to start something.

As the system was so deeply conservative and intolerant towards 'deviancy' in all its perceived forms, the 'freaks' tended to huddle together for the simple reason that they had nowhere else to go and no one to turn to. In the 1960s they would have been called creeps and no-goodniks; now punks, goths, 'swampies' and the occasional skinhead prowled between clubs along with the drunks, speed freaks, heroin users, small-time hoods, aboriginals, the armed-service jerks doing the pussy circuit, disco heads, steroid-swollen bouncers, curb crawlers, the homeless, the artistic and the insane (or both) in the city and the inner suburbs such as Spring Hill and Fortitude Valley. None of the clubs from the late 1980s survive – eighteen months is a long life in clubland. Some of the buildings still stand, others are just holes in the ground or glass and steel towers, part of Brisbane's ongoing evolution from cow town to something bigger but not necessarily smarter.

The Valley was (and still is) the Soho or 42nd Street of Brisbane, a stretch of strip clubs, cafés and discos centered on Brunswick Street. The goth DJ Sebastian Niemand was sober enough to remember the Valley in the late 1980s well: 'Brunswick Street was like a Scorsese movie.' The Chinese triads were starting to move in as Italian crime families were meant to be lying low after the Fitzgerald Enquiry, but both were running drugs and operating illegal brothels and casinos through the back doors of nightclubs, pool halls and even amusement arcades. DJs knew the police were paid off if the club wasn't raided. Cops would walk in while bands were playing and collect paper bags full of fifties from the bar. It was a great place to go out and get fucked up, if you kept your eyes open and your mouth shut.

In 1989, goths and swampies were within spitting distance everywhere you looked. 'Swampies' (named after the Scientists' song 'Swampland') wore paisley shirts, black stovepipe pants and winkle-pickers, dyed their hair black and listened to sixties rock throwbacks such as the Lime Spiders, the Triffids and the Birthday Party. Goths looked pretty much like they do today: white make-up, velvet dresses or suits, Celtic and Egyptian jewellery, medieval motifs, *Addams Family*-style cartoon death imagery. They listened to gloomy electronic music (the Cure, Bauhaus, Sisters of Mercy and Alien Sex Fiend). Both goths and swampies emerged from the post-punk ooze around 1984 and tended to hang out at dance clubs such as Morticia's at the Hacienda Hotel in the Valley. One of Brisbane's more comical sights is a goth in trenchcoat and biker boots, face melting in the forty-degree heat. There was a popular joke at the time: 'Why did the goth cross

Brunswick Street?' 'It didn't: it kept jumping in front of traffic.'

Not surprisingly in Queensland, gay culture was also marginalised. Gay clubs such as the Set and the Terminus on Brunswick Street tended to be even more underground than the 'freak' clubs, owing to the number of violent homophobic assaults (which are still terrifyingly popular in the suburbs). The gay clubs were popular among straight punks and goths because of the tolerant atmosphere, and the music – it wasn't Kylie Minogue and kitsch seventies disco at the time, more post-New Romantic pop, heavy electro, Euro loops, early Pet Shop Boys, Bronski Beat – what can only be described as 'alternative dance music'. The freaks huddled together with other freaks, bonded by music or drugs or just by being 'deviant'. It was a special time in Brisbane that can never be recaptured.

Kim Jervis and Tracey Waugh were regulars at the Set, the gay club in Brunswick Street. Jervis dressed like a typical goth, all satin and lace, purple and black, when she wasn't working as a photo operator. In black and white make-up she cut a striking image. She was also obsessed with death imagery, decked out in magic icon jewellery and covered in tattoos of occult symbols. Her girlfriend Tracey Waugh was a polar opposite: unemployed, shy and introverted, quite plain. Rarely drank or did drugs. She came from a close family but was drawn to the more forceful personality of Jervis. Then one night at the Set in August 1989 they spied a new figure. Seventeen stone and nearly six foot tall, forceful and intense.

Enter Tracey Avril Wigginton.

She was born into an affluent family in Townsville, about 1,000 kilometres (620 miles) north of Brisbane.

Her mother, child of a self-made millionaire named George Wigginton, had married a drifter named Bill Rossborough, who soon left her and her young daughter. Around the time Tracey was six her mother dumped her in the custody of her grandparents, who also had an adopted daughter and foster child in their care. George was a womanising monster who started forcing himself on Tracey when she was eight. Grandmother Avril despised her husband (although possibly unaware of the sexual abuse) and in turn punished Tracey and the other children mercilessly. Dorelle, the adopted daughter, later stated:

> We were flogged with the ironing cord. It wasn't a normal flogging . . . the beatings went on and on . . . She tried to poison our minds, telling us men were bastards.[2]

At Catholic school Tracey was known as a predatory lesbian, and was expelled from one school for 'molesting' the other pupils. Once she left school she started calling herself 'Bobby' and began to turn violent, vandalising her grandmother's house, assaulting her mother. She worked as a bouncer in a gay club further north in the popular tourist destination, Cairns. After a failed lesbian marriage, she asked the club owner to impregnate her in front of 'six close friends'. She later had a miscarriage.

In 1987 she moved to Brisbane and started living with a girlfriend, Donna Staib. They agreed to an open relationship, although the wild promiscuity both women enjoyed apparently upset Wigginton. It is unknown when her interest in Satanism started, but it was in full tilt when she met Jervis and Waugh that August evening.

In October the three met again at Club Lewmors. It was Friday the 13th. Lewmors was just around the corner from Brunswick Street and out of the mainstream club scene, an exclusively gay drinking den, with the occasional DJ, located in a dilapidated old brick building. Since Lewmors closed after the murder there were a few mediocre attempts to open a club in the space, but it is almost as if the soil were poisoned, and the building has been closed for almost eight years. Even then the downstairs bar always looked boarded up and closed to the general public. The dance area upstairs was stripped back to the concrete and felt like a World War Two bunker. The DJ, John Griffin, who ran Morticia's at the time, said Lewmors was frequented by neither the gay nor goth mainstream that he saw in his club. Perhaps with the benefit of hindsight he described the place as having 'a negative vibe or aura because of the people. It was too exclusive, too left field, too extreme, even for the gay crowd. Was it the hardcore dyke influence? Was it an S&M crowd? I just don't know.'

That night Jervis brought along a friend, a large girl she had known for eight years called Lisa Ptaschinski. She and Wigginton immediately clicked; together the four women, with a shared sexual orientation and a common interest in Satan, talked for hours about the occult significance of the full moon above the Valley on such a date.

That night was the start of a brief but intense sexual relationship between Ptaschinski and Wigginton. Ptaschinski was a deeply disturbed 24-year-old with a submissive personality and a past riddled with depression, drug abuse and numerous suicide attempts, including swallowing a stomach-load of razor blades. She had been hospitalised 82 times in five years – once for a heroin overdose. Knowing this, Wigginton instructed her new lover to tie a tourniquet around her arm and slice a vein so that Wigginton could feed on the blood. Over the next week she did this four times.

Wigginton displayed other bizarre forms of behaviour. She avoided sunlight and mirrors, and would venture out only at night. And when she wasn't lapping at Lisa's arm she drank pig's and goat's blood from the fridge.

Then on the 18th, only five days after the group bonded in the Valley nightclub, they met at Jervis's flat in Clayfield, a neighbourhood located a few kilometres north of the city centre. Under a stolen gravestone in Jervis's living room and surrounded by her collection of headless dolls and photographs of cemeteries, Wigginton told them she needed human blood to survive. They then formulated a plan to lure a victim, kill him and allow Wigginton to feed on him. Lisa and Tracey were to pose as prostitutes in an inner-city park to entice the prospective victim. Jervis and Wigginton would then drain the body of blood, and hide the corpse in a freshly dug grave under a shallow layer of dirt. In the morning a coffin would be lowered into the hole, concealing their crime for ever. A simple plan.

Wigginton already owned a small silver martial-arts-issue butterfly knife; Jervis bought an identical blade that week. On Friday, 20 October, the four women sat in Club Lewmors and ordered several bottles of champagne. In the two years Jervis and Waugh had frequented the club the owner had never served them champagne before, but otherwise their behaviour did not attract attention. They quietly celebrated their future kill, then left at 11.30 p.m.

Meanwhile, on the other side of the Brisbane River, Edward Clyde Baldock was drinking and playing darts with his mates at the Caledonia Club. At 47 he was a family man, a father of five who had recently celebrated his silver wedding anniversary. Brisbane City Council flexitime allowed him to have the Friday off from his job as a road paver, and he was spending it as hundreds of thousands of typical Aussie blokes did – in the pub.

The green Holden Commodore sedan crawled along New Farm Park and the City Botanic Gardens with no luck. Around midnight it crossed the Story Bridge into Kangaroo Point, and spotted a plump middle-aged drunk wrapped around a lamppost. The car stopped.

Wigginton and Jervis got out of the car and asked Edward Baldock if he wanted a lift. The prospect of having sex with one or more of the women was implied; Baldock climbed into the back and clung to Wigginton's hand. She told the driver to head towards the river bank near Orleigh Park in West End, a few kilometres around the bend of the river. Baldock lived nearby, but the car stopped at the South Brisbane Sailing Club. He walked with Wigginton to the river. 'I told him I'd like to have a good time,' Wigginton said later. 'He said he was all for it.'[3]

Wigginton returned to the car and said, 'I need help. The bastard's too strong.' Ptaschinski took Jervis's butterfly knife and walked with Wigginton to the river, where Baldock was sitting in nothing but his socks. Wigginton gave the order to kill, but Ptaschinski folded. She fell in front of Baldock in a mess. Wigginton took the knife from her, then walked behind him. Baldock asked what she was doing. She said nothing, and stabbed him in the neck. Then repeatedly, in the other side of the neck, again and again. She grabbed his hair, yanked back his head and stabbed him in the front of the throat. He was still alive. 'I stabbed him in the back of the neck again, trying to get into the bones, I presume, and cut the nerves.' Wigginton was unrepentant. 'I then sat in front of the tilt-a-doors and watched him die.'[4]

SO MUCH BLOOD, SO MUCH BLOOD

Baldock was stabbed fifteen times with the two butterfly blades, and his head was almost entirely severed. According to Ptaschinski's and Wigginton's statements, Ptaschinski was on the sand in front of Baldock watching Wigginton butcher him. Ptaschinski was then reportedly ordered back to the other two women in the car while Wigginton feasted on his blood. She washed herself in the river afterwards and returned to the car, and the four drove back to Jervis's flat. When asked if she had drunk Baldock's blood, she replied she did. Waugh smelled blood on Wigginton's breath, and Jervis said she looked 'almost satisfied, like a person would look if they had just sat down to a three course dinner'.[5]

No witnesses, no links to the victim. They had left the body in the open next to the river, but they would be long gone before he was discovered.

Then Wigginton discovered that her Commonwealth Bank keycard was missing. She and Ptaschinski drove back to West End. Baldock's body was still lying by the river. They checked the entire area for the keycard but no luck. Panic set in. On the drive home, Wigginton tried to convince herself she had dropped the card elsewhere. That was it – they were still safe.

Fuck! The cops!

It was a random late-night/early-morning check for drunk drivers. The police questioned a white-faced Ptaschinski behind the wheel. She had left the flat in such a hurry she had forgotten her licence. Officers took her full details, plus the green sedan's registration number. She promised to call into the local station with her licence and was allowed to go.

Back at Jervis's flat the four women tried to calm themselves and fabricate their alibis. Meanwhile, Mrs Elaine Baldock received a visit from three detectives. She had already called the police, worried that her husband had not returned home, and by 8 a.m. the naked and bloodied body of a middle-aged man had been discovered by two early walkers and a solicitor on a morning row.

Located inside Edward Baldock's sock was a Commonwealth Bank keycard. He had picked it up, perhaps believing it was his, and had kept it safe until after his romantic riverside rendezvous.

Wigginton returned to West End by herself. Police had already sealed off the area, television cameras filming the pathetic sight of Baldock's blood-caked body. It took Detective Senior Sergeant Pat Glancy less than five minutes to find a keycard in Baldock's sock. The name on it read, 'T. A. Wigginton'.

Wigginton made one final visit to the murder site at 1 p.m. Detectives interviewed her on video camera, as they did a number of curious onlookers that day. She offered the shaky alibi the four women had decided on: she and Jervis had been to Orleigh Park the day before – during the day – and had seen a suspicious couple prowling the riverbank. Shaky. Police prodded a little harder. Yes, Officer, we did go back at night-time and stumbled over a body. Must have been Baldock. But they were too scared to report it.

Oh, yes, and the keycard . . .

Meanwhile Ptaschinski had left the flat at Clayfield and, in a state of anguish and confusion, ended up 50 kilometres (30 miles) on the other side of town and surrendered herself to Ipswich police.

At 7 p.m. both women were charged with the brutal slaying of Edward Clyde Baldock. Jervis and Waugh soon joined them in custody and were also charged.

It would take fifteen months for the trial to commence. Fifteen months for the media to speculate on the four women's dark backgrounds, motives and apparent bloodlust and hatred for men. The sight of a naked middle-aged man with his head almost severed by a group of young predatory black-clad lesbians was enough to make the staunchest of thrill seekers spill their Saturday-morning breakfast cereal. Once the police raided the women's homes – particularly Jervis's batcave with the tombstone on the lounge wall – the police hinted there might be occult overtones to the murder.

Suddenly Satan was everywhere. 'Sadist Killings'[6], in which two goats and a gosling were found mutilated and killed at Southport State High School, were branded as 'satanic' with no proof other than, 'Teachers at the school believe Satan worshippers were responsible.' Forgetting, of course, that boys will, sometimes, be boys. Church groups and family organisations spearheaded the media campaign that fed off the hysteria; SATANISM LINKED WITH CHILD PORN, TEENAGE SUICIDES[7] screamed the *Courier Mail*'s headline on the Australian Federation for the Family's (AFF) campaign against pornography. The article then made vague links between porn and satanic rituals, which led in turn to suicide. Schoolgirls were at the most risk, AFF's director Jack Sonnemann stated, because of the portrayal of 'young schoolgirls as being readily accessible'. Margaret Sonnemann, Jack's wife and AFF associate director, agreed: 'The majority of people who have been in touch with us are those who have been damaged by pornography.' But probably not Satanism.

Wigginton underwent intense pretrial psychoanalysis to determine whether she was legally sane – after all, she had confessed to a brutal satanic slaying. During a total of 26 hours of hypnosis a number of personalities emerged. 'Big Tracey' seemed to be her normal depressed adult self; 'Young Tracey' was a frightened little girl of eight. Then there was 'Bobby', a deep-voiced, almost masculine brutarian who admitted to killing Baldock and was railing against 'all of them'. The fourth personality, a cool detached character called 'the Observer', calmly explained that Tracey was merely killing everyone who had ever hurt her. Her mother, her grandmother, her sister, her girlfriend – everyone.

Psychiatrists were under no doubts that Wigginton was suffering from a multiple-personality syndrome, and that she indeed had been in a state of diminished mental health. She maintained she had killed Baldock and was adamant about her interest in Satanism and the occult. But she denied she was a vampire, and refused to admit she drank the victim's blood – or any blood, for that matter.

Psychiatrists Quinn and Clarke declared that Wigginton was mentally ill, most probably from the childhood trauma of abandonment, extreme cruelty and sexual abuse. Regardless, she had planned Baldock's murder with such cold calculation; she was aware of her behaviour and its consequences, and therefore was not legally insane.

Mentally ill but legally sane, Wigginton was sentenced to life imprisonment in January 1991. The media trial of the other three lesbians was to begin soon after.

Brisbane Supreme Court was packed with the families of Baldock, Jervis and Waugh, and members of Brisbane's lesbian community who had turned out to show solidarity. Lawyers were quick to point out that the three women had not raised a hand to Baldock, but were instead under the fearful spell of Wigginton, the vicious and manipulative self-styled 'vampire' who was already serving life for Baldock's murder. All three claimed they thought the plan to sacrifice a victim and drink their blood was a 'joke' and could not believe it actually happened. Ptaschinski was diagnosed in prison with borderline personality disorder, which supposedly clouded her ability to comprehend the circumstances leading to the murder. Dr Peter Mulholland said Ptaschinski was under the delusion that Wigginton was a vampire; on the stand, Jervis said Wigginton offered to 'share some of the takings'[8] – Baldock's blood – with her. Waugh swore under oath that Jervis had fallen under the vampire's influence when her crucifix broke. She had also witnessed Wigginton disappear, leaving only her 'cat's eyes' visible.

The picture the women presented in court – three frightened girls watching helplessly and in fear of satanic retribution as their vampire guru killed and gorged herself – was torn to pieces by the prosecution. The jury reached its verdict on 15 February 1991.

Lisa Ptaschinski was handed a life sentence for the murder of Edward Baldock. Tracey Waugh was acquitted, viewed by the jury as the unwilling participant of the other three women's insane plan. That left Kim Jervis to face the judge, who stated, 'You knew what was likely to happen, you took no pity on Mr Baldock as another human being.'[9] Evidence that Jervis had purchased one of the knives that Wigginton used almost to behead their victim had damned her, and she was sentenced to eighteen years in jail for manslaughter. It was all a matter of circumstances. Wigginton used the two knives on Baldock in a cold-blooded and premeditated act of bloodlust: murder. Jervis bought one of the knives but stayed in the car: manslaughter. Ptaschinski left the car but couldn't bring herself to stab Baldock: murder. Waugh sat in the back of the car, she claimed unwillingly but under the malevolent influence of the other three: free.

The most extreme of the 'Satan hysteria' articles appeared in the *Courier Mail* during the trial. The piece headed SATANISM: A DARK SIDE OF THE SUNSHINE STATE said 'the occult, in its many and varied forms, is flourishing in Brisbane', and echoed the fear in most God-fearing citizens: 'the vampire-style murder . . . might be the catalyst for more horrific crimes committed in the name of Satan.' 'Cathy Jones', a former inmate who knew Wigginton in jail, was interviewed and claimed Wigginton and her followers had performed 'blood marriages with the Devil'.[10] Now 23, she said she was lured into the occult underworld as a nine-year-old Melbourne street kid, where she witnessed blood drinking and human and animal sacrifices. 'Tracey does have power and she can be evil,' 'Cathy' is quoted as saying. 'She is a priestess in the occult because she is married to Satan . . . Giving blood is the only way Satan can get total control. Tracey can put people under her control.'

The same article also claimed that half of the missing-persons cases were linked to satanic sacrifices ('Cathy' again), and quoted a white witch who claimed that Brisbane Satanists (numbering 'between 500 and 1,000') made up a small percentage of those involved in the occult. Bestiality, paedophilia, Walpurgis, Crowley, the Church of Satan and the Temple of Set are thrown around for shock effect. The reporter then introduces the haggard 'horror videos lead to the occult' theory, and compares Wigginton's crime to those of the vampires played by Susan Sarandon and David Bowie in *The Hunger*. 'It was a film Wigginton and her cohorts had watched repeatedly. By coincidence or otherwise, the final victim in the film is a character named Blalock – just a few letters short of Edward Baldock's name.'

Much of the media attention over the West End murder centred on the protagonists' goth and lesbian lifestyle. Yet again, they jumped to wild conclusions. Gay culture simply did not embrace death, while goths used ghoulish imagery on a superficial level. 'Most goths were designer goths,' says John Griffin, 'and to their peers they looked good, embraced their music with a passion, but at the end of the day they weren't practicing the occult.' What Wigginton (and to a lesser extent the other three women) followed were increasingly aberrant, antisocial models of behaviour. Drug taking, promiscuous sex, blood drinking as a fetish or part of sex magic, and a fixation on death imagery are nothing special, and are often merely superficial signs of rebellion. But a few goths, or pagans for that matter, are willing to transgress the outer boundaries of 'normality': cemetery desecration, church burning and grave robbing. Rape. Murder. Wigginton and her three followers were a weird hybrid of gay and gothic culture – more a death obsession with pagan and lesbian overtones.

In some ways Brisbane has grown up. Following the grunge-era youth-culture explosion in the early 1990s the city is more tolerant of what it sees as its deviant subcultures. The Queensland Film Censorship Board no longer says people are 'going to hell' for watching *Hail Mary* or *Last Temptation of Christ*, and there is less gay bashing these days. In other ways we're still ruled by peanut farmers who work on the same old linear logic: pot smoking leads to heroin addiction; watching porn leads a grown man to rape; and dressing like a goth is the Devil's Highway to satanic possession. Violent movies can lead to all sorts of trouble. Remember, the Tasmanian gunman Martin Bryant's favourite movie was *Babe*.

If we believe everything we read in the tabloid press, Satan is a diesel dyke who shares a bunk with chief vampire Wigginton in Cell Block H. The real cause of Wigginton's obsession with blood and death and the sad death of Edward Baldock – her childhood history of sexual abuse and withdrawl into fantasy – is possibly too brutally human for tabloid spin. Maybe she was the Devil's bride, but so is every other depressed schlub from the suburbs with an armful of razor scars and a permanent Trent Reznor scowl. I like to think of Wigginton like this: from poisoned soil, strange little flowers grow. The Devil may not have made Tracey Wigginton do it, no matter what the voices on the television said.

NOTES

1. See pp. 83–105 of Deane Wells' *The Deep North*, ch. 'Heirs and Beneficiaries', pub. Outback Press, Collingwood, Vic, Aus, 1979.
2. David Jessel (ed.), *Murder Casebook Vol. 6 Part 83: The Vampire Killers*, London: Marshall Cavendish Ltd, 1991, p. 2960.
3. Ibid. p. 2963.
4. Ibid. p. 2964.
5. Ibid.
6. 'Sadist Killings', *Sunday Mail*, 30 September 1990, p. 3.

7. Cindy Wockner, 'Satanism Linked To Porn, Teen-age Suicides', *Courier Mail*, 22 September 1990, p. 19.
8. *Courier Mail*, 2 February 1991, p. 3.
9. *Sunshine Coast Daily*, 16 February 1991, p. 6.
10. Jason Gagliardi and Shelley Thomas, 'Satanism – A Dark Side of the Sunshine State', *Courier Mail*, 23 February 1991, p. 10.

BIBLIOGRAPHY

Deane Wells, The Deep North, Outback Press, Vic. Australia, 1979.

David Jessel (ed.), *Murder Casebook Vol. 6 Part 83: The Vampire Killers*, London: Marshall Cavendish Ltd, 1991.

Thanks to Duane Watson, John Griffin and Sebastian Niemand.

11. BLOOD AND SAND

TRAGEDY AT MATAMOROS

JACK SARGEANT

Religion in its entirety was founded upon sacrifice.
> – Georges Batailles, *The Tears of Eros*

It was like a human slaughterhouse.
> – Cameron County Sheriff Alex Perez

There the devil did fail them,
Satanic murderers
> – 'Tragedy in Matamoros' by Suspiros de Salamanca[1]

The town of Matamoros lies just across the American–Mexican border, located across the Rio Grande (or Rio Bravo as the Mexicans call the river that flows along the border) south of Brownsville, Texas. Like other communities on the fragile, inevitably permeable, borders between rich First World and poor developing countries, Matamoros has an economy that is largely driven by the demands of its wealthy neighbour.

Matamoros is an interzone where two different peoples meet: comparatively rich Americans and dirt-poor Mexicans. It offers a cheap escape for partying American students during the college ritual of Spring Break, when an estimated 250,000 students descend on the Mexican town to enjoy a respite from their studies. The town also acts as a staging post for drug smugglers, who export narcotics to the wealthy northern neighbour. If the *gringos* have the money, somebody will always inevitably be prepared to risk capture by the various law-enforcement agencies and the border patrols in order to satisfy the demands of the market-place.

That drug trafficking is a major trade is hardly surprising: similar illicit trades flourish across most borders. However, the events that came to light in April 1989 revealed something far more disturbing, writhing and squirming in the darkness beneath the surface of the Mexican border town.

> They all started trembling
> Because that satanic gang,
> They are not afraid to kill.
> — 'Tragedy in Matamoros,
> by Suspiros de Salamanca

On 13 March 1989, among the masses of students heading south to celebrate Spring Break, were four friends: Mark Kilroy, Brent Martin, Bradley Moore and Bill Huddleston. The group partied in the local bars and, in the early hours of the morning of the 14th, they began to head back to Texas. Kilroy, a 21-year-old University of Texas student, did not make it across the International Gateway Bridge: separated from his friends on their walk back to the border, he was never seen alive again. The student was kidnapped, thrown into a pickup truck and taken twenty miles (32 kilometres) out of town, to the Rancho Santa Elena. Within 24 hours he would be killed, savagely hacked to death in a grisly ritualised slaughter.

Mark's parents – Jim and Helen Kilroy – began searching, and within days a police task force was established in Brownsville. Despite the fact that Matamoros was beyond their jurisdiction, they assisted *federales* with their enquires. Sixty people had vanished in Matamoros in the first three months of 1989, but they were Mexicans; the disappearance of an American represented a threat to the local tourist-driven economy. Life on the border may be cheap for Mexicans but – in the stark pragmatism of contemporary politics and international economics – it is not for an American. But nothing was found. Mark Kilroy appeared to have vanished into thin air.

On 1 April 1989 Mexican *federales* established a roadblock, a short drive from Matamoros, searching cars for drugs. Routine police work. Nothing special. Until a pickup truck raced past them, ignoring the warning signs that demanded drivers slow down. The stunned law-enforcement agents followed the vehicle to a nearby ranch – Rancho Santa Elena – but, rather than arrest the driver, whom they recognised as Little Serafin Hernandez, a member of a local family of known but unconvicted drug smugglers, they opted to sit and wait. After Serafin left the ranch the two agents climbed from their car and began to explore, noticing that one of the cars among the vehicles parked at the ranch – a new Chevy Suburban – was fitted with a cellular phone, and that the seats were caked with a thin layer of marijuana dust commonly associated with moving large quantities of the drug. More disturbingly to the superstitious Mexicans, they saw a statue in the car, a figure with a pointed head, its features created from seashells.

On hearing the report, Matamoros *federales'* Comandante Juan Benitez Ayala organised his agents, telling them to watch the ranch, and initiating an investigation into the apparent wealth associated with the Hernandez family, who many believed had fallen on hard times. Then he contacted the Drug Enforcement Administration (DEA) agents across the border. It appeared that a drug ring was about to be busted.

On 9 April agents made their move. Raiding a Hernandez residence in Matamoros, they arrested Little Serafin and another associate, David Serna Martinez. Shortly afterwards two other suspects were caught: Sergio Martinez and Elio Herndandez. Strangely, however, none of those arrested seemed concerned. And then Domingo Reyes Bustamante was arrested. The 'caretaker' of Rancho Santa Elena, he began to talk immediately, telling the agents that the gang had stored drugs at the ranch. He also told his inquisitors that he had seen a *gringo* at the ranch. When he was shown a photograph of Mark Kilroy, the scared caretaker confirmed that this was a man the gang had brought to the remote ranch.

Little Serafin Hernandez was interrogated again. During the lengthy questioning the youthful drug smuggler spilled his guts, willing to confess all to the police. The American had been tortured – Serafin stated – mutilated prior to being murdered with a heavy blow to the skull from a machete. The gang-cum-cult believed that the brutal sacrifices would ensure power, success and protection for the initiates. The ritual guaranteed that the smugglers would be invisible to the police. They could not be harmed by bullets. They were invincible. And in return they had given their souls. Serafin *knew* all this to be true, he had been told so by the leader of the group, El Padrino – the Godfather – Adolfo de Jesus Constanzo.

Back at Rancho Santa Elena they began to dig, slowly unearthing a graveyard like no other. The corpse of Mark Kilroy was found, alongside several other cadavers all buried in shallow graves. By the end of the investigation at Rancho Santa Elena, thirteen decomposing, mutilated male corpses were exhumed, while a further two bodies were located in a nearby orchard.[2] Many of the victims appeared to have been tortured prior to death, their bodies beaten, hacked, sliced and cut. Several of the corpses had been castrated; some had fingers amputated and nipples snipped off. Some had been decapitated; many showed massive head trauma, the skulls caved in, the brains removed. These were not the traditional victims of internecine drug feuds: rather they appeared to have been ritually killed to some arcane specifications.

In a grim wooden shack, a short distance from the ranch houses, the investigators discovered the sacred site for the killer cult. In the blood-splattered shack the *federales* found sinister traces that hinted at some form of ritualised violence: a machete, part-smoked cigars and candles forming an altar; and they found the cult's magical cauldron – a *nganga*. In this cauldron were powerful totems: the corpse of a black cat, fourteen horseshoes, railroad spikes, a roasted turtle, scorpions, 21 wooden sticks, traces of rotting blood, decomposing human flesh and a human brain.

On Sunday, 23 April – the religious symbolism of the chosen day adding to the effectiveness of the ritual – scant days after the discovery, a local *curandero*, a healer/white witch, performed a *limpia*, a cleansing ritual, on both the ranch and the land on which it lay. Entering the shack in which the sacrifices occurred, the *curandero* exorcised the dark forces: setting the wooden building on fire, destroying the residues of darkness that the locals believed lurked within.[3]

But the cult's leader, and several followers, remained at large.

> The Santa Elena Ranch,
> It looks like a cemetery there.
>> – 'Tragedy in Matamoros',
>> by Suspiros de Salamanca

In Miami on 1 November 1962, a fifteen-year-old Cuban immigrant, Delia Aurora Gonzalez del Valle, gave birth to a boy: Adolfo de Jesus Constanzo.[4] Delia believed that her son was blessed with magical powers and, according to Edward Humes's book *Buried Secrets*, Constanzo was only six months old when he was first presented to the local *palero* (a priest in the Palo Mayombe faith), and described as 'a chosen one'.[5] It is believed that as a child Constanzo was subsequently educated in various religious traditions: Santeria, Palo Mayombe and Catholicism (although, following the events at Rancho Santa Elena, his family claimed to be Catholics). Reports also suggest that in his early teenage years he experienced visions revealing the 'truth' of Marilyn Monroe's death and predicting John Hinkley's assassination attempt on President Ronald Reagan. To his mother these moments emphasised her son's developing magical powers. He was growing into a powerful man.

In 1984 Constanzo moved from Miami to Mexico City to work as a model and used his magical knowledge to work as a fortune-teller and adviser. It was here that he consolidated his reputation as a powerful magician, earning large sums of money casting spells among the glitterati of Mexico City. Setting up his home in the Zona Rosa, Adolfo de Jesus Constanzo began sexual relationships with Martin Quintana Rodriguez and Omar Francisco Orea Ochea, both of whom were seduced by the combination of Constanzo's good looks, 'spiritual' knowledge and magical skills. Over the following months Constanzo initiated Omar – and others – into his cult, instructing them in what many subsequent news reports suggest to be a twisted combination of two religions: Santeria and Palo Mayombe.

* * *

Santeria and Palo Mayombe are both syncretic religions, traditional religious beliefs brought to the Caribbean by slaves who – forced to undergo baptism and embrace the Catholicism of their 'owners' in the 'New World' – represented their old gods and spirits with the Christian saints. The two religions came from different tribal groups: Santeria emerged from the Yuruban slaves, while Palo Mayombe emerged from the Congolese slaves. The hidden aspect of both religions – the lack of any single written doctrine and the emphasis on oral communication from generation to generation – add to the apparently covert nature of these traditions, yet the secrecy associated with these faiths emerged as a response to the Catholic slave owners' evangelical brutality.

While these faiths – and other Afro-Caribbean beliefs – are different religions, they share similar beliefs in:

> blood sacrifice, spirit possession (generally
> interpreted positively as the manifestation of a deity
> in the body of a worshipper), ancestor worship,
> and herbal healing.[6]

It should be noted that the blood sacrifice these religions embrace is animal and *not* human sacrifice; moreover, the animals sacrificed (generally chickens and goats) are rapidly killed – their throats slit – and their blood is used as an offering to the gods in return for good health or in order to overcome bad luck. In many cases the animal is eaten following the ceremony.[7] The relationship between these faiths may appear muddied to adherents of the Abrahamic[8] religions by the fact that the Afro-Caribbean religions recognise the relevance of other faiths: thus, for example, followers of Santeria may also be Christian, and sometimes followers of Santeria can also follow Palo Mayombe. In his exploration of the syncretic religions George Brandon highlights the example of a follower who embraces aspects of both Santeria and Palo Mayombe because both are concerned with the spirit.[9]

Thus the two religions *can* be complementary, but do not have to be. To some followers of these religions their essence is their mutability.

Some writers on the Matamoros case have erroneously suggested that Palo Mayombe is the 'dark side' of Santeria[10] despite the fact that it is a different religion. Such statements presume to superimpose a Judeo-Christian good–evil dialectic on to faiths that have emerged from different cultures and have their own philosophical and metaphysical value systems.[11] This nature of the difference and contingent nature of 'good' is best summarised in Esteban Montejo's *The Autobiography of a Runaway Slave*, in which he suggests that, among the slaves with whom he grew up,

> There was no love lost between Congolese magic-men [practitioners of Palo Mayombe] and the Congolese Christians, *each of whom thought they were good and the others wicked.*[12] [My emphasis.]

One of the key aspects of Palo Mayombe is the use of the *nganga*, the sacred cauldron that contains the spirits of the dead – often via the presence of a human skull – which need sustenance provided by ritualised sacrifice. Such cauldrons were common among the Congolese slaves: 'they prepared big pots called *nganga* . . . and that was where the secret of their spells lay. All the Congolese had these pots for mayombe'.[13] For Christians the notion that the cauldron contains a spirit that enacts the will of the *palero* and acts as a conduit between the material world and the world of the spirits is anathema. The ethnocentric notion that Palo Mayombe is 'dark' almost certainly lies in the religion's emphasis on the spirit and magical realm manifested through the *nganga*, yet it was Christians who traded in humans across the Atlantic.

Palo Mayombe – like other syncretic religions – offers believers a way in which they can communicate with gods and a way in which they can affect events and circumstances in the world around them. Contemporary followers of the religion normally obtain the human skull for their *nganga* legally – through medical suppliers.[14] According to some experts, the cauldron is not to be tampered with and only those with experience should even attempt to possess one.[15]

Having secured a base of operations in Mexico City, Adolfo de Jesus Constanzo became increasingly ambitious and increasingly ruthless. In 1987 Constanzo began working for the drug smuggler Guillermo Calzada Sanchez – using his fortune-telling skills to predict the best time for the smuggling of drugs and casting protective spells. Knowing how much money could be made from smuggling, Constanzo suggested that Guillermo Calzada Sanchez divide the profits evenly with him. However, the offer was rejected.[16]

On 7 May two mutilated corpses were found in the Rio Zumpango, a male who had been castrated and bludgeoned, and a female whose throat had been slashed so deeply that her head had been almost sliced from the body and whose chest had been torn open, leaving a gaping cavity where the heart should have been. Over the following week, five more bodies were pulled, bloated and stinking, from the rivers and canals of Mexico City. All were savagely mutilated. Bizarrely, for a suspected drug-related homicide, two of the cadavers appeared to have had their brains removed. Eventually just three of the bodies were officially identified: El Titi, Calia Campos de Klein and Gabriela Mondragon Vargas – Guillermo Calzada Sanchez's body-guard, secretary and maid. The other four bodies – too damaged by mutilation and too rotten from time spent sunk in dirty water to be identified – were believed to be Guillermo Calzada Sanchez, his wife, his mother and his partner. Although it was never proven that these killings were the work of the cult, it is believed that the murders were the work of Constanzo.

In July 1987 Adolfo de Jesus Constanzo began to move into the drugs trade on the Mexico–United States border, in Matamoros. The Hernandez clan had fallen on hard times: the gang's leader, Saul Hernandez, had been killed in January; the new leader, Elio Hernandez, was not making a success of smuggling; and the suppliers for whom the family worked had stopped supporting the operation. Constanzo, however, had the power to help: he knew the drugs trade, and he had the magical power to protect the superstitious smugglers. All he needed was a contact.

Using a combination of manipulative seduction and magic, Constanzo impressed a young Texas Southmost College student, Sara Maria Aldrete Villareal. She would become – according to many of the followers – the godmother, and was known as La Bruja, the Sorceress, to the cult. More importantly, she knew Elio Hernandez, and shortly after meeting Constanzo she introduced the two men. Everything was falling into place: the drug smugglers had protection, and Constanzo had the leadership and power that he so craved.

The first killings at the ranch are believed to have started the following summer. In May 1988 two local men were killed, but they were simply shot and buried, and neither their deaths nor their bodies were used in any rituals. The first victim to be ritually sacrificed, and whose body parts were used in the creation of the Matamoros cauldron, was a transvestite, Ramon Paz Esquivel (a.k.a. La Claudia), who was killed in Mexico City in July 1988. La Claudia's body was dismembered in a bathtub and much of the fleshy remains were left in bloody trash bags, but the transvestite's fingers, genitals and brain were transported to the *nganga* at Rancho Santa Elena.

The sacrificial victims unearthed at Matamoros revealed that many of their bodies had been strung up above the cauldron and the blood pouring from their wounds had been allowed to flow into its depths, feeding the spirits that the cult believed lurked within, spirits that would subsequently do El Padrino's bidding. The brains and sometimes the hearts and lungs of the victims were put into the *nganga*, creating more spirits. Some of the mutilated corpses were buried with wire inserted into their exposed vertebrae, so that when decomposition had reached a critical point – the flesh and tissue flensed by worms and maggots – the segment of wire sticking above the grave could be tugged, pulling out the corpse's vertebrae in order to produce charmed talismans.

> For that satanic gang
> Black will be their sentence
>   – 'Tragedy in Matamoros',
>   by Suspiros de Salamanca

Following the discovery of the ritual slaughterhouse at the Rancho Santa Elena, Mexican and American authorities began searching for Adolfo de Jesus Constanzo, Sara Maria Aldrete Villareal, Martin Quintana Rodriguez, Omar Francisco Orea Ochoa and Alvaro de Leon Valdez, a.k.a. El Duby: the *narcosatanico*, as the Mexican press had (incorrectly) nicknamed them. Sightings were reported across the North American continent. None were accurate. The cult leader and his surviving inner circle had retreated to Mexico City, where they rented a cheap apartment and began making their plans to escape the country.

Sara too began making plans, perhaps aware of the inevitability of discovery and capture. She wrote a note and threw it into the street:

> Please call the judicial police and tell them that in this building are those that they are seeking. Give them the address, fourth floor. Tell them that a woman is being held hostage. I beg for this, because what I want most is to talk – or they're going to kill the girl.

Although the note was picked up, it was not handed in to the police until after the case had been closed.

In the end the case was solved through the stupidity of the cult members. First they attracted attention to themselves when shopping in the supermarket opposite their hideout, attempting to pay for their groceries with a hundred-dollar bill. Then, on seeing an 'unmarked' police car in the street, the increasingly paranoid Constanzo opened fire from the window of the fourth-floor apartment. Even as his shots strafed the street, it was over. Unable to escape, and with ammunition running low, Adolfo de Jesus Constanzo decided that death was his only escape, and the gang hit man, El

Duby, was given the task of killing both El Padrino and his lover Martin Quintana Rodriguez. The surviving cult members were taken into custody. It was 6 May.

Sara Maria Aldrete Villareal began her defence immediately, claiming she had been kidnapped by the cult, and that she had no knowledge of the grim findings unearthed at the ranch near the border. When questioned about her beliefs she insisted that she had only ever practised Santeria Cristiana – Christian Santeria. After months of legal stalling the trials began. Despite her protestations, Sara Maria Aldrete Villareal was found guilty of criminal association, while other members of the bloodthirsty cult were convicted of crimes that included both murder and drug smuggling.

In an unsettling twist, while investigating the crime, law-enforcement officials found numerous items of children's clothing at apartments used by the cult, and although no infant corpses were ever found it has been speculated that Constanzo may have killed as many as sixteen children.

Even as the evil was exorcised from Rancho Santa Elena and Adolfo de Jesus Constanzo's bullet-riddled corpse was shipped back to America, the cold terror fed by the cult's frenzied malevolence spread like a cancer through Mexico and beyond.

The killings that took place under the malevolent guidance of Adolfo de Jesus Constanzo were unlike those undertaken by almost all other death cults. There was no apocalyptic 'purpose' to the cult's killings, no 'great' vision or visions: instead, the victims were tortured and sacrificed in order that the cult should continue their illegal trade unmolested. As a cult, they were largely banal, self-centred and greedy.

The media's response to the killings was predictably hysterical, with talk shows and newspapers variously describing the cult as satanic, as followers of 'voodoo', as practitioners of Santeria and, eventually, Palo Mayombe. This confusion was added to by the contrary statements from the arrested cult members, who also offered differing names for the belief system they embraced, too ill-educated and manipulated, too scared and too power-hungry, to understand exactly what they were involved in.

Satanic rituals, and the belief in a massive satanic underground and other similar conspiracy theories, formed the basis for numerous right-wing evangelical fundamentalist Christian witch-hunts in the eighties and nineties. Numerous Christian groups believed that a massive Devil-worshipping occult underground was operating across America, but, despite numerous accusations, no evidence was ever found to substantiate such beliefs, which lay purely in the overactive imaginations of fundamentalist zealots. Despite this lack of evidence – and sometimes *because* of this lack of evidence – the fundamentalist belief in a satanic conspiracy continued to flourish. For some fundamentalist Christians and self-appointed cult watchdogs, Matamoros represented the proof they wanted for the existence of the satanic underground. To add to the confusion around the case, some Christians suggested that the Rancho Santa Elena was the same ranch referred to in the delusional rambling 'confessions' of the 'serial killer' Henry Lee Lucas[17] despite the chronological impossibility – Lucas described an occult snuff ranch during one of his (imaginary) confessional bouts following his apprehension in 1983, long before Constanzo established himself in Matamoros.[18]

During the media circus around the Matamoros killings, several journalists linked the cult's beliefs to those of an imaginary group presented in the film *The Believers*, directed by John Schlesinger (1987). This film follows a group of yuppies who follow a quasi-'voodoo'-styled belief system with a suitably violent (and predictable) narrative. The film merely follows in the tradition of numerous other Hollywood movies in presenting a clichéd perspective of 'malevolent' aboriginal beliefs.[19] Edward Humes dismisses this theory in his book on the case, and certainly the cult were motivated by more than a movie. However, in *Across the Border*, Gary Provost suggests that:

> Sara was helping to recruit new members of the cult. Her main recruiting tool was the film *The Believers* ... [. . .] ... it helped persuade some young people, and Constanzo's cult grew.[20]

Some students from Texas Southmost College – where Sara Maria Aldrete Villareal was a student – were shown the film by the devotee prior to her espousing the values of the 'occult'. Similarly, on his arrest, Little Serafin reportedly told law-enforcement officials that his favourite film was *The Believers*.

Constanzo's beliefs – while *appearing* to be rooted in a particularly twisted interpretation of various Afro-Caribbean syncretic religions – betray a uniquely feral temperament. Historical accounts of religious sacrifice – often written by supposedly benevolent Christians – describe brutal killings that were undertaken to appease savage gods. Notably, however, these victims often *wanted* to be sacrificed – as in descriptions of ancient Aztec rituals. Indeed, much of the power (both to a culture and as a form of religious symbolism) of the human sacrifice comes from the consensual nature of the human offering.[21] This is in stark contrast to Constanzo's crimes, which were entirely to satisfy his own bestial desires.

The killings undertaken by Constanzo and his disciples ultimately belong to no known or recognisable tradition. Of the victims exhumed from the Matamoros soil, 'most had been . . . sodomized, castrated'.[22] Further, as Sara stated during her police interviews,

> 'Before sacrificing these people, Adolfo would remain by himself in the room of the dead with them, so he could have sex with them just before the sacrifice . . . It satisfied him'.[23]

The rituals and violent fixations were Constanzo's. He disguised his interests behind what, to the uneducated Mexican drug smugglers, must have been a bewildering combination of religious doctrines and the implicit threat of imminent violence, matched by the promise of magical power and massive financial rewards. His followers were largely brutal, ugly men for whom violence was a regular occurrence – a 'necessary' part of their daily business – and Constanzo utilised this proclivity for brutality to benefit his own ends. According to evidence presented in Edward Humes's book, many of the followers were initially revolted by the exceptional brutality of the sacrifices, but their willingness to believe in El Padrino's magic meant that they soon became inured to the sacrificial rituals.[24]

The extreme brutality of the killings undertaken by Constanzo and his cult are almost unique in their pathology; indeed, in their morbid fascinations they recall the *lustmord* of sexual killers and the snuff fixation of those individuals for whom the corpse itself is nothing less than a fleshy toy and a plaything. Constanzo's fixation with rape, genital mutilation and power suggests that he shared a pathology with murderers such as Jeffrey Dahmer and Fred West. Constanzo's bloodthirsty crimes recall Colin Wilson's description of the sexually sadistic serial killer – an egocentric figure who can present a socially acceptable façade but who will manipulate people towards his own ends, and who, at base, is 'a cunning methodical killer'.[25] Thus viewed, Constanzo's ability to surround himself with a pack of weaker but similarly violent personalities was a recipe for certain mayhem.

NOTES

1. 'Tragedy in Matamoros' by Suspiros de Salamanca. The song – a *corrido* – details the Matamoros case. Historically the *corridos* detail social events and describe historical events.
2. Alongside Mark Kilroy, the deceased exhumed at the ranch were: Ezequiel Rodriguez Luna, Victor Saul Sauceda, Gilberto Garza Sosa, fourteen-year-old Jose Luis Garcia Luna, Ruben Vela Garza, Ernesto Rivas Diaz, Miguel Garcia, Joaquin Manzo, Jorge Valente del Fierro Gomez. Three corpses remained unidentified, their identities annihilated. The corpses buried at the orchard were those of Moises Castillo and Hector de la Fuente.
3. While this may appear to be an unnecessarily superstitious response to the discovery of the cult's shack, it should be observed that other sites where particularly violent murders have been committed have also been destroyed. See, for example Fred and Rosemary West's house at 25 Cromwell Street,

Gloucester, which – following the police investigation – was demolished, as if erasing all physical traces of the crime scene and the associated aberrant behaviour might cleanse the grim atmosphere.

4. According to Gary Provost, *Across The Border: The True Story of the Satanic Cult Killings In Matamoros, Mexico*, New York: Pocket Books, Simon and Schuster Inc., 1989, she was also known as 'Aurora Gonzalez Constanzo and Delia Posada' (p. 89).

5. Edward Humes, *Buried Secrets, A True Story of Serial Murder, Black Magic, and Drug-Running on the U.S. Border*, New York: Dutton, 1991, p. 48.

6. James T Houk, *Spirits, Blood and Drums: the Orisha Religion in Trinidad*, Philadelphia: Temple University Press, p. 53.

7. Sacrifice is also present in many other traditions, including Judaism, Islam and Christianity, and readers should observe the numerous sacrifices that are carried out within the Old Testament of the Bible.

8. Abraham was an Old Testament patriarch who is seen as the founder of the Hebrew people in Judaism via his son Isaac, and seen as the founder of the Arab people via his son Ishmael. Abraham is thus a key figure in Judaism, Islam and Christianity.

9. See: George Brandon, *Santeria From Africa to the New World: The Dead Sell Memories*, Bloomington and Indianapolis: Indiana University Press, 1993, p. 176.

10. See, for example, Richard Monaco and William Burt, *The Dracula Syndrome*, (London: Headline Book Publishing, 1993), which states that the Palo Mayombe is the 'evil flip-side of Santeria' and 'loathsome' (p. 189).

11. It should be observed that both Santeria and Palo Mayombe have specific codes of conduct.
12. Estaban Montejo, *The Autobiography of a Runaway Slave*, translated by Jocasta Innes, edited by Miguel Barnet, London: The Bodley Head, 1938, p. 38.
13. Ibid. p. 34.
14. Kerr Cuhulain, 'Matamoros Cult Killings' in *Cult-Watch Response* Vol. I, Issue 6.
15. See www.religioustolerance.com and www.palo.org.
16. This is according to Edward Humes, *Buried Secrets*, op. cit. p. 109, who suggests that the Calzada's business (a fire-extinguisher company) was 'a front for a cocaine storage centre' and the family were 'cocaine smugglers', while other writers on the case suggest that this is only alleged, or describe the family as 'businessmen' (Mikita Brottman, *Hollywood Hex: Cursed Movies*, London: Creation Books, 1999, p. 157).
17. Lucas clearly enjoyed the grand notoriety of being a serial killer and he 'confessed' to more than three hundred murders, although many of these confessions contained contradictory and inaccurate information.
18. See, for example, Andrew Boyd's *Blasphemous Rumours*, London: Fount, HarperCollins, 1991, which suggests that:

> Lucas said he was in possession of satanic literature. He described a ritual at a ranch which involved chanting and praying to the devil, and which ended in cannibalism: 'Towards the end, the victim would be killed and each of us would drink blood and eat part of the body'.

> More than three years elapsed before the authorities were finally to raid the ranch at Matamoros. [p. 70]

Although Boyd concedes the murders may not be satanic, his style of literary slippage between fact, rumour and imagination, and his careful exorcism of contradictory evidence (such as the 'three years' between Lucas's confession and Matamoros – largely irrelevant, as Constanzo didn't move to Matamoros till a year before the cult was uncovered) mean that little genuine information is presented, although the more gullible Christian reader can infer much from hiš vaguely conspiratorial writing.

19. Similarly clichéd presentations of syncretic faiths can also be seen in eighties movies such as *Angel Heart*.

20. Gary Provost, *Across The Border*, op. cit. pp. 128–9.

21. See Brenda Ralph Lewis, *Ritual Sacrifice: A Concise History* (Thrupp: Sutton Publishing, 2001), who states that:

> To be sacrificed to the Sun was, to them, a great honour, a means of achieving divinity and something else that might never have otherwise come their way – translation after death to the Paradise of the Sun normally reserved for great warriors or women who had died in childbirth. On occasion, the Spaniards were able to save victims from death on the sacrificial altar, only to be utterly confounded when these same victims proved ungrateful and demanded to be sacrificed. [p. 83]

Similarly, early Christian martyrs willingly went to their deaths at the hands of the Romans in the arena rather than renounce their faith, an action that surely should be regarded as a form of self-sacrifice. To die for one's faith must always be a viewed as a form of religious offering: a sacrifice.

22. Edward Humes, *Buried Secrets*, op. cit. p. 43.

23. Ibid. p. 351.

24. Of course, the confessions of various cult members – such as Omar Francisco Orea Ochoa – which detail their initial fear and reluctance to torture, dismember and kill the cult's sacrificial victims, must also be seen from the context of attempting to appease the court and receive more lenient sentences.

25. Colin Wilson and Donald Seaman, *The Serial Killers: A Study In The Psychology Of Violence*, London: Virgin, 1998, p. 65.

BIBLIOGRAPHY

Georges Batailles, *The Tears of Eros*, San Francisco: City Lights Books, 1989.

Gavin Baddeley, *Lucifer Rising: Sin, Devil Worship and Rock 'n' Roll*, London: Plexus, 1999.

Andrew Boyd, *Blasphemous Rumours*, London: Fount, HarperCollins, 1991.

George Brandon, *Santeria From Africa to the New World: The Dead Sell Memories*, Bloomington and Indianapolis: Indiana University Press, 1993.

Mikita Brottman, *Hollywood Hex: Cursed Movies*, London: Creation Books, 1999.

Kerr Cuhulain, 'Matamoros Cult Killings' in *CultWatch Response*, Vol. I, Issue 6.

James T Houk, *Spirits, Blood and Drums: the Orisha Religion in Trinidad*, Philadelphia: Temple University Press, 1995.

Edward Humes, *Buried Secrets, A True Story of Serial Murder, Black Magic, and Drug-Running on the U.S. Border*, New York: Dutton, 1991.

Arthur Lyons, *Satan Wants You: The Cult of Devil Worship in America*, New York: Mysterious Press, 1988.

Richard Monaco and William Burt, *The Dracula Syndrome*, London: Headline Book Publishing, 1993.

Estaban Montejo, *The Autobiography of a Runaway Slave*, translated by Jocasta Innes, edited by Miguel Barnet, London: The Bodley Head, 1968.

Gary Provost, *Across The Border: The True Story of the Satanic Cult Killings In Matamoros, Mexico*, New York: Pocket Books, Simon and Schuster Inc., 1989.

Brenda Ralph Lewis *Ritual Sacrifice: A Concise History*, Thrupp: Sutton Publishing, 2001.

Colin Wilson and Donald Seaman, *The Serial Killers: A Study in the Psychology of Violence*, London: Virgin, 1998.

INTERNET
www.palo.org.
www.religioustolerance.com.

12. WHAT THE WORLD NEEDS NOW IS FEAR

LANCE SINCLAIR

Man is, and always will be, a simple creature. Huddled about the diminishing campfire of logic and moral rightness, looking ever inwards with back turned to the horrors and wonders surrounding it. Localised, tribal, insular. The Western world at the turn of this century, knowing little of real fear or oppression, has grown fat and self-righteous, a directionless and pampered behemoth whose basic duties in life (to hunt, gather and create shelter) are automatically provided for, and who has taken only tentative steps into the next levels of evolution, to create and explore. Mathematically speaking, the great majority of people hit the suburbs and found its lukewarm morass the most painless and least thought-provoking way to see in extinction.

When one exists in a state of flatness and conformity, it is important to have a justification for doing so, and this is why we need the suggestion of horror in our lives. Put another way, if we are 'Good', we can only be so because, somewhere, there is 'Evil'. There's got to be something exciting, nasty and dangerous out there to justify the self-induced narcosis we've brought upon ourselves.

The Cult has been a popular scapegoat and buzzword through the latter half of the twentieth century, in that it offers us not merely an aberrant member of our society to shudder at, condemn and promptly forget, but an entire community that is anathema to the norm, an alien world that exists primarily to define ourselves against. Jim Jones, Charles Manson, David Koresh, Adolf Hitler and Shoko Asahara are a few of many that have provided the world with talismanic figures that we are able to frame or deify as one would a rendering of Jesus Christ, holding them before the tribe and proclaiming, 'Here it is – this is Evil, this is not of us. Because of this, we are righteous.'

In a direct parallel to Christ the details are unimportant: it's the flashing lights and the promotional campaign that count.

MCMARTIN PRESCHOOL

> 'The McMartin case has poisoned everyone who
> had contact with it'
> — Superior Court Judge William Pounders. [1]

On 18 January 1990, to all intents and purposes, a case that would set the benchmark for mass delusional paranoia came to its bitter end. Dozens of lives on both sides of the argument would be left shattered, and the germ of suggestion successfully planted in a nation's consciousness.

Six years before, the charges had been laid: that seven adults connected to the McMartin Preschool in Manhattan Beach, California, were ritually abusing hundreds of the children who had passed through their doors in a variety of fashions, ranging from the horrific to the ludicrous. The lion's share of accusations fell on one Ray Buckey, part-time care worker at the school and son of Peggy McMartin Buckey, owner of the institution. Incidents included the 'Naked Movie Star Game', in which child pornography was produced; children were forced into coffins and buried alive as punishment for resistance; satanic rituals involved blood drinking and the sacrifice/burning of babies; and there were nightmarish journeys through the labyrinth of tunnels that swarmed beneath the school, leading into a variety of chambers where the children would again be sexually abused. More outlandish claims were the reports of flying witches, visits from movie stars and local politicians, Ray Buckey killing a sea turtle by piercing its shell with a knife, trips in hot-air balloons and the testimony of children who claimed to have been flushed down toilets, to have travelled through the sewerage system to locales where they were, once more, sexually molested, before being cleaned up and transported back to school in time to be picked up by their parents.

The McMartin Preschool incident would become a national event, its gorier aspects beamed into every home willing to receive them, and tying the notions of those who care for our children and those who prey on them together into a nightmare vision ecstatic in its outrage.

It was a mentally unbalanced alcoholic named Judy Johnson who ignited the initial firestorm of panic. In August 1983, Ms Johnson brought to the attention of local law authorities claims that her son was being molested while at school. In September of that year Ray Buckey was arrested, although promptly released owing to a total lack of evidence against him, despite Ms Johnson's expanding list of alarming claims: that an elephant and a lion had injured her son during a McMartin-organised field trip; that he had been physically pierced with staples and other classroom implements by his carers; and, on an unrelated note, that her ex-husband had raped not only her son but her unfortunate canine house pet.

After being diagnosed as suffering from acute paranoid schizophrenia, she died from alcohol-related liver
failure. This could have been the beginning and end of
a particularly bitter, nasty story, were it not for the
intervention of local law authorities. The acting chief of
police took it upon himself to distribute unofficial
warnings to local parents that Ray may have forced
children into acts including 'oral sex, fondling of
genitals, buttocks or chest area or sodomy'[2] Of course,
this supposedly confidential secret warning would spill
directly on to local television, and the connection in the
public mind between the phrases 'McMartin Preschool'
and 'ritual child abuse' was established. The rantings of
a disturbed woman had been established, through
media exposure and sloppy procedure, as fact.

Through leading, manipulative interrogation carried
out by the CII (Children's Institute International), more
than 360 children in the Manhattan Beach area were
diagnosed as having 'suffered' 'ritual abuse'. A total of
nine other care and learning institutes were dragged into
the sordid pit of accusation with dozens of teachers
implicated, and it was at this time that the words 'satanic
cult' made their progressively more common appearance.

The charges mentioned above were reported as
though factual, and a telephone survey of the local area
found that 90 per cent of the population was convinced
of Ray's guilt.

Fingered schools were searched for traces of the
crimes. No bodies, no tunnels, no kiddie porn, no flying
witches were found.

In March of 1984 it went to trial anyway. Seven staff
members from McMartin were to be charged with sexual
offences involving forty of their students. As part of its

struggling case, the prosecutors at one point produced a pair of severed rabbit ears, a cape and a set of black candles to impress upon us the fact that there was an underground satanic cult operating under the surface of the community – indeed, most likely the entire country. The actual props had no physical connection to the case at hand, but their appearance served as another trigger effect in the popular consciousness. If a theory or an accusation is merely repeated loudly and frequently enough, a lot of people are going to believe it. The reason is that we want to.

The floodgates were open. Even as the McMartin trial ground to an end, and all involved were acquitted of their charges (cold comfort in the face of the financial and moral hell the accused suffered and suffer still), similar cases were springing up across the country (and, shortly after, across Europe as the satanic panic spread). With time, the great majority of accusations have been debunked, but for a long, dark time there were satanic cults operating all across the face of the US wearing the mask of the educator and spiriting innocent children through subterranean, cruelly cold mazes into bleak candlelit dungeons. They would rape, eat, burn and bury the innocent in an orgy of primordial lust. Any fantasy that we could imagine was true. It walked among us. A glorious time for the faceless, morally stupefied public deep in the void of Regan-era smirking righteousness. A devil to burn can be the uniting event for a shuffling, apathetic village, and the eighties gave them more than enough.

That so many lives were maimed in the process hardly matters when one steps back and looks at the bigger picture. For a while we were entertained, and, through our manufactured insecurities, felt secure.

THE HAND OF DEATH

> From now on, you will do everything you are told.
> Make sure you cut him clean because we'll be
> needing him later.
>
> — Don Meteric[3]

> When she woke up she was at the Ranch Diablo
> looking into the faces of the Dagonite women with
> filed teeth.
>
> — Kenneth 'Mad Dog' McKenna[4]

The undying fascination we have with random death and carnage has found its catalyst in many varying figures. From Vlad the Impaler to Charles Starkweather, from the Marquis de Sade to Marlon Brando in *The Wild One*, we have made icons of the libertine, who places above all else their own satisfaction, be it sexual, financial or territorial. These figures of power, unfettered by conscience or law, all have at the very core of their being the same deity. Satanism demands of its practitioners only rigorous self-examination. It asks not for empathy or reason, only evaluation and action, without regret or retraction.

One of the most pathetic examples of such impulses turned towards waste and despair is the modern trading-card and comic-book hero, Henry Lee Lucas, and to a lesser extent his partner in crime, Ottis Toole. Their well-documented tale is one of pointlessness and inanity magnified to such a disproportionate level that it would cost the lives of many, many unfortunate by-standers to satisfy the short-term interest spans of a couple of cracker jail punk drifters. It's from Lucas that the legend of the Hand of Death seems to have been made public. During his post-arrest confessions (in which the number of victims left in his wake fluctuated between 75 and 500) mention was made of his and Toole's involvement in contract murders farmed out to them by a man by the name of Don Meteric.

Starting at the beginning is probably the best way to reach the end, so we begin with the birth of Henry Lee on 23 August 1936 in Blacksburg, Virginia. Son of Viola and Anderson 'No Legs' Lucas (so named after the result of his drunken brawl with a freight train), Henry would suffer the indignities of dirt-level poverty, brutal physical and mental abuse and the public humiliation of being forced to attend school barefoot in a petticoat dress before discovering the joys of bestiality and torture at the age of fifteen. It was around then that he began to long for the intimacy only another human could give, and his first rape/murder was committed. A long and well-documented life followed: essentially, a fluctuating series of robberies, murders and prison time were to be Henry's lot in life, until he crossed paths with the arsonist and murderer Ottis Toole in 1976.

Their story has become the stuff of modern legend, more so because the details of their adventures were verifiable only by Toole and Lucas themselves, lending them an exciting air of variable plausibility, leaving the door open for any number of revisions or embellishments either might wish to make (one of Lucas's more bizarre claims was his brief period of employment under the wing of his friend Jim Jones, for whom he would personally deliver the poison to be used in the Jonestown mass-suicide ritual). They travelled across the United States for six years, and they killed a lot of people for little or no reason. Those are the facts of which we can be reasonably certain.

The tale that concerns us occurs some time during the middle of their nationwide tour of bloodshed, when

Meteric came into their small lives. Meteric initially offered the two a gig delivering stolen cars to their respective new owners. When Lucas declined the offer, Meteric upped the stakes to $10,000 per hit for dispatching marked enemies of an organisation known as the Hand of Death (a.k.a. the Hands of Death). The two seasoned killers had few qualms about going about the business they were already engaged in, especially with the promise of hard cash.

'You have to join our religion' was the only condition added by their new employer. 'And there is only one way out.'[5]

Weeks later, deep in the gothic haze of the Florida Everglades, the two would be given entry into the Hand. Transported by airboat deep into the swamps, they were given their first task: the murder of a man whose time had been chosen at the whim of the blackest depths of the Hand of Death. It was a simple task for the two equally simple men, although the kill itself was merely the preliminary stage in a greater evil. In all reports that have surfaced concerning the Hand of Death, one of the consistent motifs has been the act of cannibalism. That evening, previously hidden members of the Hand would make themselves known to Ottis and Henry, as their victim became the centrepiece of a frenzy of flesh rending and satanic delirium. They were in.

The Hosts of the Hand reside in the highest seats of power, and their army must contain no weakness, so over the next two months the hapless duo would have their skills in the fields of death, kidnapping, devil worship and improvised mayhem honed beyond their previous capabilities. Set loose, they proved to be ruthless and swift in the execution of their orders, be it the smuggling of narcotics and/or children, wiping those who oppose the Hand of Death from the face of the earth, or any number of varied tasks required by their masters.

This is Henry's story, and as much as he could, he was sticking to it. Henry Lee Lucas was, as well as the blank killer most of us are familiar with, a pathological liar with a flair for self-aggrandisement matched only by his capability to retract seemingly random statements that he had already attested to. Henry may have killed a lot of people, but he also talked a lot of bullshit, and the nature of his unfocused, selfish, undisciplined personality makes you wonder why any Dark Lord didn't consider it safer just to let him be, to carry on his random acts of petty evil, rather than assign seemingly important tasks to a man who was just as likely to fall asleep in a park, take the wrong highway bypass and strangle the wrong target.

At one point Henry recanted his contradictory, often fabricated confessions, until he realised the opportunities presented to him by such statements. Lucas was able to travel from state to state, relieving the boredom of incarceration, as numerous sheriffs' departments brought the murderer to their particular jurisdiction in the hope of clearing up unsolved crimes. It was a former FBI agent, Robert Ressler, who best described Lucas and his post-capture modus operandi: 'He's a serial liar, rather than a serial killer.'[6]

That testimony comes from an unreliable source is no reason to dismiss it completely, although, as illustrated in the unfortunate McMartin Preschool case, too little fact checking and a righteous, overzealous attitude can result in wasted time at best, catastrophe at worst. Reports independent of Henry's have appeared over the last decade, however, from those who claim to be closer to the dark heart of the Hand than any mere assassin.

Gerard John Schaefer, better known in certain circles as the 'Sex Beast', was an incarcerated former police officer linked with the murders of more than twenty people before his demise at the hands of another inmate. Schaefer's main hobby while behind bars was the writing of several novels that could very loosely be referred to as 'true crime', mostly dealing lovingly with the debasement and extermination of nubile female victims. Like Lucas, in fact like most cons, he was a master of overstatement, egotism and barefaced lying. During the mid-1990s Schaefer conducted a series of interviews with a variety of fascinating characters for the Australian magazine *Fatal Visions*. The Hand of Death would be a recurring topic through the majority of this work, and the light shed on it from this standpoint was previously unseen. Lucas had let the cat out of the bag, but it seemed that the Sex Beast was tenuously grabbing and examining said feline.

Schaefer's discussions with one Ken 'Mad Dog' McKenna are the most revealing of the offered glimpses into the Hand of Death and its workings, providing fleeting snatches of a landscape, if real, almost too terrible to contemplate.

According to Mad Dog, the infamous serial murderer Ted Bundy had strong connections to the Hand, whose tutelage would help the fledgling killer blossom from a fairly standard example of his type into the vampiric beast he was at the time of his final capture. His strangest contribution to Hand of Death folklore would come after his death by electrocution in February 1989. Out of gratitude to his mentor McKenna, who refers to himself as a Fourth Prince of the Hand of Death (an exact breakdown of the chain of command has yet to appear), Bundy handed over a detailed map outlining the location of a secret cave in Washington State. It was here that Bundy had been able fully to indulge in the barbaric power rituals that had been passed on to him by the satanic coven. Rape, prolonged torture, strangulation, necrophilia and cannibalism were standard fare in the isolated cavern of perversion. The spirit of one unfortunate victim had been bound to guard Bundy's haven from intruders, while her earthly shell decayed under the cold, stained cave floor, following the lessons taught and examples set by the Hand.

McKenna was fond of Bundy, and appreciated his work, but found him lacking as a student. 'You should be careful not to confuse what Bundy did with what a Fourth Prince does,' he warned Schaefer.

> Bundy had that cave where he took his captive women. He got that idea from the Hand of Death cave of skulls where we deposit the heads of our enemies. The cave Ted had was just a place where he took those women for the purpose of torture and murder. Ted was a sadist when he started out and a depraved necrophile when he finished. Bundy was given good information about cannibalism and ended up a filthy vampire. You cannot compare me to Ted Bundy – I'm a Fourth Prince of the Hand of Death and Bundy was a murderous out-of-control killer punk.[7]

Despite such disappointment, the two were still close enough for the map to change hands, and all the evil captured within, along with whatever trinkets and keepsakes Bundy had secreted, became the property of Mad Dog.

The year 1991, and enter Molly Von Heydreich, freelance journalist and pursuer of the secrets that lay behind the wall of smoke that was the Hand. Working primarily for the *Justice Now Newsletter*, a slapped-together, right-wing, photocopied 'zine that pretends to be repulsed by the violence it so willingly bathes in (to which Schaefer was a regular correspondent), Von Heydreich was somehow able to convince McKenna that, if he shared the secrets of Bundy's cave with her, both would be wealthy and revered through the inevitable television specials and movies that would follow the publication of her exposé.

'It was sounding terrific to me, so I sent her a copy of Bundy's map. She went out to Washington State and found the cave. All Ted's stuff was still there,' recalls McKenna. 'The ghost couldn't keep Molly out, that tells me that Ted didn't do the ritual correctly. The ghost has no power. Ted was a fuck up.'

The correspondence continued, quickly hitting a dark and sour note: 'She turned on me when she found out that I had a hobby as a serial killer. At first she didn't believe me so I gave her a list of 52 women I'd murdered.'

The killings had been conducted as part of an Abraxian blood-cycle ritual, and the list apparently checked out. Molly would then make the greatest and last mistake of her life.

She published the list [the fortunate publication is not named, and is seemingly untraceable] and put big heat on me – then she tried to blackmail me. Molly told me to sign over my claim to the story of Bundy's cave or she'd turn my letters over to the Seattle cops and I'd find myself swinging at the end of a rope at the State Penitentiary out there.

McKenna was serving a life sentence for rape, conspiracy to murder and possession of narcotics, and the release of his confessions was not what he needed at that time.

I contacted my friends in the Satanic underground and they paid Miss Molly a visit. These are avowed Satanists who want to show that they are worthy of induction into our organisation. We call them the 'Servants of the Hand'. They are all coven members but mostly minor league types. What I did to get them moving was write a letter to the leader of the coven. The letter was written in runes. Runescript is the official written symbol of advanced Satanists. The runic message is sent to the Chief Witch of the coven selected to serve the Hand of Death. The chief witch is called a Hellbitch. I sign it in blood with the mark if the devil and mail it. The Hellbitch then convenes the coven and they do a magickal ceremony which involves the casting of the runes; and what this involves is tossing certain small lacquered sticks before a demonic image. The coven members who cast the series called the Death rune carry out the terms of the message. We call the message the Edict. My edict was sent to the Hellbitch of Vampira in Atlanta, Georgia. Four marked witches of coven Vampira cast the Death rune. The Vampira coven is a subcult within the ancient society of the Daughters of Anath, they're very powerful witches who worship the Satanic Goddess Anath. The four witches went south to find Molly Von Heydreich and they did find her. Molly was kidnapped, bound, gagged, put in the trunk of a car and driven directly to Mexico. Molly was drugged to keep her quiet; when she woke up she was at the Ranch Diablo looking into the faces of Dagonite women with filed teeth. They stripped Molly down to her bare ass, washed her so she didn't stink up the council, then dragged her before the tribunal. They don't believe in wasting time down there. Molly was not important. They just wanted to hear her admit she was guilty before they killed her. Von Heydreich stole from me and ratted on me to the cops; today she is reduced to pig shit. Yes, she was fed to the swine. Molly doesn't cause me problems anymore.

Perhaps unwisely, McKenna gives out more secrets regarding the Hand of Death and its make-up:

The Dagonites are a major Neo-Baalist cult that worships the God Dagon. Dagon is another name for Satan. Their women have filed teeth because they are cannibals. The Hand of Death is a Trinity, an unholy Satanic Trinity comprised of the three primary Satanic Forces in Western Civilization: The Sons of Dagon, The Ancient Society of the Daughters of Anath, and the sisterhood of Asherah. These are the three major forces in demonic Satanism at work in the world today. The world headquarters of the Hand of Death is located in the mountains of Northern Mexico not all that far south of the Texas border. All Satanic cults are sub-cults of these three.

Why would a Fourth Prince in the Hand of Death reveal such secrets? During the course of his conversations with Schaefer he reveals an up-front dislike of the interviewer, and one wonders what the purpose was in the dispatching of Molly Von Heydreich, seeing that McKenna is more than willing to pontificate on the inner workings of the Hand of Death in an international print forum. The remainder of his earthly life will be spent in prison, but the punishment awaiting him for spilling the beans would surely far outweigh more worldly concerns. Schaefer's connection to the three main players in the tale is awfully convenient (he claims to have been a close personal confidant of Bundy's, as well as acting as his legal research assistant during their ten years together on death row), although it does offer him a one-of-a-kind perspective to aid the writing of books such as *The Horrors of Bundy's Cave*.

Schaefer is dead now, and the mysterious Ms Von Heydreich long gone from this mortal coil. Henry Lee Lucas and Ted Bundy have been returned to the void, and Kenneth McKenna has not appeared in print since the mid-nineties. Little has been heard of the Hand of Death since. Were these players silenced by the far-reaching Hand, or is the explanation a little more mundane?

Aside from Schaefer's own tales, this writer has been unable to uncover any connection between the deceased 'Sex Beast' and Ted Bundy, whose life and deeds have been extensively covered by every media format current-ly available. Of greater interest is the lack of any paper trail that will even confirm the existence of the doomed Molly Von Heydreich or the Satanic Prince McKenna. It is as though their tale were so revealing, so dangerous, that it would be for ever relegated to the nether regions of masturbatory violence-obsessed fanboys. The Hand of Death, if it wishes truly to spread fear and evil throughout the world, will have to rethink profoundly its approach to public relations.

GHOST STORIES: THE DELIGHTS OF FEAR

> Our comics are for 'Mature Readers Only' and are
> done in a very tasteful manner.
> – Editorial from *Psycho Killers*[8]

The McMartin Preschool case was absorbed eagerly and
without question by a society eager to identify the germ
of evil that existed in its midst. If we think of
conventional society as a family unit, then the McMartin
case exists as the warning, etched in stone, of the
darkness that waits beside the garden path. An adult
fairy tale, sombre and grim.

The most harmless, loud and predictable element of the
family is the rebellious child, whose brash, prurient and
obnoxious habits serve to annoy all and sundry while
filling the child with a sense of experience and worldliness.
The Hand of Death is the comic book this brat will be
reading. Dog-eared and incomplete, the tale of the cult
seems to come about through a chain of Chinese Whispers,
starting with the 'True Crime' paperback that introduced
the reader to the malefic Mr Meteric and his vague
overlords, their goals seeming to be only the proliferation
of an already healthy wave of malice sweeping the globe.
Expanded on by Gerard John Schaefer, the author whose
primary concerns revolve around the inflation of his own
ego and the pornography of murder, the Hand of Death
has become an all-encompassing organisation that functions as a Legion of Superheroes for the criminally insane.
Theorists have linked Charles Manson, David 'Son of Sam'
Berkowitz and the uncaught Green River Killer[9] to the
Hand of Death and its unknowable grand plan.

No Ranch of the Devil has ever been found south of
the Texas–Mexico border, and no boot camp for the

training of satanic foot soldiers has been found in the Florida Everglades. 'They were probably tipped off you were looking for them' was the excuse provided by Henry Lee, master of the grey line between fact and fiction. Convenient enough for those of us who want to believe. Just as the majority are able to feel justified and decent when hearing the McMartin debacle shouted through the evening news, so those of us who would like to think of ourselves as bad, different, superior or confrontational can wallow vicariously in the supposedly true and verified accounts of madness, cannibalism, slaughter and black lust offered up by the most dubious of sources.

We love the idea of the Cult, the great Other whose structure so closely resembles our own. There must be a leader, a council of superiors, and, of most importance, there must be the faceless mass, the followers and soldiers and simple workers who reflect the skewed vision of ourselves and who, through their study or their incineration, give definition to the blank slate that we are.

NOTES

1. www.religioustolerance.org/ra82mcmar.htm
2. www.religioustolerance.org/ra82mcmar.htm
3. *Henry Lee Lucas: Deadly Drifter* by Patrick Bellamy (transcription at www.crimelibrary.com).
4. Gerard John Schaefer, 'Mad Dog MacKenna Interviewed by . . .', *Fatal Visions* #18, 1995.
5. *Henry Lee Lucas: Deadly Drifter*, op. cit.
6. Robert Ressler cited in Gavin Baddeley, *Lucifer Rising: Sin, Devil Worship and Rock 'n' Roll*, London: Plexus, 1999, p. 145.
7. All McKenna quotations from *Fatal Visions* #18, 1995.

8. *Psycho Killers Mailman Special* Vol. 1, No. 1, November 1992.
9. Although the motives and reasons behind the killings of an unknown and still-at-large murderer are obviously pure guesswork, with no evidence for the existence of the Hand of Death, that hardly matters.

BIBLIOGRAPHY

Gavin Baddeley, *Lucifer Rising: Sin, Devil Worship and Rock 'n' Roll*, London: Plexus, 1999.

Patrick Bellamy, *Henry Lee Lucas: Deadly Drifter*, transcription at www.crimelibrary.com.

Gerard John Schaefer, 'Mad Dog MacKenna Interviewed by . . .' *Fatal Visions*, #18, 1995.

Psycho Killers Mailman Special, Vol. 1, No. 1, November 1992.

INTERNET

www.religioustolerance.org/ra82mcmar.htm

THE CONTRIBUTORS

Jack Sargeant is the author of numerous highly acclaimed books on avant-garde and underground culture, including *Deathtripping: The Cinema Of Transgression*, *Naked Lens: Beat Cinema* (both Creation Books), and *Cinema Contra Cinema* (Fringecore). He is editor of the journal *Suture*, and contributes to numerous publications, including *Headpress*, *Black Ice* and *Sleazenation*. Sargeant has toured widely, and his underground-and-outlaw-culture lectures and film shows mix a twisted academic perception with occasional outbursts of virulent nihilism. He is fascinated by extremes of human behaviour, and is currently working on several book and film projects.

Chris Barber is a freelance journalist and regular contributor to *QX* magazine, in particular on true crime and history. He also works as a legal representative for solicitors and barristers on criminal defence trials.

Mikita Brottman is professor of literature at Maryland Institute College of Art. She is the editor, most recently, of *Car Crash Culture* (Palgrave/St Martin's), and the author of *Hollywood Hex* and *Meat Is Murder* (both Creation Books).

Monte Cazazza is a musician, filmmaker, artist, writer and provocateur. Among other aesthetic outrages, he coined the term 'industrial music', collaborated with Throbbing Gristle and Factrix, produced the mondo film *True Gore*, contributed to the cult tome *Apocalypse*

Culture (Feral House) and worked at the Museum of Death. He refuses to curtail his interests in the malevolent, strange and downright amusing. Cazazza views contemporary society as an extension of the surveillance-based prison, and he prefers to live a long way from most of the other inmates.

Andrew Leavold has owned and managed Trash Video, the largest cult-video rental store in Brisbane (and Australia), since 1995. For the last six years he has curated the 'Eat My Schlock' Bad Taste Short Film Festival. Never bored, he also writes for various magazines and book projects, fronts the cow-punk cabaret combo They Might Be Vaginas, co-runs the Turkeyneck Records label, and churns out lurid posters and record covers for bands around the country.

John Harrison is a freelance writer based in Melbourne, and contributes to publications such as *Headpress*, *The Eros Journal*, *Is it Uncut* and the *Something Weird Video* catalogue updates and website. In his spare time, he runs a small mail-order company called the Graveyard Tramp – specialising in offbeat items of pop culture memorabilia – and is currently writing a book on vintage adult paperbacks.

Marzy Quayzar is an excellent painter of the macabre and perverse. She published *Polka Dot* and *Pain* fanzines, is a gourmet cook and exceptional tarot reader. In her spare time she enjoys taxidermy and embroidery.

Lance Sinclair is a thirty-year-old former music journalist operating from Queensland. His twin lifelong passions of film and true crime ephemera have given him a unique insight into the milieu of the contemporary lazy voyeur.

When not running Xochi Publications, **Michael Spann** can be found at the Vulkano Diskotek in Ougadougou, Burkina Faso.

Look out for other compelling, all-new True Crime titles from Virgin Books

September 2002

My Bloody Valentine – Couples Whose Sick Crimes Shocked the World

Edited by Patrick Blackden

Good-looking Canadian couple Paul Bernardo and Karla Homolka looked the epitome of young, wholesome success. No one could have guessed that they drugged, raped and murdered young women to satisfy Bernardo's deviant lusts. Nothing inspires more horror and fascination than couples possessed of a single impulse – to kill for thrills. Obsessed by and sucked into their own sick and private madness, their attraction is always fatal, their actions always desperate. The book covers a variety of notorious killer couples: from desperados Starkweather and Fugate, on whom the film *Natural Born Killers* was based, right through to Fred and Rose West, who committed unspeakable horrors in their semi-detached house in Gloucester, England. With contributions from a variety of leading true crime journalists, *My Bloody Valentine* covers both the world-famous cases and also lesser-known but equally horrifying crimes.

£7.99 ISBN: 0-7535-0647-5

September 2002

DANGER DOWN UNDER

Patrick Blackden

Australia is one of the most popular long-haul tourist destinations for Britons, but its image of a carefree, 'no worries' BBQ, beach and beers culture set in a landscape of stunning natural beauty tells only one side of the story. *Danger Down Under* lets you know what the tourist board won't – the dark side of the Australian dream. The mysterious vanishing of Briton Peter Falconio in summer 2001 is just one of many puzzling unsolved cases of tourist disappearances. With a landscape that can be extremely hostile to those unfamiliar to its size and extremes and an undying macho culture – not to mention the occasional psychotic who murders backpackers, or crazed gangs of bikers and cultists – there is much to be cautious of when venturing down under.

£7.99 ISBN 0-7535-0649-1

October 2002

DIRTY CASH – Organised Crime in the Twenty First Century

David Southwell

There was once only one Mafia: now every country seems to have its own. Until fairly recently gangsters kept to their territories, but crime – like every other business – has been quick to take advantage of the new global economy. Business, it seems, is good, with over $150 billion laundered each year in Europe alone. As links are formed between the Mafia, the Triads, the Yardies, the Yakuza, the Russian Mafiya and the South American cartels, a tide of misery spreads throughout the world. The book looks in detail at the specific groups involved, the horrifying crimes they commit, and the everyday lives of their members.

£7.99 ISBN: 07535 0702 1

November 2002

TEENAGE RAMPAGE – The Worldwide Youth Crime Explosion

Antonio Mendoza

Columbine High School, Colorado, Spring 1999. 12 of its school-children and one teacher lay dead. Two boys have gone on a killing spree, venting their anger at their classmates before turning their guns on themselves. Cases such as Columbine are occurring with increasing regularity – and guns are not always involved. In Japan in 1998, a 13-year-old schoolboy murdered his teacher in a frenzied knife attack. What is happening in society that young people are running amok, fuelled by hatred and nihilism, with little regard for their own lives and the lives of those around them? Expert crime writer Antonio Mendoza investigates this worldwide problem and comes up with some shocking findings that call for a global rethink on how we bring up – and punish – those responsible for the worldwide teenage crimewave.

ISBN: 07535 0715 3

December 2002

FEMALE TERROR – Scary Women, Modern Crimes

Ann Magma

Statistics show that female crime and female violence is on the rise, particularly in America where, in 1999, over two million violent female offenders were recorded and the rise was cited as 137 per cent. Women are becoming an ever-growing presence in crime statistics, becoming a major force in both organised crime and terrorism. In the last ten years they have also come to the fore as homicidal leaders of religious sects and gun-toting leaders of Los Angeles street gangs, whose members are every bit as tough and violent as their male 'gangsta' counterparts. From Ulrike Meinhof to Wafa Idris; from IRA terrorists to Mafia godmothers, this book will look at the rise and rise of female terror.

ISBN: 07535 0718 8

January 2003

MONSTERS OF DEATH ROW – America's Dead Men and Women Walking

Christopher Berry-Dee and Tony Brown

From the cells of Death Row come the chilling, true-life accounts of the most heinous, cruel and depraved killers of modern times. At the time of writing, there are 3,702 inmates on Death Row across the USA, many of whom have caused their victims to consciously suffer agonising physical pain and tortuous mental anguish before death. These are not normal human beings. They have carried out serial murder, mass-murder, spree killing, necrophilia, and dismemberment of bodies – both dead and alive. In these pages are to be found fiends who have stabbed, hacked, set fire to, and even filleted their victims. So meet the 'dead men and women walking' in the most terrifying true crime read ever.

ISBN 07535 0722 6

The best in true crime from Virgin Books

How to order by mail:

Tick the box for the title/s you wish to order and complete the form overleaf. Please do not forget to include your address.

From Cradle to Grave	Joyce Eggington	0 86369 646 5	£6.99	☐
Perfect Victim	C. McGuire & C. Norton	0 352 32561 5	£6.99	☐
Precious Victims	Don Weber & Charles Bosworth	0 86369 598 1	£6.99	☐
The Serial Killers	Colin Wilson & Donald Seaman	0 86369 615 5	£6.99	☐
The Last Victim	Jason Moss	0 7535 0398 0	£6.99	☐
Killers on the Loose	Antonio Mendoza	07535 0681 5	£6.99	☐
Crossing to Kill	Simon Whitechapel	0 7535 0686 6	£6.99	☐
Lone Wolf	Pan Pantziarka	0 7535 0617 3	£6.99	☐
I'll Be Watching You	Richard Gallagher	0 7535 0696 3	£6.99	☐
Unsolved Murders	Russell Gould	0 7535 0632 7	£6.99	☐
My Bloody Valentine	Ed. Patrick Blackden	0 7535 0647 5	£7.99	☐
Death Cults	Ed. Jack Sargeant	0 7535 0644 0	£7.99	☐
Danger Down Under	Patrick Blackden	0 7535 0649 1	£7.99	☐
Dirty Cash	David Southwell	0 7535 0702 1	£7.99	☐
Teenage Rampage	Antonio Mendoza	0 7535 0715 3	£7.99	☐
Female Terror	Ann Magma	0 7535 0718 8	£7.99	☐

Please send me the books I have ticked above.

Name _____

Address _____

_____

_____

_____

Post Code _____

Send to: Cash Sales, Virgin Books, Thames Wharf Studios, Rainville Road, London W6 9HA.

US customers: for prices and details of how to order books for delivery by mail, call 1-800-343-4499.

Please enclose a cheque or postal order, made payable to Virgin Books Ltd, to the value of the books you have ordered plus postage and packing costs as follows:

UK and BFPO – £1.00 for the first book, 50p for each subsequent book.

Overseas (including Republic of Ireland) – £2.00 for the first book, £1.00 for each subsequent book.

If you would prefer to pay by VISA, ACCESS/MASTER-CARD, DINERS CLUB, AMEX or SWITCH, please write your card number and expiry date here:

_____

Signature _____

Please allow up to 28 days for delivery.